The Ark of Millions of Years

of Years

Volume Four

Book of Updates

by

E. J. Clark

&

B. Alexander Agnew

authorHOUSE®

AuthorHouse™
1663 Liberty Drive
Bloomington, IN 47403
www.authorhouse.com
Phone: 1-800-839-8640

Published by AuthorHouse   08/17/2015

ISBN: 978-1-4567-2528-0 (sc)
ISBN: 978-1-4567-2529-7 (e)

Library of Congress Control Number: 2008903057

Print information available on the last page.

This book is printed on acid-free paper.

The Ark of Millions of Years
Volume Four

Contents

Dedications

This book is dedicated to my wonderful
Grandchildren, namely, William, Ashton,
and Janet Kimsey and to my Maya
Grandson, Jorge Luis Dzib May.

E. J. Clark

After a lifetime of studying time and the involvement
of consciousness in creation, I have concluded that it is the
accompaniment of family that makes the experience unique. This
book is dedicated to the special souls who came here to the Earth
with me. Each of them is a vital contributor to the outcome of this
experience. April, Ben, Mike, and June, and Marlene are foundation
souls in a grand transition from another world.

Brooks A. Agnew

Foreword

When we finished the writing of *The Ark of Millions of Years* trilogy, we were certain that the books were finished. However, more and more things kept popping up that confirmed our writings and added to our knowledge of the 2012 events. So much, that we decided to do another book that would contain updates to the trilogy which would keep the books current.

Because this book is a book of updates to the trilogy, it is necessary to first read the trilogy in order to understand this book. The Table of Contents is divided into three sections; General Updates, Archaeological Updates, and End Time Updates. Each update will be placed in the section deemed the most appropriate. A few of the updates will appear as additional chapters. Because the updates are categorized, it will be easy to locate their contents therefore eliminating the need for an index. The reference chapter titled *The Beginning* in Volume One, will serve this book as well. As you read this book, if you have the three books of the Ark trilogy handy and available for a quick search of pictures and story content, the updates will have more meaning. In addition, if you have a computer available to look up several online pictures of murals and stele images, it will help to better understand the written content of two chapters.

We believe this book is the last of the series because time is running out...only one year and ten months left at the writing of this book till the End of the Age and associated 2012 events. Please enjoy these updates. They will add so much more to our understanding of the nature of the creation and of its ultimate 2012 destiny.

While the more than 1,500 pages of history, archaeology, and science we have documented and explained tells a foreboding story of the 2012 Endtimes, they also empower the reader to be able to choose a different future for themselves. With this knowledge, you may not only survive the cataclysms predicted to befall planet Earth, you will be able to thrive and even lead others to a more enlightened understanding. Now that you know the cliff is coming, you don't have to walk over it with those who are still asleep.

General Updates
Book Cover Redesign

The first most noticeable change that has taken place is the re-design of the covers of the first two books. When *The Ark of Millions of Years* became a trilogy, we wanted the books to look like a matched set using the same cosmic themes. Graphic artist Roy Young captured our vision for the cover of the third Volume in such an amazing way that we asked him to re- design the covers of the first two books. The trilogy book covers are now eye catching, intriguing, and beautiful to behold.

On the front cover of Volume Two (Figure 1) there is a Greek style snake ouroboros swallowing its tail with the symbols of the Cardinal Constellations surrounding it. These four Cardinal Constellations will align to form a cross on December 21, 2012.

An Egyptian winged sphinx stands above the head of the snake. It is the symbol of the four Cardinal Constellations. Most of the ancient people could not read or write but they could understand symbols. Whenever they saw a winged sphinx it was a reminder of the four Cardinal Constellations due to re-align to form a cross at the End of the Age which we know is December 21, 2012.

The winged sphinx is comprised of parts of all four of the Cardinal Constellations as it has the body of a lion (Leo), the feet of a bull (Taurus), the head of a man or woman (Aquarius) and the wings of an eagle (Scorpio). Note: Scorpio the scorpion is also represented as an eagle.

Winged Egyptian sphinx thrones were also guardians of time during a king's reign. The upside down U with 2012 inside of it is an Omega Symbol. It has always been a symbol for the End of the Age which translates into December 21, 2012.

Figure 1: The Ark of Millions of Years: Volumes One and Two covers.

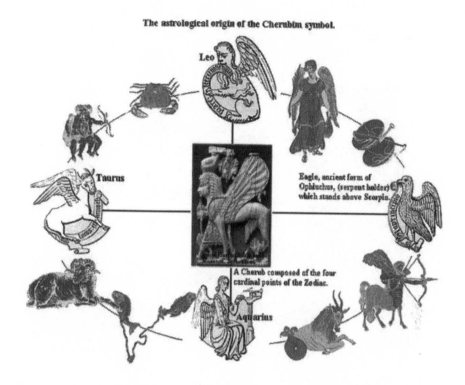

The astrological origin of the Cherubim symbol.

Leo

Taurus

Eagle, ancient form of Ophiuchus, (serpent holder) which stands above Scorpio.

A Cherub composed of the four cardinal points of the Zodiac.

Aquarius

Figure 2: The Astrological Origin of the Cherubim.

This Volume Four Book of Updates front cover shows the two bronze columns of Solomon's Temple, Jachin and Boaz. Jachin has the globe of the Temporal Earth on its capitol and Boaz has the celestial globe of the Spirit Earth on its capitol. Many Masonic Temples use these columns with exact globes in their lodges and temples. The black and white checkerboard squares represent the porch of Solomon's Temple. The symbol of the winged sphinx has been explained. The rest of the symbolism will be revealed elsewhere in the text.

The Pomegranate

Figure 3: Notice the calyx on this amazing fruit.

The pomegranate or "punica granatum" figures prominently in four of the world's major religions. We will answer why this fruit held such devotion in ancient times and why now has recently had resurgence as a healthy food

Based on excavations of the Early Bronze Age (3500-2000BC.), it is believed that the pomegranate was one of the first cultivated fruits. It originated in Mesopotamia in the regions of Persia and Iraq. In 1600BC. the pomegranate was brought to Egypt from Syria during the rule of the Hyksos. There it became an important food source and was part of the supply of fruits required in a pharaoh's palace. Nothing of the fruit is wasted. Pomegranate blossoms were crushed to make a red dye for coloring textiles and the peel was used for dying leather and the bark used for making medicine. In addition the pomegranate tree has very hard wood that was used in making woodcrafts and walking sticks. Moreover, the juice from the fruit and the bark of the tree was used to cure practically everything from memory loss, treatment of fevers, treatment of urinary disorders, and for increased fertility. You name it and it cured it. Of course, the best appeal is the fruit itself. It is beautiful in color which ranges in various intensities of reddish pink. When the fruit is opened, the juice and seeds, called arils, are delicious to the taste. You can feel your salivary glands watering up in expectation of the sweet juice and tart seeds that will titillate your taste buds to climax in an explosion of mouth watering delight. It's a mixed taste sensation of erotica and exotica at the same time.

This one fruit became so revered by the Egyptians that pomegranates are found depicted on Egyptian wall paintings in tombs as early as 2500 BC., symbolizing life after death. In fact, King Tut took a pomegranate vase into the afterlife with him. The pomegranate is mentioned in the inscriptions of Tutmos 1 (1547 BC.) and symbols of the fruit were found in the tomb of Ramses 1V (1145BC.). Large dried pomegranates were found in the tomb of Djehuty, the butler of Queen Hatshepsut.

The pomegranate was important enough to be mentioned in the Bible twenty-five times. One reference to the Promised Land is found in Deuteronomy 8:8 that read as follows:

"A land of wheat and barley, of vines and fig trees and pomegranates, a land of olive oil and honey;..."

Even God wanted the pomegranate to hold a special place in Jewish temple worship because he told Moses how to make and decorate the robe of the e-phod of the Levitical high priests. Moses was instructed to decorate the hems of the e-phod as follows in Exodus 28:33-34:

"And beneath upon the hem of it thou shalt make pomegranates of blue, and of purple, and of scarlet, round about the hem thereof; and bells of gold between them round about:

A golden bell and a pomegranate, a golden bell and a pomegranate, upon the hem of the robe round about."

Thereafter, even Jewish kings had pomegranates embroidered on the hems of their robes. Later on King David received specific instructions from God on how to build His temple. King David had hoped to build it, but was told by God that his son, Solomon, would be the one to construct the first temple. The temple was to serve two purposes; a place to house the Ark of the Covenant and to serve as a place to worship the God of Israel.

The two bronze columns of Jachin and Boaz at entry to Solomon's Temple were adorned with wreaths of pomegranates on their capitols. The pomegranates numbered one hundred per column capitol. It is said that King Solomon designed his coronet based on the pomegranates "crown" which has a calyx shaped like a crown. Pomegranates are one of the few images which appear on ancient coins of Judea as a sacred symbol. In addition, when the scrolls of the Torah are not in use, they are stored in dual silver cylinders with silver clasps that have pomegranates engraved on the clasps. Judaic tradition asserts that every pomegranate holds 613 seeds, representative of the 613 commandments of the Torah.

In Buddhism, the pomegranate is one of the three blessed fruits (pomegranates, olives and dates). Pomegranates decorate the temple of the founder of Zen Buddism, which was built in 1195 in China to honor Bodhidharma.

Between 600-700 BC., Zoroastrianism became the major religion of ancient Persia. Pomegranate trees were planted in the courtyard of Zoroastrian temples because their leaves remained green most of the year which stood as a symbol of eternal life.

All the above is very interesting but it doesn't tell us why the pomegranate held such high status, even to be favored of God. To find the answer, one must turn to the religion of Islam. Pomegranates are mentioned three times in the Qur'an. According to Surah 55:068 in the Qur'an, pomegranates grew in the gardens of paradise along with date palms, all kinds of fruit trees and olives. This was a great aha light bulb moment. How did the pomegranate get from the Spirit Earth to the

Temporal Earth? Noah, of course, who else? He brought the seeds with him on the ark. When he settled down permanently in Mesopotamia, he planted and grew the seeds as did some of his children who scattered at the Lord's command. The pomegranate originated in that area and later the seeds have been spread over most of the planet.

Islam tradition says to eat every seed of a pomegranate because one can't be sure which aril came from paradise. Mohammed encouraged his followers to eat plenty of the fruit because he taught that pomegranates protect the eater from envy and hatred.

When you research the origins of the date palm and the olive tree, one will find that these plants have the same origins as the pomegranate. The Sumerians, Noah's people, were cultivating the date palm by about 4000BC. This finding adds credence that these varieties of plants were brought here by Noah. Although palms and olives trees were here before Noah's arrival, they were inferior varieties, producing poor quality tasteless, often inedible fruits. Noah introduced new, better varieties of these plants. It was an olive branch that the dove of Noah carried in its beak when it returned to the ark. The olive tree and date palms are among the oldest known cultivated trees and like the pomegranate, considered sacred. Olive oil is often referred to as "Holy oil" in Christian churches and used for anointment during baptism and in other religious ceremonies. One Muslim tradition describes the date palm as the chief food created by God to nourish Adam in the Garden of Eden.

In Judaism, the first books of the Torah argue that the forbidden fruit was not an apple but rather a pomegranate. Now we can understand why Buddhism refers to the three fruits, pomegranates, dates, and olives, as blessed because they were found in the garden of paradise. Many believe the pomegranate was the forbidden fruit from the Tree of Knowledge that led to the expulsion of Adam and Eve from the Garden of Eden. The fact that God instructed Moses to have pomegranates embroidered on the hem of the e-phod and gave specific instructions to David to have pomegranate wreaths adorn the capitols of the two bronze columns of Solomon's Temple certainly lends credence to that story.

Since the Bible doesn't identify what kind of fruit the Tree of Knowledge of Good and Evil bore, how did the notion come about that the forbidden fruit was an apple? It is probably because one early Latin translation of the Bible uses "apple" instead of fruit. In classical Latin where "malum" was broadly applied to many apple-like fruits, the pomegranate name was malum punicum or malum granatum meaning "apple having many seeds." The name apple stuck and thus became the favored representation of the forbidden fruit in Christian art. Early Christian burials in catacombs often had scenes of Adam and Eve eating of the apple from the Tree of Knowledge carved on their tombs as a reminder that Adam and Eve's transgression brought death into the world. The early Greeks enforced the belief by saying that the forbidden fruit was similar to their apple, noting that apple trees do not grow in the Middle East. Christians later adopted the pomegranate as a symbol of the resurrection and the hope of eternal life. The fruit is often found in devotional statues and paintings of the Virgin and Child. Most biblical scholars now agree the forbidden fruit was most likely the pomegranate.

Today, the pomegranate is being hailed as the new super fruit. Preliminary studies indicate that the juice may possess almost three times the antioxidants of red wine or green tea. Its health benefits boast of being loaded with vitamins, potassium, folic acid and iron. Culinary arts use the seeds and juice to garnish salads and deserts. Glazes made from the juice are used to glaze turkeys. Pomegranate cocktails have become popular. Just Google pomegranate recipes and see the long list of recipes out there. Grenadine syrup is made from the juice of the pomegranate. Inks and insecticides are made from the bark and leaves. Lastly, a large bowl of pomegranates sitting on buffets and tables make great holiday decorations. If you have never tasted of its juice, try it. You can even find juices blended with it such as cranberry pomegranate juice, blackberry pomegranate juice, cherry pomegranate juice, mango pomegranate juice or even blueberry pomegranate juice. There is a flavor or mix for every palette.

In conclusion, having read this story, whenever you see a pomegranate in a grocery store, drink its juice or eat of its seeds, this story will come to mind and you will wonder if it indeed was the forbidden fruit that led to the temptation of Adam and Eve to eat and thus become the first mortals subject to death on our Spirit Earth, the original creation. Subsequently, as promised by Lucifer in the Garden of Eden, we became wise having our eyes opened and we have become as the gods, knowing the good from the evil. No wonder the fruit has been so revered and commemorated throughout the ages.

The Sacred Feminine

Fans of author Dan Brown will remember his highly popular best seller, The Da Vinci Code, which was later made into a movie. Although his book is a fictional novel, he developed a plot based on an old story that has been in circulation since 50 AD. The legend is that Mary Magdalene, sister of Lazarus and Martha, married Jesus at their second Messianic marriage ceremony in Bethany as the Cana first marriage ceremony was a Betrothal. Born of high-ranking royal Hasmonaean stock, she was the *Magdal-eder* or apostle, acting in her capacity as a bridal high priestess, that anointed Jesus at this second marriage rite as was customarily done by the Essenes in Messianic marriages as Mary Magdalene was an Essene. At the time of Jesus' crucifixion, Mary was three months pregnant with his first child.

According to the legend, Jesus survived crucifixion and joined his wife, Mary. Mary gave birth to their first born child, a girl that was named Tamar the Sarah, Sarah meaning princess. Due to eroding politics, unfair taxation, torture and loss of trading liaisons under Roman rule, the Essenes launched a Zealot guerrilla movement against Roman overlords that eventually led to the Jewish revolt in 66 AD. The climate of oppression forced Mary to flee to the Provence area of France for safety. It is said that Joseph of Arimathea, Lazarus and Martha went with her. Mary Jacob, the sister of Jesus, and other members of Jesus family may have followed also. Mary Magdalene was now pregnant with the second child of Jesus. In 37AD. she gave birth to Jesus' son, named Jesus after his father. Later Jesus joined Mary in France. In 44 AD., Mary gave birth to their second son and third child named Josephes.

Jesus and Mary Magdalene's priestly home and heirs and the heirs of Jesus' extended kinsmen bloodlines became known as the Fisher Kings who ultimately founded the French monarchy known as the Merovingian dynasty.

Jesus' brother James held the office of the Nazarene Bishop of Jerusalem. As such, he became the Divine Highness or the Joseph *ha Rama-Theo* that translates literally into the better known title of Joseph of Arimathea. Legends say that Joseph of Arimathea/James was given a large land grant of tax-free land by King Arviratus at Glastonbury in England where he built a church. His daughter, Anna, married into the Camelot dynasty and from them descended a great line of Celtic kings.

According to the legendary story, the royal lineages of the House of David were considered to be God's offspring, not Jesus' lineage alone but included his immediate kinsmen and heirs of his family. These Messianic heirs were called the *Desposyni*, meaning heirs of the Lord. This is confirmed by Eusebius of Caesarea in his *Ecclesiastical History* that included the third century writings of historian Africanus. The annuals of Africanus relate that King Herod-Antipas ordered the genealogical records of Jesus' family burned and later under Roman occupation, the governors burned all remaining Messianic records pertaining to the family's pedigree to prevent future access to this knowledge. Only private records were carefully preserved by family descendants as a reminder of their proud and noble heritage. There were at least three well-known authentic lines of legitimate blood descent from Jesus' own family.

Laurence Gardner states the following in his book, *Lost Secrets of the Sacred Ark:*

"The 2nd-century Palestinian historian Hegesippus reported in his *Hypemnenata* (Memoirs) that Emperor Vespasian (A.D. 69-70) went so far as to order that no member of the Messianic house should be left alive and that 'all descendants of King David should be ferreted out.'"

Thereafter the Desposyni began to be persecuted, hunted down like animals and put to death by the sword by Imperial orders. After Vespasian's reign which was followed by the reign of Emperor Domitian (A.D. 81-96), by Imperial decree, among the Desposyni seized were the sons of Jesus' brother Jude, Zoker and James, who were later released and became leaders of the Jewish Christian Church. Emperor Domition's reign was followed by the reign of Emperor Trajan (c.

AD. 110), when the Desposynos Simeon was crucified in 106 AD. for belonging to the family of Jesus.

Obviously, as the Desposyni descendants increased in number, they presented a potential threat to the Holy Roman Church because many of them held high positions of special honor in the early Jewish Christian Church. Should the Desposyni hereditary heirs make a rightful claim to be the legitimate leaders of the Holy Roman Church and succeed; the present leadership would be divested of all power and deposed. Actually in 318 AD., a Desposyni delegation did just that; it is a well documented fact. They journeyed to Rome and insisted that the Church should be centered in Jerusalem and not in Rome. They argued that the Bishop of Jerusalem should be a true hereditary heir of the Lord's family and bishops should be appointed from the Lord's family to head other churches in surrounding major city centers. Their demands were heard in vain as their demands never reached the ears of the Emperor Constantine who had already relegated the power of salvation away from Jesus to rest in the Emperor himself. Those who opposed his decree were be-headed, thus in this manner, the bishops were enabled to reinforce their claim to holy authority through their heritage from St. Peter *(Lost Secrets of the Sacred Ark* by Laurence Gardner, pp.223-225).

Nevertheless, as the story goes, Jesus died in France ca. 66AD. and Mary Magdalene died ca. 63 AD. at Aix-en-Provence, France. Several locations have been given for her tomb but St. Maximin La Sainte Baume, Provence, is generally the recognized place of her sepulcher. Because it is said that Mary Magdalene converted many French to Christianity, she is highly venerated there as many shrines have been built in her honor. Mary Jacob, Jesus' sister, also had a large following in medieval England during the 13th century. Supposedly, the Holy Grail is the royal bloodlines of Mary and Jesus' family and not the chalice Jesus used to institute the Holy Eucharist at the Last Supper. According to author Lawrence Gardner, this was the big secret the Knight Templars were protecting in order to save the Desposyni royal bloodlines from destruction. Those who believe this story contend the bloodlines from the children of Jesus and Mary Magdalene lives on to this day in secret. In a nutshell, that is the legendary story of Jesus and Mary Magdalene. Books have been written on the subject.

Is there any truth to the legend? In our opinion, there is always a little truth to every story. Books written on the subject relegate the statue of Jesus to that of a great prophet of God born of an ordinary birth to Mary and Joseph, his parents. He was crucified for being an insurgent and ultimately survived crucifixion to live out the remainder of his life with Mary Magdalene in France. The religion of Islam contends Jesus was not the son of God but born of mortal parents however, Jesus is recognized as a great prophet of God. The Qur'an teaches Jesus was never crucified and he never died a mortal death but ascended into heaven; no mention of a marriage.

There is sufficient documentation to support Jesus was indeed a historical figure. And there is sufficient documentation recorded in historical records to note there were Desposyni royal bloodline descendants from the brothers and sisters of Jesus. It is also possible and highly probable the Desposyni descendants could number between one and two million today; most not aware of their royal bloodlines and connection to Jesus. As intriguing as the story is, there is not one religious or historical record in existence that states Jesus was ever married.

The Gnostic Gospel of Philip in the Nag Hammadi Library is a third century writing which states that Mary Magdalene was a companion of Jesus. Some argue that the Greek word **Koinonos,** from which the word companion was translated, implies consort or marital partner. In a broad sense it could, but in the context the word was used most likely it meant associate or disciple of Jesus. Because the third century Gnostics viewed sex and marriage as defilement, it is doubtful the word meant consort or implied Jesus, who was viewed as their perfect risen Savior, was married.

We do acknowledge the Bible has been severely altered and it is generally agreed by religious theologians that possibly one-third of the original Bible text is missing. It could be argued because Jesus was a

Rabbi, he would be married as required by Jewish law; others argue this requirement came later. Even if Jesus were married and sired offspring, it would have been in accordance with Jewish thinking. Jesus did not teach that sex was defiling, in fact he sanctions marital unions by which the two become one flesh as God intended. A married Jesus would have affirmed his natural human side; not violated his divinity. Ascetical piety came later (second and third century) in the early church that had problems with these things. Therefore due to lack of documentation, this scenario cannot be proven at present.

As to the divinity of Christ, excluding the Qur'an, there is much more documentation, outside of the Bible, to support he was the son of God who died by crucifixion for the sins of the world, was resurrected on the third day and ascended into heaven then not. The third century Gnostic Gospels in the Nag Hammadi Library teach esoteric wisdom conveyed to them by a Divine risen Jesus. We must take into account those saints, maybe numbering in the hundreds, who were resurrected along with Christ; who right away appeared to many of their friends and family members as recorded in the Bible. The resurrected Christ also appeared to many thousands in Mesoamerica during ancient times. Oral traditions say he visited the Native American Indian tribes and the Tahitians in the South Pacific. As late as 900 AD., the Muskogean Indians say he came to dedicate their temple built in his honor and most likely lit the eternal sacred fire on top of the pyramid temple located in what is now called the Etowah Mounds in Cartersville, Georgia. Then, there are those many thousands of early Christian converts who believed in the divinity of Christ and in an upcoming future resurrection, therefore they humbly submitted themselves to be savagely torn apart and eaten alive by lions in the Roman Coliseum rather than deny their belief. They sealed their testimony with their blood. Throughout the ages and under different circumstances, thousands of other Christian martyrs have done the same.

What stirs men and women to die rather then deny their belief? The answer is simple......FAITH. This thing called Faith came about by eye witness accounts of the Savior's teachings, healings, resurrecting the dead, his death, his resurrection, and his ascension into heaven which spread like wildfire. Most of Christ's apostles were martyred for their belief in his resurrection. The apostle Peter and even his wife were both crucified for their belief. They could have denied Christ and perhaps lived; but they didn't because of their eye witness to the resurrected Christ; a truth they could not deny. From these eye witness accounts of the ministry of Christ and from the teachings of the early apostles who also were eye witnesses to the resurrected Christ, Christianity took root and spread. An eye witness to an event is a powerful testimony. By the unshakable eye witness testimonies of Christ, even to death by martyrdom, spurred other Christians, who did not have an eye witness, to believe or have Faith in the resurrection of Christ and to believe he was the son of God who died for sins of the world. Could a mere mortal man have instantly healed the sick and lame, restored sight to the blind, reattached an apostle's severed ear, turn water into wine, feed 5,000 people from a mere one basket of fish and bread at his sermon given on the Mount, raise the dead, walk on water, command the elements of a raging storm to cease and be still, and on the third day following crucifixion was resurrected from the dead? Could a mere mortal man have inspired millions, over a two thousand year time span, to endure to the end in Faith and follow him? We don't think so.

Back to the Da Vinci Code. We realize that Dan Brown's novel is a work of fiction based on an old legend that resurfaces from time to time about Mary Magdalene's close association with Jesus which has been interpreted as marriage. The plot thickens when he concludes the Knight Templars were hiding the truth about Jesus' family bloodlines, described as the Holy Grail, to protect the Desposyni descendants from assassins. It is a story woven around Mary Magdalene, whose womb became the cup bearer of the seed of the Holy Grail. Supposedly, the Templars were guarding her tomb to protect it from desecration and the Roman Church. During the course of the story, he has wrongly assumed the Templars were using the terms "the sacred feminine" and "sacred union" in reference to Mary Magdalene and her marriage to Jesus. In truth, the Templars were referencing the Spirit Earth and its union with the physical Earth. The spiritual creation has always been called sacred. When Native Americans say Mother Earth, they are referencing to the feminine spiritual creation or simply the Spirit Earth.....and they say she is sacred. According to ancient belief, all spiritual planets from higher universes are feminine gendered. They are considered sacred because they were created directly by God in higher spiritual universes or heavens. All planets in the physical universes are male gendered and were created directly by the son of God, under his Father's direction. Thus the term "the sacred feminine" used by the Templars was a way to speak of the Spirit Earth or even other planetary spiritual creations. The vaulted ceiling of Rosslyn Chapel, a Templar church in Scotland, is decorated with hundreds of five pointed stars which represent the many spiritual planetary creations or Spirit Earths located in higher spiritual dimensions. Of course, the Templars had discovered this knowledge from the Jerusalem Scrolls found in the hollow bronze columns of Solomon's Temple. They learned the spiritual creation or original creation had united with our physical planet in the days of Noah and thereafter the Templars called the event the "sacred union." Anciently the event was viewed as a sacred marriage sexual union between planets. Large stone penis's were erected on this male gendered planet (some still stand, pardon the pun) to attract and hold the feminine gendered Spirit Earth in a spiritual union. Archaeologists have found groves of these upright stone phalluses all over the world. They believe some sort of fertility rite was performed in those locations when in fact; it was a way to express belief in a sexual "sacred union" of planets between the feminine and masculine. The ancient mystery schools called the planetary union the "one mystery" which we re- named the Union of the Polarity. The Templars used the term "the sacred feminine" and "sacred union" to protect themselves, during the Inquisition, from being accused of teaching false doctrines and heresy by the Roman Church which was punishable by death. It was sort of a code…a Da Vinci Code, if you will, understandable only to the Templars. In this way, they did secretly protect and preserve the knowledge of the Union of the Polarity which was passed down to their later off shoots namely…..the Freemasons, The Knights of Columbus, and the Rosicrucians. These organizations knew the Zohar end time prophecy and knew the prophecy would be fulfilled just prior to the end time date of December 21, 2012; information found in the Jerusalem scrolls or Divine Book of Wisdom, scrolls preserved by Noah, and the Zohar, a writing preserved by the Jews which most likely was originally part of the Jerusalem Scrolls or one of the many scribed copies of the Divine Book of Wisdom given to the children of Noah. The Zohar prophecy was fulfilled with the publishing of *The Ark of Millions of Years* trilogy along with this fourth *Book of Updates* which restores the knowledge of the "one mystery" or "sacred union" (the Union of the Polarity) and the "sacred feminine" (the Spirit Earth) back to the world right before the imminent return of the Savior.

The Bermuda Triangle

Addition to Volume Three
Chapter The Tetrahedron

The Bermuda or Devil's Triangle, dubbed The Sea of Lost Ships, encompasses a large area in the western part of the North Atlantic Ocean. One tip of the triangle touches Bermuda; another tip of the triangle touches Miami, Florida, and the third tip of the triangle projects down to Puerto Rico.

Gian J. Quasar, author of **Into the Bermuda Triangle**, wrote the following:

"The list of eyewitnesses and survivors of extraordinary and unexplainable events in the Triangle is impressive. Airliner pilots have encountered unexplained and severe "jolts" and "pulses" out of nowhere that have sent big jumbos dashing to the surface in precipitous dives. Clouds have "come out of nowhere" and caused compasses to spin and engine RPMs to drop off. Objects and luminous phenomena have sped past. All electronic equipment has ceased for no known reason; cell phones, radios, navigational equipment, LORAN. There are dead spots, bending of space, loss of horizon, that have been reported by accomplished pilots and shipmasters, not cranks or crackpots."

Christopher Columbus was the first person to notice and document something strange in the Triangle and recorded it in his ships log book in October 11, 1492. He and his crew observed "strange dancing lights on the horizon," flames in the sky and bizarre compass bearings.

There is another place on Earth that has the same phenomena as the Bermuda Triangle but is not as well known because the Japanese view occurrences in the Triangle as natural events rather than supernatural events. It is called the Devil's Sea, Devil's Triangle, and Dragon's Triangle, located in a large area off the coast of Japan. The Bermuda Triangle and the Devil's Sea are the two places on Earth where the compass will point at true north rather than magnetic north. This compass variation can be as much as 20 degrees, enough to throw one catastrophically off course. To add to the mystery, scientists cannot find any measure of electromagnetism in the Triangles.

Lawrence David Kusche, author of **The Bermuda Triangle Mystery: Solved,** in 1975, came to the following conclusion as follows:

"Some believe the legend of the Bermuda Triangle is a manufactured mystery perpetuated by writers who either purposely or unknowingly made us believers of misconceptions, faulty reasoning, and sensationalism."

I agree with Kusche that many writers have fostered misconceptions mixed with sensationalism for profit but again, the testimonies of numerous credible survivors tell very similar stories of strange and unexplainable happenings in the Triangle that cannot be dismissed as coincidental. Over a period of 100 years, 1000 persons have disappeared in the Triangle and are presumed dead. That breaks down to 10 persons a year; not a significant number for the large area involved. However, it is not the number that is significant but rather the manner in which they disappeared. So what is going on here?

This is what we believe is happening in the Triangles. Two of the eight Dual Star tetrahedrons project to the Earth's crust in those locations. As described in this chapter, the tetrahedrons are the engines, Charkas, or power points of the Earth. Where ever those eight tetrahedrons project to in the Earth's crust, there is high earthquake and volcanic activity that can include tectonic movement in those areas. The power points are energy points or vortexes filled with the spiraling Life Force low-density electromagnetic energy. The best and most well known example of a strong vortex on land is Stonehenge. The site was chosen because it is a large very powerful land vortex. Because vortexes are filled with Life Force energy, the ancients considered them sacred and often referred to them as Dragon Lairs, the dragon or serpent being the universal symbol of the Life Force energy, especially if the Life Force energy emanated from a cave. Reference to the Devil's Sea as the Dragon's Triangle reinforces this ancient belief of a powerful underwater vortex filled with Life Force energy.

Powerful undersea vortexes behave differently than powerful land vortexes because water is the natural and best conductor of the spiraling Life Force electromagnetic energy than land. Water amplifies the strength of the undersea vortexes many times over, making them super power points; whereas powerful land vortexes never achieve super stardom because they lack large body water amplification. Land vortexes are often found near rivers and streams in caves but the water volume is insufficient for super stardom. Energy swirls in vortexes like a hurricane. Survivors of the Triangles often report seeing the seas swirling violently in a circle, like water going down a drain, and clouds swirling above in violent circles, exactly as a vortex would do. The vortexes of the Triangles can best be described as acting like the Old Faithful geyser in Yellowstone National Park. When the underground water pressure is sufficient, there will be a tremendous eruption. So it is with undersea vortexes. When the Life Force energy or low-density electromagnetic energy builds up around the tetrahedron power point in the Earth's magma, it cannot easily escape due to the tremendous pressure of ocean water above. When the Life Force builds up sufficient pressure, it will explode like an undersea volcano blasting into the air; then the water will amplify the explosion many times over. Unlike Old Faithful whose eruptions are predictable, nearly hourly, the Triangle vortexes are unpredictable and appear to take a long time, many years, between eruptions. This makes the phenomena difficult to study from a scientific stand point.

When a Triangle vortex begins to activate, methane gas escapes to the ocean surface, bubbling like a witch's caldron. The methane gives the water an eerie underwater green glow and when it escapes into the air, the air will have a greenish glow. When the Life Force energy blasts into the air, long air currents, shooting upward in a spiraling motion, will have a reddish glow that appear to be flickering flames of fire. If a ship is unfortunate enough to be caught in a bubbling methane caldron, the surface tension of the water will change; the ship will lose its buoyancy and sink like a rock in a matter of minutes without warning

During a Triangle release of Life Force energy into the atmosphere, a fog will suddenly appear that blends the horizon to the water surface or in other words one cannot see where the sky is separate from the water surface; all is fog. The fog is a low-density misty white hyperspace energy that is created by the release of circular (swirling) Life Force magnetic energy into the atmosphere which then collides or crosses into the surface electric force field of Earth. If airplanes, caught up in these white out fogs, have a surface charge with an electric field normal to the surface should encounter a circular magnetic field crossing the electric field, then there is a radial curvature of space created toward the top and bottom of the craft. This pulls the hyper-space energy over and around the body of the craft. A powerful vortex eruption can produce a larger and stronger magnetic field sufficient enough to produce enough space-time curvature to move the craft into another dimension. Slightly weaker eruptions can create time warps rather than dimensional changes. The discharge of magnetic energy from the vortex interferes with navigational and electrical instruments causing them to mal-function. With loss of navigational instruments, pilots become disoriented in the white fog and become lost.

We believe this is what happened to the five aircraft of flight 19 on December 5, 1945. These aircraft were Grunman Avenger Torpedo Bombers on an authorized navigational training flight, departing from the U.S. Naval Air Station in Fort Lauderdale, Florida, into the Bermuda Triangle. The U.S. Navy doesn't believe that the Triangle exists so there is no designation on their maps defining this area. Around 4 pm of that training flight, the flight instructor radioed that they were experiencing mal-function of their compasses and were lost. Due to static and radio interference no contact could be established with the planes. They simply disappeared without a trace in spite of an extensive search operation. A search aircraft was lost during the operation on the same day. It may have exploded as an oil slick was found in the vicinity of its search operation and a ship in the area reported seeing an explosive fireball in the sky. During a powerful vortex eruption, Flight 19 may have flown into another dimension and were unable to return. Can living humans survive in another dimension? Yes, if they are translated and as long as they remain in a state of translation, death has no power over them. In our opinion, the process that brings about translation may be the interaction of Life Force swirling magnetic energy on the electric force field surrounding human beings in sufficient strength to raise their vibrational level high enough to endure higher dimensions. As strange as it may seem, this same process described above may have moved Flight 19 into another dimension by "rapture" via a wormhole. We will compare it to 2012 when the Spirit Earth will be removed from the Temporal Earth by a similar process via the Ouroboros portal wormhole. Many pilots who have survived Triangle events tell of their compasses spinning wildly, lost of radio contact, and flying through what appears to be a time warp. What should have been an hour of flying time in reality have been only minutes. These pilots were lucky that the vortex discharge was not strong enough to move their craft into another dimension. Is this provable science? Quiet possibly, yes! The new science of Hyper Dimensional Quantum Physics best supports this theory.

Then, there is the Atlantis crystal. If the Atlantis crystal exists in the Bermuda Triangle vortex, as many believe, it could be activated by Life Force energy during a vortex eruption. If anything, the crystal could amplify the vortex eruption to the extent that it would open a wormhole or portal into the next dimension. This of course is pure speculation as no proof has surfaced that the crystal exists. However, the Bermuda Triangle vortex appears to be the most powerful in the world so this lends some credence that the crystal may exist which can amplify vortex eruptions. A strong vortex eruption, coupled with crystal amplification, could open worm holes or portals into the next dimension. A weaker vortex eruption, coupled with crystal amplification, may produce only time warps.

Volume Three Additions

Chapter: The Other Worlds
Page 214
At end of first paragraph...add the following:

But are we actually in hell? Yes, it appears that we are living in a degree of hell. The Sumerians, Assyrians, Babylonians, Egyptians, and Hebrews all believed in seven layers or dimensions of hell. Volume One, page 58, gives the name of each hell universe or dimension from the Hebrew ideology. Erez/Aretz or the ancient name of "Earth" meaning the Temporal Earth is listed as a second degree of hell. Volume One, pages 466 and 467, identifies the name and location of Erez/Aretz as being the lowest earth (lowest level of earths) in the physical universe. From this perspective, the physical or temporal universe called Assiyah is the first named degree of hell called Adamah meaning "ground or physical." By being located in a physical hell universe, all Temporal Earths become second degrees of hell; degrees being different than levels or layers. The Mesoamericans all believed hell had nine layers, levels or compartments. In view of this light on the creation, it is quite possible that there are two lower hell universes below this present hell universe which could be sub-divided into three separate divisions within each universe. That would make six hell universes below us. Add our hell universe to those below; it adds up to seven hells, layers, or dimensions. Within each level or dimension of hell universes are various degrees. Maybe there are more divisions as the Mesoamericans believed? The Pyramid of Inscriptions, Pakal's tomb, is built in nine levels which represent the nine levels of hell or Xibalba that he has descended into.

The Buddha teaches that everything on the Temporal Earth is burning with the fires of ambition, lust, greed, desire, pleasure, happiness, etc; everything is on fire. It is not combustible fire but a spiritual fire designed to refine, purify, teach, or punish, depending on our karma. Therefore according to ancient Judaism, Buddhism, and Hinduism ideology, in a sense we are living in a second degree of a burning hell fire.

Regardless of the number of hell universes or even the number of degrees of hells, remember that Earth is a co-dimensional planet. Heaven or the Spirit Earth, which is ruled over by God, united with this planet. Therefore we are living in a degree of hell and heaven at the same time. The Spirit Earth is veiled or invisible to our natural eyes but we do feel its effect on us. That is why some days are simply pure heaven which makes us feel so good to be alive. Then there are days all hell appears to break loose that puts us in turmoil and torment. We are experiencing samples of the two dimensions to see which god we choose to follow.

Page 212 correction second paragraph in The Other Worlds chapter:
11ᵗʰ line should read:

By lowering their already lowered vibrational rate, they could materialize into human form and by raising their vibrational rate they could disappear into thin air without a trace.

Page 381 correction second paragraph in Update chapter:
8ᵗʰ line.....should read:

There is evidence that other Yucatán cities such as Tulum, Chicana, Ek Balam, Itzamna, and even further north to El Tajin, located above LaVenta, became Christianized and converted to the new religion of Quetzelcoatl, the feathered serpent.

Page 367 Figure 150
Add to bottom:

Note: Pictured are a white Toltec Indian (Nephite) and a dark skin Nonoalca Maya Indian (Lamanite) eating of the fruit of the tree. In this case it is cocoa pods from which chocolate is made.

Page 143 Figure 77
Beneath the Library of Congress window add the following:

There are a series of twelve windows down each side of the front entrance; each window representing an Age.

Please check out the book's website as book three's illustrations are already installed on the website so that you may see them in higher resolution and in color for those that are in color.

Maya UFO Pilots

Update to chapter: The Other Worlds

Volume Three
Page 229 end of last paragraph
Maya UFO pilots

When the year 2008 passed without the Maya UFO pilots returning to remove the modern day Maya, I called my remote viewers to ask them to do another remote viewing to see why the Maya had not been removed by them in 2008. My friends obliged me, did the remote viewing, and made contact with the Maya UFO pilots. The following is their reply back:

They came to remove the Maya in 2008, however, there were many more Maya now than they had calculated. It would require more space craft to do the job. They reassured the remote viewers that the Maya would be removed, probably in the year 2011, but definitely before the catastrophic events awaiting planet Earth due to occur in the year of 2012.

Their reply seemed reasonable enough to me however, I still remained a skeptic until the following information recently surfaced. The Hopi Native American Indian tribe believes the same thing! They say that in ancient times, beings from other worlds came to visit them in "ships without wings" which they further describe as wingless, dome-shaped crafts. These beings walked among them for a period of time. The

Hopi learned many things from these off worlders about the cosmos, including the coming cataclysm awaiting Earth which they call the Day of Purification. Before the aliens departed in their UFO's, they made a promise to the Hopi that they would return and remove them from this planet, either before or on the Day of Purification. The tradition of a flying shield also appears in an ancient petroglyph, found near Winslow, Arizona. The rock carving shows a triangular delta-winged spacecraft which is identical in description to the 1997 Phoenix sightings in Arizona. The Hopi say the Kachinas were spiritual beings who could materialize into human form. In addition the Kachinas were sometimes known to marry and mate with Hopi women. Their elders continue to watch and wait for the UFO's that will take them to other planets in this universe. The Hopi call these aliens Kachinas. I call them the Nephilim.

This piece of information caught my attention because it is another verification of the same story from two apparent different sources. It certainly bears watching. My remote viewing friends had no knowledge of the Hopi beliefs or the Aztec prophecy of the sons of the Sixth Sun. It does suggest that the Hopi are related to the Aztec or had roots in ancient Mexico because they speak the Shoshonean dialect which is a Uto-Aztecan language. Some researchers believe they are descendants of the Totonacas who were once part of the Aztec triple alliance. The Day of Purification and December 21, 2012, the Maya last day, are certainly one and the same.

The Fall of Babylon the Great

Update to the Update chapter
Volume Three
Last paragraph, page 387
Prophecies

It appears another prophecy was fulfilled in November 2008. That is when the world's economy collapsed. It was a global collapse that started in the United States and spread like the Domino effect, seemingly overnight. The World economy was described in the Bible by John the Revelator as Babylon the Great. In our opinion, Babylon the Great fell in November 2008 as the collapse happened globally. According to John's revelation, the fall of Babylon the Great was due to happen either on or a few years after the *harvest* at the last day. As written in Volume Two and Three of our trilogy, two scenarios were presented as to how and when this could happen. We thought possibly the year 2012 or sometime after the opening of the Seventh Seal, so 2008 caught us off guard completely. The economy of Earth never recovered from that collapse. The bureaus and departments of the United States ordered Congress—yes that is the true chain of authority in Washington—to write checks they could not possibly cover. There are only two reasons why anyone, including governments, write bad checks. They either expect they will never have to make the check good, or they are expecting a windfall profit by which they can beat the check to the bank. We report to you that the latter never happened. The soiling of the faith and credit of the United States was the fall of Babylon the Great. As we pen these words, the American dollar is barely worth the paper it's printed on. In fact, there is a global push as we outlined in *Volume Two – The Watchers* to complete the Alchemy design by turning simple ones and zeroes into gold. Plastic is rapidly replacing cash. Banks have placed daily and transactional limits on how much a person can purchase with their plastic, thus mitigating their exposure of being caught without cash in the bank to cover the transaction and to prevent an economic tsunami similar to the massive withdrawals of 1929. FDIC membership is a rouse, and protects only the first $100,000 of any account. Even then, the bank only has to return the principle, and they can take up to ten years to complete the process.

In Revelation, it implies that the fall of Babylon the Great occurs after the opening of the Seventh Seal. However, it may not be the case. Biblical scholars know that John's revelations were not given in chronological order; they jump around. This jumping around has created confusion and inability to understand the proper time frame of the revelation. Therefore, the Fall of Babylon the Great could happen anytime. John makes the point that he saw it happen sometime in the future by recording it in Revelation.

In Volume Two, we wrote the fall of Babylon the Great would most likely happen from the cataclysmic effects of 2012. In Volume Three we presented a possible second scenario as happening sometime after 2012 when the Seventh Seal was opened. It now appears that this prophetic event happened in November 2008.

What is even more amazing is that your authors, along with Rolf A.F.Witzshe whose editorial analysis was based on the ideas and presentations by the American Economist Lyndon H. LaRouche Jr., written in 2002, accurately predicted the economic woes and collapse of the global economy at least five years before it happened! Readers are referred to Volume Two in *The End Times* chapter, pages 184-189, and in the chapter, *The Watchers*, for the story. It is there in black and white. Prophecy doesn't get any better than this....to accurately predict the Fall of Babylon the Great is beyond phenomenal to say the least!

The interesting thing is that I haven't heard one preacher preach a sermon on this or correlate the collapse of the World's economy to John's revelation. Please add prophecy number 14 to the list (10 in Volume Two pp. 203-204, and 3 more in Volume Three, p.387) as follows:

14. In the fall of 2008, Babylon the Great fell when the World's economy collapsed globally.

If Babylon the Great truly fell, then this so-called "recession" is worse than what we have been led to believe and it is here to stay. The economy will improve some but it will not fully recover before the End of the Age. People have lost jobs, homes, possessions, healthcare, and money in the stock market. Europe and Asia are even worse off than the US. At the beginning of President Obama's term, he sounded an urgent warning that quick financial action was necessary to save this country and even all that we can do, it may not be enough. His "bailout" stimulus plan, which included the rescuing of financial institutions and companies with billions of tax payers dollars, was an unprecedented effort to reverse collapse. There is no historic precedent or any comparison with previous situations on which to base or solve this crisis. In other words we are sailing unchartered waters. Will Obama's stimulus plan work or is it too little too late? He recently said in an address to the nation that the recession appears to be leveling out and correcting itself. Then, the new jobless statistics rose to 10.2 per cent. It is estimated that those who have given up looking for jobs and those who are working low paying part time jobs fall in the 17.5 per cent range. Only time will tell if the stimulus plan works. Fasten your seat belt because we haven't hit the bottom yet; the worse is still to come as there probably will be another fallout phase of economic collapse.

According to Revelation, the Fall of Babylon the Great precedes tribulation. One pre-tribulation prophecy that has not been fulfilled is Iran's and Russia's attack on Israel. We wrote in Volume Two, Israel stands alone maybe because Israel strikes first to defend herself. No county comes to her defense. This scenario certainly could happen any time because Israel has threatened to take out Iran's nuclear making plants in order to defend herself. But why does Israel stand alone? This question may have been answered recently. Israel is standing alone now. Her long standing European allies and the United States have distanced themselves from her politically over her Palestinian policy. Peace making efforts are at a stalemate. For the first time in Israel's history, she is standing alone. The stage is being set for an attack on Israel. All these events were recorded by John in Revelation. If we are right in the time line of events prophesized in Revelation, the attack on Israel is prophetically imminent and will happen before 2012.

Nostradamus

Michele Nostradamus (1503-1566) really needs no introduction. Unless you are an alien from another planet, have lived under a rock, or resided in a cave somewhere as an ascetic hermit, you have heard of Nostradamus. Born in France, he was a brilliant man ahead of his times. The totality of his knowledge was expressed as a philosopher, humanist, poet, linguist, and man of science. He was a French physician and surgeon. In addition, he dedicated himself to the study of astronomy and astrology. He spoke French, Italian, Spanish, Greek, and Latin. As a poet, he is best known for his prophetic quatrains which have endured to this day. Although he is called a 16th century prophet, Michele refrained from the use of that term and maintained he was more of a clairvoyant. Nevertheless, so great was his esoteric and astrological knowledge, others consulted him about the future. Among his many consultants was the widow of Henry 11, Catherine de Medici, who wanted to know about the future of her sons and the future of the popes. She was so impressed with his knowledge; she showered him with gifts and granted him a pension. In 1564, she and her entire court visited him in Salon whereon Nostradamus presented her with a talisman engraved with esoteric symbols

Nostradamus came about his esoteric knowledge legitimately through his Jewish father, who was a scholar of the ancient Kabbalah

(Zohar) and from his paternal grandfather, Giovanni Nostradonna, a Jew from Sicily. His maternal Jewish grandfather, Jean, was a renowned esotericist and kabbalist who served as councilor to King Rene. For certain, he inherited his esoteric knowledge from his forebears, including the many esoteric prophetic text books, which some may have been scrolls. At some point in time, Nostradamus explicitly states that he destroyed the prophetic texts; most likely because he was a practicing Catholic and to avoid retribution from the Church during the Inquisition. Some have speculated that he deliberately circulated the story around to protect himself and merely hid the texts. Regardless, he really no longer needed the ancient texts as Kabbalah was deeply ingrained in him; it flowed through his veins. The root of Kabbalah lies in the ancient text called the *Zohar*. It is unfortunate that he destroyed those prophetic texts, if indeed he did, as they may have been more complete then the *Zohar* version we have today. It is clear that Nostradamus derived much of his prophetic knowledge from the *Zohar*, therefore he knew about the Union of the Polarity, 2012, dimensions, and parallel worlds, as did the Knight Templars who had built, during the 11th-14th centuries, the heavily encoded French cathedrals with the same esoteric knowledge derived from identical *Zohar* manuscripts which were scribed from the original *Zohar* texts in possession of the Templars. We can now safely conclude the *Zohar* manuscripts were once part of the Divine Book of Wisdom, manuscripts preserved by Noah and later found, by the Knight Templars, in the hollow bronze columns of Solomon's Temple (pictured on front cover of this book).

Michele Nostradamus is most famous for his extraordinary poetic cryptic prophetic quatrains which he wrote in the last nineteen years of his life following the deaths of his first wife and two sons from the dreaded, highly contagious bubonic black plague. So cryptic are the quatrains, they can be interpreted to mean almost anything. For centuries the public and scholars have been fascinated by his quatrains; each trying to decode the hidden cryptic messages. Nostradamus cleverly chose to veil his prophecies in this manner to protect him from accusations of practicing magic, witchcraft, and heresy for which the punishment was severe. He wrote his quatrains with great dynamic flair using symbolism and symbolic words to describe future events in far off places, naming cities and powerful leaders who were born years, even centuries after his death. Many of his prophecies and predictions have come true. His quatrains seem to predict World Wars 1 and 11, Hitler, the Civil War, the Kennedy killings, Civil rights, racial strife, integration, illicit drug use, moral decay, food shortages, famine, heart transplants, the rise of China's influence on the world economy, earthquakes, natural disasters, moon landings, and space exploration. It is evident Nostradamus meant his quatrains to be prophetic and not just empty rhetoric for amusement because at the end of his quatrains, in his own words, he states...... " Then is fulfilled and ends my prophecy."

Recently a previously lost manuscript, believed to be written by Nostradamus, was discovered in the Italian National Library in Rome. The English translation was published in 1998. The work is titled *Nostradamus The Lost Manuscript* by Ottavio Cesare Ramotti. The book contains 80 hand drawn symbolic pictures that are prophetic. The History Channel aired a segment on the lost manuscript where several of the symbolic pictures were shown and interpreted by Nostradamus experts. We do not fully agree with their interpretations and would like to offer our analysis. First, the prophecies and symbolic pictures in this book deal mainly with the Popes of The Restoration. We are only interested in two of the pictures that deal with 2012, namely plates numbered in the book as no. 70 and no. 72, pictured below.

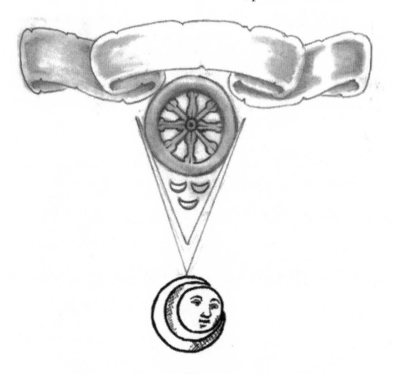

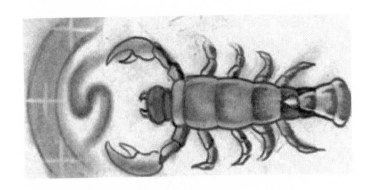

Figure 4: Plate 70.

Figure 5: Plate 72

Please note that these are my own hand drawn copies of the plates. Plate no. 70 shows a ribbon or partial moebius strip with a wheel of time or destiny underneath it. The ribbon is a stylized omega sign or upside down U which has always meant the end time date of December 21, 2012. It is pictured on the front cover of this book. Inside the wheel of time or destiny, which really represents a stylized Earth, is found the 8 spokes or rays of the three-dimensional, dual star tetrahedron which radiate from a small center circle that contains a dot. The dot within a circle is a symbol of Precession. Thus, the wheel of time is referring to the end of Precession or Great Year which ends on December 21, 2012. Beneath the wheel of time hang the united Earths. The spiritual Earth has a face which represents Mother Earth or the sacred feminine. Above the united Earth symbol are three crescent moons, inside a chevron, which represent the three days of darkness during Earths' transit through the dark rift. The united Earths are attached by a chevron ribbon to the wheel of time that indicates movement or transit and the three crescent moons indicate the length of time of three days in darkness in the dark rift. Below the united Earths is a spiral which represents the spiraling vortex/portal opening contained in the dark rift; the three stars represent the three day transit when Earth is under the astrological sign of Cancer represented by a crab disguised as a lobster.

Plate no 72 shows an extended connected moebius strip as in a circle which has dual meaning. This symbolizes the cycle of one eternal round (Precession) and symbolizes the transdimensional portal (Ouroboros) through which the Spirit Earth will pass into the 4th dimension. Inside the moebius strip, representing 2012 is the wheel of destiny or stylized Earth, now empty of the three-dimensional, dual star tetrahedron. Only one small two-dimensional, six spoked or six rayed star remains. The true Earth, the original creation or Spirit Earth (Mother Earth) is now positioned in the Ouroboros to return to another dimension leaving behind its physical counterpart, the planet we know as Earth. In other words, the dual star tetrahedron has separated. One Earth, the true Earth, has ended its existence in the physical universe and moved into the 4th dimension through the dark rift portal by a process called "rapture." The single star tetrahedron, remaining inside the wheel of time or stylized Earth, represents the physical Earth left behind.

Below the moebius strip is a figure holding an empty open book for all to see. The figure is Nostradamus with the Cartesian spatial coordinates of x, y, and z, visible on his forehead which symbolizes the Spirit Earth now departed from this three dimensional plane and a way of escape from the cataclysm awaiting the physical earth and those left behind. Cartesian coordinates are used to define the geometry of higher-dimensional spaces. In other words, it is a pre- tribulation "rapture" of not only the Spirit Earth but of the qualified righteous people to go. Below the figure are two smaller moebius strips that indicate this event will take place at the end of Precession or 2012. The smallest moebius ribbon is over the deer. The symbol of a deer is often used to represent Christ. We can interpret this as… Christ teaching the *harvest* events due to happen at end of the age or December 21, 2012; his audience being women, who were probably pagan worshippers, but who represent the world. The empty book held up by Nostradamus symbolizes the end of time for the true Earth, the original creation, or Spirit Earth in this dimension.

Nostradamus was a noted physician and healer during outbreaks of the black plague. It is reported that he saved many lives during the epidemics but unfortunately was not able to save the lives of his first wife and two sons; a burden of guilt he carried for the rest of his life. After their deaths, he wandered from place to place for eight solitary years until he finally settled in Solon, France, and married a second wife. Nostradamus confides that during this grief stricken eight years, he became more clairvoyant which enabled him to write his famous prophetic quatrains. He would see in flashes, what was to come in the future. To the end of his life, Nostradamus denied any association with knowledge derived from ancient "mystery" texts but the evidence shows he was influenced, from the cradle up, by the teachings of his kabalistic forebears. Thus, his knowledge from the ancient texts, combined with teachings from his forebears, was mixed with his Catholic views and personal tragedy; in turn it compounded his gift of clairvoyance which produced his amazing prophetic quatrains.

Therefore we can conclude with certainty, the two above symbolic pictures indicate that Nostradamus was knowledgeable of the events associated with 2012; knowledge passed down to him from his Jewish forebears and from the esoteric *Zohar* texts he inherited from them. Plate no. 70 shows what is to happen at the end of the age and the message of plate no. 72 is a warning to prepare for 2012.

Update to Volume One

Balloon Universes

On pages 60, 130 and 523 of Volume One, I drew pictures of the theorized multi layered stacked up balloon universes that float in outer darkness. Using descriptions found in the Bible, Book of Moses and other ancient texts, I was able to draw them. I believe that I, E.J. Clark, am the first person to advance this theory in Volume One of the trilogy which was published about five years ago however; the idea was conceived of several years prior to publication of the book during the writing of the text. Recently, I was surprised to find others who were working on this same theory along with parallel universes. The notion of parallel universes is not new but the science involved in trying to detect and prove their existence is new.

In the June 09 edition of *Astronomy* magazine there is a wonderful six page article illustrated with marvelous color pictures written by Steve Nadis titled **How We Could See Another Universe** that lends credence to my theory. His opening remarks state "Our universe may form one bubble of many in a vast multiverse. Cosmologists are now searching for signs of another bubble universe colliding with ours." His article envisions single layer universes floating in bubbles in space whereas I theorized the great universes are multilayered stacked up like balloons floating in outer space or outer darkness. His bubble universes are very similar to my balloon universes. Steve Nadis questions whether or not there is any danger of these bubble or balloon universes colliding with ours.

In my opinion, there is no danger of any of these universes colliding with each other ever. Outer darkness or outer space is a vast area beyond our comprehension. It lies outside the perimeters of our universe and has no bounds; it is infinite. The rules of time and space do not apply there however there does exist a kind of hyper-time where events can occur in a logical sequence. It is a realm outside the time continuum where the concept of time does not exist at all and the expression "eternity of eternities" is beyond even such hyper-time. Furthermore our laws of physics do not apply there. Outer darkness or outer space does not expand because it is infinite or endless. I believe these stacked up multilayered balloon universes float and slowly rotate in this endless space in a fixed position far from one another therefore there is no danger of them ever colliding. Expansion occurs only within the universes themselves. The distance between balloon or bubble universes is great enough to allow for expansion within the universes without collision into other balloon or bubble universes.

Steve writes that cosmologists are searching for signs of another bubble universe. With our present technology, I believe that it is impossible to see signs of another bubble or balloon universe from Earth's vantage point because they are simply too far away. An ancient text called the *Zohar* states that one would have to travel for 500 years, presumably at the speed of light, to reach the edge of our universe. Unless we can discover a wormhole to take us to the edge, it will be impossible to see them. But, if and when we can finally manage to enter the outer space or outer darkness and look around we may find millions, if not billions, of distant balloon or bubble universes floating in fixed suspension and slowly rotating much like looking at distant galaxies in our own universe.

I conclude that outer space or outer darkness is just that. It is infinite dark space outside our own universe but not empty. I believe that it is home to countless other multilayered stacked up balloon universes. In fact, string theory better supports a multilayered or multidimensional balloon universe rather than a single layered bubble universe. According to sacred scriptures, the wicked who will not repent, even after spending one thousand years in hell, will not inherit any kingdom of glory but are cast into outer darkness. Origen taught that the wicked in outer darkness would be devoid of intelligence, and will possess bodies stripped of all glory. According to the Gnostic Christian Gospel of Philip and the Pastor Hermas, those cast into outer darkness are those souls of men who have made a conscious and specific choice to rebel against God. In outer darkness they will languish powerless in this state forever.

Recently the History Channel presented an excellent animated film on parallel universes and bubble nucleation universes that further validates my theory on balloon universes comprised of stacked up parallel multidimensional universes. Two of the world's top theoretical physicists, Dr. Michio Kaku and Dr. Clifford Johnson who specialize in string and quantum field theories, were presenting and narrating their theories in the documentary film. Of particular interest to me was an upcoming experiment to prove the existence of other dimensions as presented in the documentary film. The experiment involved atom smashing in particle accelerators and then measuring the amount of energy produced from the smashed atoms. If some of the calculated amount of energy appears to be missing or unaccounted for, then scientists will know it crossed into another dimension.

I'm thrilled that cosmologists are now searching for these balloon or bubble universes because there are others out there who apparently agree with my theory and believe there is a good possibility that they do exist. If I am not the first to come up with the theory of balloon or bubble universes, then we all arose simultaneously and independent of each other's findings by coincidence. I do think however, that I was the first to write, illustrate and describe them in a published book.

The Twin Feathered Serpents

Further research indicates the concept of dualism originated with the Sumerian Enki; the Christian counterpart of Lucifer. His concept of dualism is based on scriptural truth as "there is an opposition in all things" (2 Nephi 2:11). Examples of dualistic opposites or opposing forces in nature are hot and cold, day and night, and male and female.

Likewise Enki's version of the creation story and origin of the twin or two headed serpent is founded on biblical teachings in Genesis where God curses the serpent by putting "enmity between thee and the woman, and between thy seed and her seed; it shall bruise thy head, and thou shalt bruise his heel" (Genesis 3:15).

Feathered serpents were creator gods, as conceived by Enki. He taught Enlil (Christian equivalent to Christ) was his twin brother and they both were feathered serpents who shared in the creation in all of Earth and of man. They were the two creator gods symbolized by the two headed feathered serpent, sons of Anu (Lord of Heaven or God). The biblical reference in Genesis to a serpent tempting Eve to "eat of the fruit" was probably just that, a wise spiritual being symbolized as a serpent and not an actual snake. Another analogy; a "wise old serpent" is a very intelligent spiritual being.

In the Sumerian texts, Enki plotted to overthrow his father and become like the "Most High" God. This story is also based on biblical scripture as reported in Isaiah 14:13-14 when Lucifer declared he would ascend into heaven, exalt his throne above the stars of God, and would be like the most High. It was Lucifer's plot to take over heaven; instead he was defeated in battle and cast out into this dimension or universe. Not to be outdone when his plot failed, Enki conceived another plan to take control of this planet. By mixing a little truth with deception through the use of dualism, Enki cunningly elevated himself to the equal of Enlil. Thereafter, both gods were worshipped with equal status. Each god had his own attributes attached to him. Enlil was the god of day, peace, life, and goodness; Enki was the god of night, war, death, and trickery. Both gods were deemed necessary to keep the forces of nature and the cosmic forces of the universe in sync. From Sumeria, the concept of dualism spread into Babylonia, Egypt, Iran, Iraq, Ireland, England, Peru, Bolivia, Ecuador, Chile, Mesoamerica, and the Mississippian culture in North America. It was later defined by Asians as the Yin and Yang using male and female to represent dualism. Eventually Enki was dethroned by the assembly of gods in favor of his son, Marduk, as recorded in the Sumerian texts, but the concept of dualism had already taken root and spread; only names were changed.

The following is a Maya account of the creation story. Note, Tezcatlipoca and Quetzalcoatl are the Aztec names given to these entities. At present their Olmec names are unknown. The account begins with a great war in Heaven where two brothers battled,

Tezcatlipoca (Enki) and Quetzalcoatl (Enlil). In the ensuing battle Quetzalcoatl hit Tezcatlipoca over the head with a club (bruised his head) causing Tezcatlipoca to tumble into the ocean. When he emerged from the ocean, Tezcatlipoca was transformed into a jaguar. Thereafter, the jaguar became the Mesoamerican symbol of Tezcatlipoca who ruled the underworld abode of the dead. The name Tezcatlipoca means smoking mirror. He is usually portrayed with a mirror attached to his head or chest. His mirror enabled him to see the present and future, influence men, perform sorcery, and devise trickery. We now believe the picture on page 109 in Volume Two is that of Tezcatlipoca because the helmet like hat has now been identified as his smoking mirror. The name Quetzalcoatl means Lord or "most precious feathered serpent." He was known as the Lord of Penitence.

In Mesoamerica, the two headed serpent first appears in the capitol city of the Olmecs, now called La Venta, Mexico, located in La Venta Park, pictured below on altar 4. This altar is heavily encoded with hidden meaning.

Figure 6: Altar 4

When one shades the top part of the altar, the two headed feathered serpent images appear face to face with noses touching and tongues crossing each others which symbolize harmonic union of the two forces; each being equal for the cosmos to remain stable. The images are shown as part of a sky band which signifies these two forces are cosmic in nature.

Figure 7: Altar 4 top section.

There is no mistake in our interpretation of this monument because nearby is a stone identified as altar 5 (not pictured). On its right side, the figure to the right is carved the image of Tezcatlipoca wearing his smoking mirror hat. He is holding an active were jaguar baby in his arms. This child would have been his son and perhaps had died and is now in the underworld with his father. Note the figure to the right of the Tezcatlipoca image is damaged and unreadable. Image can be seen on Google; just Google altar 5 La Venta.

When one removes the shaded section, the image of a jaguar appears. Below the sky band is a cave with a jaguar priest holding on to a chain like rope. Surrounding the cave entrance are images of water flowing out of openings. The images have eroded with time and are dim to see, nevertheless this altar honors Tezcatlipoca. The jaguar priest sits in the entrance of the opening to the underworld watery abyss. On the side of the altar is a captive person, perhaps a king, held captive by the chain like rope which indicates this person has died and is being held captive by the bands of death. By holding on to the rope, the jaguar priest shows he is acting as a priest representative of the lord of the underworld and lord of the dead, Tezcatlipoca. In the La Venta Olmec archeological site, a large pyramid was built in honor of Quetzalcoatl which indicates Quetzalcoatl was the principal god they chose to follow.

According to Olmec myth, the People of the Rubber or Olmecs (Book of Mormon Jaredites) were a race of giants who were created by the mating of a woman and a jaguar. They were called the Quinametintzoculithicxime or Quinametzin for short. Does this sound familiar? Tezcatlipoca was Nephilim. The babies and adults spawned by this union are called were jaguars because they possess features of both human and jaguar; the jaguar being the symbol of Tezcatlipoca. Many Olmec pottery pieces, jade pieces, statues, and stone altar carvings show were jaguar infants and adults.

Figure 8: Were jaguar adult statue with almond shaped eyes, down turned lips, flame eyebrows, pleated hair do, and crossed-bars quincunx icon on chest and waist wrap. The four points of the quincunx symbolizes life, breath, spirit, wind; the center fifth point symbolizes death. These were aspects of the twin serpent gods. Statue found in San Lorenzo Tenochtitlan museum.

Figure 9: Were jaguar infant amulet

As written in Volume One, pp. 361-362, the giants were destroyed, and their civilization came to an end as a result of great calamites and punishments from heaven for some grave sins that they had committed. We speculate the sins were the cross breeding of Nephilim with humans which produced the giant Quinametzin race and choosing to follow Tezcatlipoca instead of Quetzalcoatl. They became an evil corrupted race. Ixtlilxochitl, the Mexican historian, gives the date of their destruction as 240 BC.

By the time of the destruction of the Olmec giants, the dual serpent religion had spread over most of Mesoamerica, ancient northern South America, and even into the Mississippian culture of North America.

The Guatemalan Chichimec Quiche Maya have a different slant on dualism as presented in their sacred book, the *Popol Vuh*. Dualism in the cosmic creative forces expressed as Serpent Twins evolved into twin boys, Xbalenque and Hunapu, who really were gods and who were the sons of the Heart of Heaven or God. The book contains many myths associated with them. Practically all cultures had a name for the twin forces (see Volume One, pp.263-264). But, the rest of the Mesoamerican tribes worshipped both gods equally until the appearances of the pre-mortal and post-mortal Christ (Quetzalcoatl, Virachocha, Kukulcan, Itzamna, etc.) in ancient Sumeria and in the Americas. He taught the Plan of Salvation, taught against human sacrifice, and taught there was only one way into the highest heaven....through him. He brought division in religious thinking. Thereafter, the people had to choose which god to follow, the lord of the underworld or the lord of heaven. Religious division brought religious wars. It appears the ancient Mesoamerican cities of Tula and Teotihuacán became unrighteous, abandoned the teachings of Quetzalcoatl, and chose to follow Tezcatlipoca. They wanted to reinstate human sacrifice, a demand of Tezcatlipoca. This demand was expressed in Mesoamerican art as a jaguar eating the hearts of men. Around the fourth century, in Teotihuacán, a temple was built to Tezcatlipoca directly in front of the temple of Quetzalcoatl that dramatically over shadows the prominence it once held which indicates the Teotihuacán's chose to follow Tezcatlipoca. All that remains of the temple to Tezcatlipoca is a large platform now called the Adosada Platform. In Tula, located 50 miles northwest of Teotihuacán a priest of Quetzalcoatl and his Toltec followers were driven from the city because the people of Tula wanted to worship only Tezcatlipoca and re-instate human sacrifice. There is evidence of political and religious uprising at Teotihuacán around 750 AD. because only the residences of the priests were destroyed and burned. And, archeologists have recently found pictures of feathered jaguars around the base of the Great Pyramid. When the Aztecs arrived, they assimilated the religion of the Olmecs (Book of Mormon Jaredites) and the Toltecs (Book of Mormon Nephites) into their religion. The Florentine Codex recounts Tezcatlipoca inflicting harmful acts upon the Toltecs, Huemac (their king), and Quetzalcoatl, which indicates political and religious unrest with possibly religious conflict in the Teotihuacán region.

The Aztecs and Maya worshipped many gods and goddesses, however; Tezcatlipoca, Huitzilopochtli, and Tlaloc, were the main gods of the Aztecs. In Tenochtitlan, present day Mexico City, a lofty and magnificent temple, Templo Mayor, had twin pyramids on the top of its platform that represented duality and polarity union. One temple pyramid was dedicated to the rain god Tlaloc, which is an aspect of Quetzalcoatl, and the other temple pyramid was dedicated to Huitzilopochitli; several smaller temples in the city complex were dedicated to Tezcatlipoca and one to Quetzalcoatl. Although the

Aztecs revered Quetzalcoatl as a god, his status was relegated to that of a lesser god. Their calendars honored different aspects of these gods as days were assigned to the wind god, the rain god, the death god etc. Other gods were worshipped such as K'inich Ahau, the Maya sun god and Tonatiuh, the Aztec sun god who rules over the 5th and present world. Nevertheless, many Mesoamericans were converted believers and followers of Quetzalcoatl, but there were also those who continued to worship the old pagan gods. Sometimes Quetzalcoatl was worshipped under the name of Ehecatl, the Lord of the Winds or Wind God. Temples to Ehecatl were built in a circular fashion. Likewise, another aspect or name for his twin brother was Xolotl. The planet Venus, which passes through its alternating phases of morning star and evening star, was also associated with duality. Hence, Quetzalcoatl ruled over the morning star Venus during the morning phases and during the day, and his dark twin, Xolotl, ruled over Venus in the evening phases and during the night.

There are many numerous and somewhat gruesome myths about the serpent twins which developed as the result of superstition and apostasy. So it was until the arrival of the Spanish conquerors in 1519. Their conquerors didn't recognize the Christian liturgy in many parts of Mesoamerica. They deemed their form of Christianity as pagan which tragically resulted in the deaths of many thousands of Mesoamerican Christians at the hands of the Christian Spanish. Under pain of death, the survivors were forced to accept another form of Christianity. That ended the concept and belief in dualism of feathered serpent gods in Mesoamerica. Likewise, when St. Patrick visited Ireland, he is said to have killed all the snakes when he stuck his Sheppard's staff in the ground. It is a symbolic way of saying that the Holy Roman Church replaced the old dual feathered serpent religion with Catholicism. All that remains of the dual feathered serpent religion are carved images in stone, two headed thrones, a few yin yang symbols, some murals on walls, myths associated with the twin forces, and paintings on pottery.

The ancient Mesoamericans took the "bruising of the head" of Tezcatlipoca literally while the Genesis account implies that Christ counters the teachings of Lucifer with Christianity thereby in doing so "bruises his head" which is a symbolic expression. Likewise, each time Lucifer (Tezcatlipoca) attacks Christianity, in any form or manner; he symbolically "bruises the heel" of Christ (Quetzalcoatl). It is the Christian form of dualism; only the names have been changed. The battle between these two entities, Christ and Lucifer, is ongoing in spiritual warfare. Regardless, it is evident that ancient Mesoamerica understood the biblical account of good and evil as defined in Genesis which later became corrupted by apostasy.

The Cataclysms Arrive

Earth's Thermosphere Collapses

NASA-funded researchers are monitoring a rarefied layer of gas around the Earth called "the thermosphere," because it recently collapsed and now is rebounding again. "This is the biggest contraction of the thermosphere in at least 43 years," says John Emmert of the Naval Research Lab, lead author of a paper announcing the finding in the June 19th issue of the *Geophysical Research Letters* (GRL). "It's a Space Age record."

The collapse happened during the deep solar minimum of 2008-2009. The thermosphere always cools and contracts when solar activity is low; however, the magnitude of the collapse was two to three times greater than low solar activity could explain.

"Something is going on that we do not understand," says Emmert.

The thermosphere ranges in altitude from 90 km to 600+ km and is also where solar radiation, and as it turns out galactic radiation, makes first contact with our planet. The thermosphere intercepts extreme ultraviolet (EUV) photons from the sun before they can reach the ground. When solar activity is high, solar EUV warms the thermosphere, causing it to puff up like a marshmallow held over a camp fire. (This heating can raise temperatures as high as 1400

K—hence the name *thermo*sphere.) When solar activity is low, the opposite happens.

Lately, solar activity has been very low. In 2008 and 2009, the sun plunged into a millennium-class solar minimum. Sunspots still are scarce, solar flares almost non-existent, and solar EUV radiation at a low ebb. Researchers immediately turned their attention to the thermosphere to see what would happen.

How do you know what's happening all the way up in the thermosphere? Emmert uses a clever technique: Because satellites feel aerodynamic drag when they move through the thermosphere, it is possible to monitor conditions there by watching satellites decay. He analyzed the decay rates of more than 5000 satellites ranging in altitude between 200 and 600 km and ranging in time between 1967 and 2010. This provided a unique space-time sampling of thermospheric density, temperature, and pressure covering almost the entire Space Age. In this way he discovered that the thermospheric collapse of 2008-2009 was not only bigger than any previous collapse, but also bigger than the sun alone could explain.

One possible explanation is carbon dioxide (CO_2). When carbon dioxide gets into the thermosphere, it acts as a coolant, shedding heat via infrared radiation. It is widely-known that CO_2 levels have been increasing in Earth's atmosphere. Extra CO_2 in the thermosphere could have magnified the cooling action of solar minimum.

"But the numbers don't quite add up," says Emmert. "Even when we take CO2 into account using our best understanding of how it operates as a coolant, we cannot fully explain the thermosphere's collapse."

About 60% of the thermosphere collapse is not accounted for, considering the loss due to CO2 cooling, and other usual causes.

Authors of the GRL paper acknowledge that the situation is complicated. There's more to it than just solar EUV and terrestrial CO2. The overall sensitivity of the thermosphere to solar radiation could actually be increasing. There could be effects that we only see in this neighborhood of the galaxy, one that is visited every 26,000 years as the solar system travels through the Precession.

"The density anomalies," they wrote, "may signify that an as- yet-unidentified climatological tipping point involving energy balance and chemistry feedbacks has been reached."

Scientists who were not fortunate enough to read the first three volumes of *The Ark of Millions of Years,* are left surprised and grasping for theories after the Voyager Spacecrafts emerged from the heliosphere far ahead of their schedules. What was even more amazing is waiting for the exploration vehicles on the outside was not the quiet, cool microwave hum left over from the theoretical Big Bang. They found instead something that should not have been there at all.

The solar system is passing through an interstellar cloud that physics says should not exist. In the Dec. 24th issue of *Nature*, a team of scientists reveal how NASA's Voyager spacecraft have solved the mystery.

"Using data from Voyager, we have discovered a strong magnetic field just outside the solar system," explains lead author Merav Opher, a NASA Heliophysics Guest Investigator from George Mason University. "This magnetic field holds the interstellar cloud together and solves the long-standing puzzle of how it can exist at all."

Voyager flew through the outer bounds of the heliosphere en route to interstellar space. A strong magnetic field reported by Opher et al in the Dec. 24, 2009, issue of Nature is delineated in yellow. Image copyright 2009, The American Museum of Natural History.

The discovery has implications for the future when the solar system will eventually bump into other, similar clouds in our arm of the Milky Way galaxy.

Exactly as predicted by the authors in the chapter called *The Cataclysms Arrive,* Astronomers discovered what they are calling the Local Interstellar Cloud or "Local Fluff" for short. It's about 30 light years wide and contains a wispy mixture of hydrogen and helium atoms at a temperature of 6000 C. The existential mystery of the Fluff has to do with its surroundings. About 10 million years ago, a cluster of supernovas exploded nearby, creating a giant bubble of million-degree gas. The Fluff is completely surrounded by this high-pressure supernova exhaust and should be crushed or dispersed by it.

"The observed temperature and density of the local cloud do not provide enough pressure to resist the 'crushing action' of the hot gas around it," says Opher.

So how does the Fluff survive? The Voyagers have found an answer.

"Voyager data show that the Fluff is much more strongly magnetized than anyone had previously suspected—between 4 and 5 microgauss*," says Opher. "This magnetic field can provide the extra pressure required to resist destruction." This clearly supports the prediction made by the authors that the Solar system would pass through a plane of highly magnetized gaseous matter in the year 2012, and that it was the result of alignment with the rift in the Milky Way Galaxy.

NASA's two Voyager probes have been racing out of the solar system for more than 30 years. They are now beyond the orbit of Pluto and on the verge of entering interstellar space—but they are not there yet.

"The Voyagers are not actually inside the Local Fluff," says Opher. "But they are getting close and can sense what the cloud is like as they approach it." The space explorers will reach the edge of the cloud sometime in the year 2011, with the Solar system not far behind,

The Fluff is held at bay just beyond the edge of the solar system by the sun's magnetic field, which is inflated by solar wind into a magnetic bubble more than 10 billion km wide. Called the "heliosphere," this bubble acts as a shield that helps protect the inner solar system from galactic cosmic rays and interstellar clouds. The two Voyagers are located in the outermost layer of the heliosphere, or "heliosheath," where the solar wind is slowed by the pressure of interstellar gas. But in recent years, the Solar wind has dropped to around 300 km/sec, making a weak challenger against this new more powerful galactic wind.

Voyager 1 entered the heliosheath in Dec. 2004; Voyager 2 followed almost 3 years later in Aug. 2007. These crossings were key to Opher *et al*'s discovery.

The fact that the Fluff is strongly magnetized means that other clouds in the galactic neighborhood could be, too. Eventually, the solar system will run into some of them, and their strong magnetic fields could compress the heliosphere even more than it is compressed now. Additional compression could allow more cosmic rays to reach the inner solar system, possibly affecting terrestrial climate and the ability of astronauts to travel safely through space. On the other hand, astronauts wouldn't have to travel so far because interstellar space would be closer than ever. These events would play out on time scales of tens to hundreds of thousands of years, which is how long it takes for the solar system to move from one cloud to the next.

"There could be interesting times ahead!" says Opher.

Space Storm Damage

It is midnight on 22 September 2012. Observers from skyscrapers all over New York are looking out at the city that never sleeps when they notice the night sky fill with a color aurora. Within seconds the billions of lights across the metro area flicker slightly, then seem to grow nervously bright for what seems like a minute before going black. Within a minute every light on the Eastern seaboard is cool and quiet. The panic of being on the 40th floor of a building that hums with electric power 24 hours a day dropped into a blackout is almost commonplace for New Yorkers. This shouldn't be a problem.

A year later and millions of Americans are dead and the nation's infrastructure lies in tatters. A solar storm, 150 million kilometers away on the surface of the sun, has evaporated three hundred years of nation building. A world that could scarcely remember rotary phones is relearning how to rub to sticks together to make fire.

An extraordinary report funded by NASA and issued by the US National Academy of Sciences (NAS) in January of 2010 claims it could do just that.

The projections of just how catastrophic make chilling reading. "We're moving closer and closer to the edge of a possible disaster," says Daniel Baker, a space weather expert based at the University of Colorado in Boulder, and chair of the NAS committee responsible for the report.

It is hard to conceive of the sun wiping out a large amount of our hard-earned progress. Nevertheless, it is possible. The surface of the sun is a roiling mass of plasma - charged high-energy particles - some of which escape the surface and travel through space as the solar wind. From time to time, that wind carries a billion-ton glob of plasma, a fireball known as a coronal mass ejection. And when the Earth aligns with the dark rift in the Milky Way—the plane of gravity rippling through space from the super-massive spinning black hole in the center of the galaxy—a solar flare, CME, induced by a galactic gravitational wave, it will be susceptible to a solar tsunami of devastating proportions. The incursion of the plasma into our atmosphere causes rapid changes in the configuration of Earth's magnetic field which, in turn, induce currents in the long wires of the power grids. The grids were not built to handle this sort of direct current electricity. The greatest danger is at the step-up and step-down transformers used to convert power from its transport voltage to domestically useful voltage. The increased D.C. current creates strong magnetic fields that saturate a transformer's magnetic core. The result is runaway current in the transformer's copper wiring, which rapidly heats up and melts.

This is exactly what happened in the Canadian province of Quebec in March 1989, and six million people spent 9 hours without electricity. But things could get much, much worse than that.

How bad can it be?

The most serious space weather event in history happened in 1859. It is known as the Carrington event, after the British amateur astronomer Richard Carrington, who was the first to note its cause: "two patches of intensely bright and white light" emanating from a large group of sunspots. The Carrington event comprised eight days of severe space weather, although the temporary loss of telegraph communications was the only effect to the commerce of the world. The loss of the microelectronic world of today would be cataclysmic.

Though a solar outburst could conceivably be more powerful, "we haven't found an example of anything worse than a Carrington event", says James Green, head of NASA's planetary division and an expert on the events of 1859. "From a scientific perspective, that would be the one that we'd want to survive." However, the prognosis from the NAS analysis is that, thanks to our technological prowess, many of us may not.

There are two problems to face. The first is the modern electricity grid, which is designed to operate at ever higher voltages over ever larger areas. Though this provides a more efficient way to run the electricity networks, minimizing power losses and wastage through overproduction, it has made them much more vulnerable to space weather. The high-power grids act as particularly efficient antennas, channeling enormous direct currents into the power transformers.

The second problem is the grid's interdependence with the systems that support our lives: water and sewage treatment, supermarket delivery infrastructures, power station controls, financial markets and many others all rely on electricity. Put the two together, and it is clear that a repeat of the Carrington event could produce a catastrophe the likes of which the world has never seen. "It's just the opposite of how we usually think of natural disasters," says John Kappenman, a power industry analyst with the Metatech Corporation of Goleta, California, and an advisor to the NAS committee that produced the report. "Usually the less developed regions of the world are most vulnerable, not the highly sophisticated technological regions."

According to the NAS report, a severe space weather event in the US could induce ground currents that would knock out 300 key transformers within about 90 seconds, cutting off the power for more than 130 million people (see map). From that moment, the clock is ticking for America.

First to go - immediately for some people - is drinkable water.

Anyone living in a high-rise apartment, where water has to be pumped to reach them, would be cut off straight away. For the rest, drinking water will still come through the taps for maybe half a day. With no electricity to pump water from reservoirs, there is no more after that.

There is simply no electrically powered transport; no trains, underground or overground. Our just-in-time culture for delivery networks may represent the pinnacle of efficiency, but it means that supermarket shelves would empty very quickly - delivery trucks could only keep running until their tanks ran out of fuel, and there is no electricity to pump any more from the underground tanks at filling stations.

Back-up generators would run at pivotal sites - but only until their fuel ran out. For hospitals, that would mean about 72 hours of running a bare-bones, essential care only, service.

The truly shocking finding is that this whole situation would not improve for months, maybe years: melted transformer hubs cannot be repaired, only replaced. "From the surveys I've done, you might have a few spare transformers around, but installing a new one takes a well-trained crew a week or more," says Kappenman. "A major electrical utility might have one suitably trained crew, maybe two." Manufacturing new transformers without the high-voltage supply to the plants that construct them, would be simply impossible. In fact, the vehicles it would take to transport the replacement transformers would not start, because the microelectronics of the vehicles would be destroyed in the geomagnetic storm.

Even when some systems are capable of receiving power again, there is no guarantee there will be any to deliver. Almost all natural gas and fuel pipelines require electricity to operate. Coal-fired power stations usually keep reserves to last 30 days, but with no transport systems running to bring more fuel, there will be no electricity in the second month.

Nuclear power stations wouldn't fare much better. They are programmed to shut down in the event of serious grid problems and are not allowed to restart until the power grid is up and running.

With no power for heating, cooling or refrigeration systems, people could begin to die within days. There is immediate danger for those who rely on medication. Lose power to New Jersey, for instance, and you have lost a major centre of production of pharmaceuticals for the entire US. Perishable medications such as insulin will soon be in short supply. "In the US alone there are a million people with diabetes," Kappenman says. "Shut down production, distribution and storage and you put all those lives at risk in very short order."

Help is not coming any time soon, either. If it is dark from the eastern seaboard to Chicago, some affected areas are hundreds, maybe thousands of miles away from anyone who might help. And those willing to help are likely to be ill-equipped to deal with the sheer scale of the disaster. "If a Carrington event happened now, it would be like a hurricane Katrina, but 10 times worse," says Paul Kintner, a plasma physicist at Cornell University in Ithaca, New York.

In reality, it would be much worse than that. Hurricane Katrina's societal and economic impact has been measured at $81 billion to $125 billion. According to the NAS report, the impact of what it terms a "severe geomagnetic storm scenario" could be as high as $2 trillion. And that's just the first year after the storm. The NAS puts the recovery time at four to 10 years. It is questionable whether the US would ever bounce back. Even moderate recovery would take between 10 and 20 years to accomplish.

"I don't think the NAS report is scaremongering," says Mike Hapgood, who chairs the European Space Agency's space weather team. Green agrees. "Scientists are conservative by nature and this group is really thoughtful," he says. "This is a fair and balanced report."

Such nightmare scenarios are not restricted to North America. High latitude nations such as Sweden and Norway have been aware for a while that, while regular views of the aurora are pretty, they are also reminders of an ever-present threat to their electricity grids. However, the trend towards installing extremely high voltage grids means that lower latitude countries are also at risk. For example, China is on the way to implementing a 1000-kilovolt electrical grid, twice the voltage of the US grid. This would be a superb conduit for space weather-induced disaster because the grid's efficiency to act as an antenna rises as the voltage between the grid and the ground increases. "China is going to discover at some point that they have a problem," Kappenman says.

Neither is Europe sufficiently prepared. Responsibility for dealing with space weather issues is "very fragmented" in Europe, says Hapgood.

Europe's electricity grids are highly interconnected and extremely vulnerable to cascading failures. In 2006, the routine switch- off of a small part of Germany's grid - to let a ship pass safely under high-voltage cables - caused a cascade power failure across western Europe. In France alone, five million people were left without electricity for two hours. "These systems are so complicated we don't fully understand the effects of twiddling at one place," Hapgood says. "Most of the time it's alright, but occasionally it will get you."

By far the most important indicator of incoming space weather is NASA's Advanced Composition Explorer (ACE). The probe, launched in 1997, has a solar orbit that keeps it directly between the sun and Earth. Its uninterrupted view of the sun means it gives us continuous reports on the direction and velocity of the solar wind and other streams of charged particles that flow past its sensors. ACE can provide between 15 and 45 minutes' warning of any incoming geomagnetic storms. The power companies need about 15 minutes to prepare their systems for a critical event, so that would seem passable.

However, observations of the sun and magnetometer readings during the Carrington event shows that the coronal mass ejection was travelling so fast it took less than 15 minutes to get from where ACE is positioned to Earth. "It arrived faster than we can do anything," Hapgood says.

There is another problem. ACE is 11 years old, and operating well beyond its planned lifespan. The onboard detectors are not as sensitive as they used to be, and there is no telling when they will finally give up the ghost. Furthermore, its sensors become saturated in the event of a really powerful solar flare. There is no spare detector, and recent budget cuts in manned U.S. spaceflight mean it will be at least 10 years before one could be put into place.

Readers of *The Ark of Millions of Years* are informed enough to be able to do something about this exposure. They know that storage of food, water, and the design of an emergency preparedness plan is important. They know that there are things we can do as humans to prevent the effects from being so devastating to life on Earth.

The Wavering Sun

The sun is in the pits of a century-class solar minimum, and sunspots have been puzzlingly scarce for more than two years. Now, for the first time, solar physicists might understand why.

At an American Astronomical Society press conference today in Boulder, Colorado, researchers announced that a jet stream deep inside the sun is migrating slower than usual through the star's interior, giving rise to the current lack of sunspots.

Rachel Howe and Frank Hill of the National Solar Observatory (NSO) in Tucson, Arizona, used a technique called helioseismology to detect and track the jet stream down to depths of 7,000 km below the surface of the sun. The sun generates new jet streams near its poles every 11 years, they explained to a room full of reporters and fellow scientists. The streams migrate slowly from the poles to the equator and when a jet stream reaches the critical latitude of 22 degrees, new- cycle sunspots begin to appear.

Extreme Weather

While Pakistan has been hit by catastrophic flooding, Russia has endured a lethal heat wave.

Some 1,200 people have been killed in the deluges sweeping Pakistan, but in Moscow more than 30 are reported to have died in wildfires as temperatures have soared to a new record for the region of 38C (100F).

It marks out 2010 as the year of extreme weather - and experts predict the pronounced conditions will continue across the globe. Last month alone the UK was hit by a hosepipe ban, saw tarmac melting on roads and the population was issued health warnings about the dangers of too much sun.

Yet despite the heat wave, it was also the wettest July ever recorded.

According to provisional statistics from the Met Office, the country was 46 per cent wetter than average and some areas faced devastating floods. Britain was not alone. The mercury climbed to its highest point in decades in other parts of Europe, the U.S. and Japan as record temperatures were recorded.

In Russia the army was drafted in to battle the wildfires which threatening dozens of towns and villages. Thick smoke and ash slowed firefighting efforts and thousands of people were being evacuated. A state of emergency was declared after swathes of the country were engulfed in flames and thousands were left homeless. The city has been veiled in acrid smoke causing landmarks to disappear from view and meteorologists expect the scorching temperatures will continue to rise.

More than 2,000 people are said to have died in the region since the beginning of July as they tried to cool down in lakes and rivers. And in Greece dramatic blazes on the island of Samos have wreaked havoc.

Hundreds of tourists were evacuated as the fires spread and helicopters along with more than 150 firefighters were brought in to tackle the flames.

The fire, which broke out in a ravine on Monday, is the second to strike the island in a week.

But Met Office climate change scientist Peter Stott insisted the extreme weather patterns were not unexpected and in keeping with climate change theories.

'What we have observed generally is a tendency for more heavy rain fall, a tendency towards a greater risk of flooding and also a greater risk of drought as well.

'These are consistent with what we know about climate change,' he said.

Man-Made Weather Warfare

As Muscovites suffer record high temperatures this summer, a Russian political scientist has claimed the United States may be using climate-change weapons to alter the temperatures and crop yields of Russia and other Central Asian countries.

Andrei Areshev, deputy director of the Strategic Culture Foundation, wrote, "At the moment, climate weapons may be reaching their target capacity and may be used to provoke droughts, erase crops, and induce various anomalous phenomena in certain countries." The article has been carried by publications throughout Russia, including "International Affairs," a journal published by the Foreign Ministry and by the state-owned news agency RIA Novosti. During the summer of 2010, Moscow sweltered under record temperatures. On July 29, 2010 Moscow suffered its hottest day ever, with temperatures hitting 39 degrees.

But Russia isn't the only country that suffered from a heat wave. Indeed, the United States is also experiencing record temperatures. On July 24, temperatures in Washington, D.C., hit 37.7 degrees. Areshev agrees that it is also hot in the United States, but notes that the United States is significantly farther south than Russia, meaning that such high temperatures are not so surprising there.

The U.S. National Oceanic and Atmospheric Administration, however, announced in July that land and ocean temperatures throughout the world were the highest ever, since they began tracking global temperatures in 1880. In the article, Areshev voiced suspicions about the High-Frequency Active Aural Research Program (HAARP), funded by the U.S. Defense Department and the University of Alaska. HAARP, which has long been the target of conspiracy theorists, analyzes the ionosphere and seeks to develop technologies to improve radio communications, surveillance, and missile detection.

Areshev writes, however, that its true aim is to create new weapons of mass destruction "in order to destabilize environmental and agricultural systems in local countries." Areshev's article also references an unmanned spacecraft X-37B, an orbital test vehicle the Pentagon launched in April 2010. The Pentagon calls X-37B a prototype for a new "space plane" that could take people and equipment to and from space stations. Areshev, however, alleges that the X-378 carries "laser weaponry" and could be a key component in the Pentagon's climate-change arsenal.

The Pentagon was not immediately reachable for comment, although reported earlier in the year that the X-37B was a former NASA project that ran out of money. The Air Force showed high interest, placing it into their rapid Deployment Program with an unlimited budget. To date, no mission criteria or budget has been released for the spacecraft already in orbit for its 9-month mission orbiting the Earth.

Asked whether or not Russia was also experimenting with climate-control methods, Areshev said since he was not a member of the government, he did not have information about such projects

New Earth Discovered

Earth is rare. The authors agree, but have maintained since the chapter *The Dimensions* that is was possible that other Earths could exist and could support life as we know it.

One of the most remarkable discoveries in astrobiological history was announced recently by a team of European astronomers, using a telescope in La Silla in the Chilean Andes. It forced bookies to slash odds on the existence of alien beings.

The Earth-like planet that could be covered in oceans and may support life is 20.5 light years away, and has the right temperature to allow liquid water on its surface. That is barely 1.5 year travel time for a craft accelerating at one *gravity* for half the time and decelerating at the same rate for the other half with a propulsion technology tested by the U.S. as far back as 1968.

This remarkable discovery appears to confirm the suspicions of most astronomers that the universe is swarming with Earth-like worlds. We don't yet know much about this planet, but scientists believe that it may be the best candidate so far for supporting extraterrestrial life.

The new planet, which orbits a small, red star called Gliese 581, is about one-and-a-half times the diameter of the Earth. It probably has a substantial atmosphere and may be covered with large amounts of water - necessary for life to evolve - and, most importantly, temperatures are very similar to those on our world. It is the first exoplanet (a planet orbiting a star other than our own Sun) that is anything like our Earth.

Of the 220 or so exoplanets found to date, most have either been too big, made of gas rather than solid material, far too hot, or far too cold for life to survive.

"On the treasure map of the Universe, one would be tempted to mark this planet with an X," says Xavier Delfosse, one of the scientists who discovered the planet.

"Because of its temperature and relative proximity, this planet will most probably be a very important target of the future space missions dedicated to the search for extraterrestrial life."

This new planet - known for the time being as Gliese 581c - is a midget in comparison, being about 12,000 miles across (Earth is a little under 8,000 pole-to-pole). It has a mass five times that of Earth, probably made of the same sort of rock as makes up our world and with enough gravity to hold a substantial atmosphere.

Astrobiologists - scientists who study the possibility of alien life - refer to a climate known as the Goldilocks Zone, where it is not so cold that water freezes and not so hot that it boils, but where it can lie on the planet's surface as a liquid.

In our solar system, only one planet - Earth -lies in the Goldilocks Zone. Venus is far too hot and Mars is just too cold. This new planet lies bang in the middle of the zone, with average surface temperatures estimated to be between zero and 40c (32-102f). Lakes, rivers and even oceans are possible. It is difficult to speculate what - if any - life there is on the planet. If there is life there it would have to cope with the higher gravity and solar radiation from its sun.

Just because Gliese 581c is habitable does not mean that it is inhabited, but we do know its sun is an ancient star - in fact, it is one of the oldest stars in the galaxy, and extremely stable. If there is life, it has had many billions of years to evolve.

The real importance is not so much the discovery of this planet itself, but the fact that it shows that Earth-like planets are probably extremely common in the Universe. There are 200 billion stars in our galaxy alone and many astronomers believe most of these stars have planets. The fact that almost as soon as we have built a telescope capable of detecting small, earth-like worlds, one turns up right on our cosmic doorstep, shows that statistically, there are probably billions of earths out there. "There is a protocol, buried away in the United Nations," says Dr Shostak. "The President would be told first, after the signal was confirmed by other observatories. But we couldn't keep such a discovery secret."

Archaeological Updates

Etowah Mounds

Update to Volume Three
Chapter The Oldest City in the Americas
Page 183 end of first paragraph

New research indicates the builders of the Etowah Mounds in Cartersville, Georgia, may indeed be distant cousins to the Mesoamericans. The Etowah Mounds complex consists of six earthen mounds all in the traditional Mississippian truncated pyramid shape. They were built between 950 AD. and 1450 AD. with most of the major construction done around 1250 AD. The site is surrounded by a deep moat on three sides with the Etowah River on the fourth side. Just behind the moat was a palisade wall that afforded added protection, probably from other hostile Indian tribes who inhabited the area thousands of years before the arrival of the Muskogean tribe. The Etowah Mounds are believed to have been built by the Muskogean Indians who would later be known as the Creeks. The Muskogean Indians are thought to be the builders of a previous site, Ocmulgee, which was abandoned when they moved further north and inhabited the Etowah region.

The Great Temple Mound structure is the largest at the site and is the tallest mound in Georgia, rising to 67 feet and oriented to the cardinal points as were the other mounds at the site. In the book titled, *He Walked the Americas*, by L. Taylor Hansen, the great white God (Quetzalcoatl), arrived for the dedication of the Great Pyramid Temple and gave the dedication speech along with a prophecy for the future. He spoke of the coming of white men and of an invading tribe called the Serpent People. At the end of his dedication speech, He most likely lit the sacred eternal fire at the top of the temple.

The Creeks belonged to a southeastern alliance known as the Creek Confederacy. According to Creek traditions, the Confederacy migrated to the southeastern United States from the Southwest. The original name of the Creeks was Ocheese Creek that was shorten by the English to simply Creeks because these native peoples were living along the Ocheese Creek or Ocmulgee River. In time, the name was applied to all groups of the confederacy. Most of the groups of the confederacy shared the same Muskogean language, types of ceremonies, and village lay-out. The tribes of the Creek Confederacy in Georgia were the Apalachicola, Chiaha, Creek, Guale, Hitchiti, Icaful, Kasihta, Oconee, Osochi, Olmulgee, Tacatacuru, Tamathli, Yemasee, and Yui.

The Muskogean tribes have legends that their tribe originated in Mexico. It appears that the Muskogeans migrated from western Mexico into central Mexico where they came under the influence of Teotihuacán. The down fall or problems arising at Teotihuacán may have inspired the Muskogeans to migrate northward out of central Mexico into what is now the southwestern United States.

The archaeological record supports their migration legend as the Chontal tribe of western Mexico simply disappears around 600 AD. only to show up 50 years later in central Mexico to inhabit Xochitecatl which had been abandoned centuries earlier. They had close ties with nearby Cholula where they met the Cussitaw/Chickasaw tribe who joined with them. From these sites they migrated to Teotihuacán. The Creek legends say that their group was comprised of four tribes, two of which have been identified as Chontal and Cussitaw. The problems that arose in Teotihuacán (could have been the nearby volcano Popocatepetl erupting around 745-800 AD., or perhaps civil war or civil unrest, could be a religious revolt, maybe food shortages?) caused them to migrate northward to the southwestern part of the United States. Please note that not all the Chontal's migrated northward. Many stayed in Mexico but a significant number of them did migrate northward. In fact, around 700 AD., new ethnic groups appear in the Yucatán Puuc sites, the main center being Uxmal. The new groups are generically identified as Chontal Maya who reached the peninsula from the southwest. Something going on at the time apparently forced the Chontal to divide into groups and leave Teotihuacán for other parts.

The influence of Teotihuacán through trade routes was broad and wide. They traded with the Gulf Coast Olmec, the Zuni in New

Mexico, the Hopi in Arizona, the Adena Mound Builders of Ohio which predate the Mississippian Culture, the coastal regions of the state of Chiapas, the city of Kaminaljuvu in highland Guatemala, Tikal in Guatemala, and as far southeast as Costa Rica. The point I want to get across is the Chontal, and the other three tribes who joined with them, were not traveling unchartered waters when they migrated northward to eventually settle in Etowah, Georgia. They were following well established centuries old trade routes. The Adena Mound builders, as well as the Mississippian Culture, had their roots in ancient Mexico.

Likewise, most of the Native American Indian tribes, are descendants of Mesoamerican tribes who migrated northward during some time in history; the exception being the Eskimo-Aleut (the Inuit), and Yupiks of Alaska, Canada, and the Artic. Add to this list, the Navajo and the Apache, who are related and speak a language related to the Athabaskan language group spoken by those who migrated via the Bering Strait into Alaska and Canada.

The great cultures of Mexico, the Mayans, Toltecs, and Aztecs, appear to have had northern outposts that stretched into Arizona and New Mexico...perhaps other states as well. The best and largest example is found at the site of Wupatki, Arizona, located northeast of Flagstaff, Arizona. It has been labeled "Hohokam" and called "Northern Toltecs." The ruins date from 900-1200 AD. It even has a ball court and a serpent petroglyph which marked the site as a powerful vortex containing sacred Life Force energy that emerges from a blow hole on the site. The Hopi note that it was a northern migration of the Toltec that created the Hohokam culture. By 1225 AD., Wupatki had been abandoned. Few people know that over two-hundred ball courts, all built between 700 and 1200 AD., have been discovered in southern Arizona. Other well known Arizona sites are found at Snake Town and Casa Grande. The Snake Town site dates earlier from 300-1200 AD., and appears to be the actual centre of the Hohokiam culture, having a population of around 2,000 people. It could be that the Chontals migrated to one of these southwestern sites for a time before migrating east to Etowah, Georgia.

The Muskogean language belongs to the Hokan family. This language has its origin in Mexico and Central America where the Chontal and Yuman group are still spoken in western Mexico. Additionally the Muskogean tribe wore the same style of headdress and shoulder sash as the Mexican Chontal tribe. The Chontal tribe was also noted for their making of funeral statues such as was found in a tomb in Etowah. And they built their city fortification, using moats and palisades of tree trunks on top, exactly as was done in many ancient Mesoamerican cities such, for example, as in the more popular sites of Edzna in the state of Campeche, Dzibanche Yucatán site in Quintana Roo, and in Becan located in the middle of the Yucatán peninsula.

Upon their final arrival to what is now Georgia, they built their first town called Ocmulgee, after killing a tribe of hostile Flat Head Indians who inhabited the area. It was patterned after the site plan of Xochitecatl. Nearby they also built a spiral pyramid at Lamar Mounds. There are only three spiral pyramids in the Americas. One is in western Mexico, one is in central Mexico, and the third is at Lamar Mounds near Ocmulgee. The building of these spiral pyramids match the migration route recounted in the Creek migration legend.

It took 500 years for them to migrate out of Mexico into the southwest and then into the southeast to build their first site of Ocmulgee, then Etowah. They brought with them the Feathered Serpent religion, the Long Nosed God, and the Eagle Warrior ideas which are still found in Mesoamerican sites in Mexico. Two small funeral statues were found in an Etowah tomb of a man and woman. The effigies and face paintings on them are almost identical to those effigies from the Chinesco culture found in the western Mexican state of Nayarit. Most of their art work designs also have strong Mesoamerican influences. These findings certainly lend credence to their legend of a western Mexico origin.

Another recent find was made by archaeologists at the Etowah site. The find has not been made public yet because it was found on private property close to the Etowah site; therefore not secured by the park system. I will disclose the find but not the exact location. The find was an underground kiva. Kivas were used by the southwestern

Indians, so it is safe to conclude that during their migration northward into the Arizona and the New Mexico areas, they were influenced by the Hohokam and Hopi cultures. This find supports their migration legend.

Another note worthy recent find is that the oldest city in the Americas, Caral, had a religious ceremonial perpetual fire that burned continuously night and day on top of its largest and main pyramid, which was maintained day and night by priests. Later, the same thing was done on many other Mesoamerican pyramids as well as on the Great Temple pyramid in Etowah. I believe that the perpetual fires were symbolic of the Union of the Polarity as the fire of the spiritual creation united with the water of the physical creation...fire united with water. An Andean cross symbol was found in Caral and later nearby city sites started building their pyramids in the shape of an Andean Cross with perpetual fires burning on top of them. It is said that the great white God (Christ) frequently attended temple dedications that were built in his honor, gave a dedication speech and then lit the sacred fire. Since Caral was the prototype of all future Mesoamerican cities, I personally believe he made the first dedication appearance at this particular temple in the Americas. He most likely lit its eternal flame.

The Cherokee have an interesting legend that tells of an outside "missionary" priesthood group whose great spiritual power was used to control the tribe even to the extent of abusing their power by demanding sexual rights to both unmarried and married women. There were many other abuses but ultimately this priesthood clan was overthrown and violently massacred. Afterwards, the Cherokee returned to a more egalitarian society with all religious ceremonies now conducted by common medicine men. This opens the questions...Did the fall of the Mississippian societies of the southeast result from an internal revolt of the societies against this same evil controlling priesthood? Was the fall of Etowah due to an internal revolt against similar priestly abuses or was it an attack from outsiders? If it were an internal revolt against the controlling priesthood then this would be very similar to the fall of Teotihuacán from whence these evil priests originally came. And it would indicate that the entire Mississippian Culture had its origins in Mexico, which I think it did. It appears that after the fall of Etowah, a great social revolution occurred. The practice of hereditary status was replaced by the Hitchiti/Woodland tradition of earned status which from pottery finds indicates the Mississippian and Woodland cultures merged. Elitist symbols were rejected and symbols associated with the Southeastern Ceremonial Complex faded away.

Nevertheless, after 125 years of prosperity (1250 AD. to 1375 AD.), a devastating attack on Etowah resulted in the abandonment of the site. The greatest Mississippian center in Georgia was now in ruins and would never rise again to the days of its former glory. However, the

Muskogeans remained one of the most powerful and organized tribal groups in the southeast even into the historic period and contact with Europeans. Eventually they banded together and moved to Oklahoma where they created a new nation with a capital named Okmulgee. After nearly 900 years of dominating Georgia, another immigrant group from the British Isles forced them back towards the western direction from whence they had originally come.

The Giants

Update to Volume One
Chapter The Union of the Polarity
Page 226

On Saturday, August 5, 2009, Fox News aired a story about archaeologists, digging in Jerusalem, who discovered an ancient foundation wall built of huge 3-4 ton stones. They were perplexed as to who could have built this wall and with what technology?

The Bible states that the Hittites were founders of Jerusalem. Among the Hittites were Hittite giants. These giants laid the foundation stones for the ancient original Jerusalem wall that archeologists have recently discovered. Nearby Jerusalem is the megalithic city of Ba'albek which is one of the largest stone structures in the world. Its wall, called the Trilithon, is comprised of hewn stones that are the largest hewn blocks ever used in construction on this planet. Ba'albek is in the territory of the Hittite giants who were the most likely tribe to have built this city. Had the archeologists, who discovered the ancient wall in Jerusalem, read pages 350-351 in Volume One, they would have found their answers. Volume One, first edition, was published nearly five years ago.

The *Zohar* relates that when King David went to find a site to build the city of Jerusalem, the site he chose to build present day Jerusalem

on each winter solstice, a shaft of light enters the tomb for 17 minutes. Why in a tomb? Because at the end of the age or on December 21, 2012, that winter solstice was believed to be the day of the resurrection of the just. They may not have known the end of the age was December 21, 2012, but they knew a resurrection was to take place on a future winter solstice date else why would they illuminate a tomb on the winter solstice with a shaft of light? Irish legends tell us the foundations of Christianity were laid there.

The third purpose of Stonehenge and the "mini" Stonehenge was to mark or herald the day of resurrection on a winter solstice, else why were the remains of the dead scattered around Stonehenge? Stonehenge was built to mark the summer and winter solstices of each year, sort of a calendar, not only to time the seasons of planting etc., but to herald the resurrection of the fallen warriors on a future winter solstice. Also the henge site is built directly over a strong energy vortex or Earth chakra filled with spiraling Life Force energy which early Christians equated to the energy of the Holy Ghost. It is by the power of the Holy Ghost that people are resurrected therefore the early Christians wanted to be buried in places where the Life Force energy was strongest. And Stonehenge was built to warn of an impending cataclysm. Like cross symbolism, Stonehenge has deep symbolic meaning, some of which we are just now learning.

Newgrange Ireland Site

Update to Volume One
Chapter The Union of the Polarity
Page 268

The megalithic Newgrange Irish site is an early Stonehenge. What makes this site so interesting is that it predates Stonehenge by a thousand years dating back to 3200 BC., and carbon 14 dating places the site 600 years older than the Giza Pyramids. Built on top of an elongated ridge, the cairn is 250 feet across and 40 feet high. To see pictures of the site, just Google Newgrange or New Grange as it is spelled both ways. The circular cairn was a sacred site which strong vortexes were in ancient times marked by mounds, henges, pyramids, and temples. Newgrange was an early circular temple mound marking the sacred site of creative Life Force energy. Concentric swirls on two kerb stones mark the entrance to the cairn that indicates this site was chosen because it was a powerful vortex. On the back side of the kerb stones, which are not visible, are what appear to be two maps that show other sites nearby that are strong vortexes. There was great effort made to carve the more than 100 motifs on each stone. Concentric swirls mark these powerful vortex sites which possibly included the nearby sites of Knowth and Dowth. Some of the S shaped lines could indicate the paths of the Life Force energy or ley line paths that connected to other vortex sites and linked to the Newgrange site. Besides marking the site as a powerful vortex, it was an early Stonehenge used for astronomical and calendrical functions. Originally thirty-eight large standing upright stones, each weighing about one ton, were placed in a circle surrounding the round mound which represented the male principle of the Life Force. Only twelve upright stones still remain in place. As in Stonehenge the site also monitored the movement of the sun and moon to predict season change and to warn of an impending cataclysm. The light of the rising winter solstice sun enters the rooftop and penetrates the passage, shining and illuminating the floor of the inner chamber for just seventeen minutes.

At present there are 75 stones with engravings but the total is not yet known due to ongoing exploration however, they are distributed as follows:

31 in the Kerb

16 in the passage

18 in the chamber

10 in the passage roof

Most certainly the Boyne Valley builders of Newgrange knew about the Union of the Polarity because a stone phallus was near the entrance to the cairn. The stone phallus indicates that the Temporal Earth was male which attracted the Spirit Earth (female) in a bond that they perceived as a sexual union. Inside the huge cairn were found some conjoined marbles or spheres carved out of a single piece of white chalk. This was their way of illustrating the Union of the Polarity....two spheres joined together and thought of as a sexual union. Two cupmarks or sockets were manmade and incorporated into the ornament, one in the kerb and one in the passage. These sockets contained marbles that fit perfectly into the cupmark which was just another way to illustrate the Union of the Polarity. The round mound (circle) temple represented a yoni or female sexual part and the male stone phallus outside the entrance was the uniting factor of the Union of the Polarity as in a sexual union.

The part I found most interesting was this knowledge was known as early as 3200 BC., and could have come from none other than some descendants of Noah who scattered earlier before the Tower of Babylon or possibly even the Nephilim. Irish legends tell us the foundations of Christianity were laid here. The site was also used as a tomb as two burials and three cremated bodies were found in the inner chamber. Archeologists call this site a passage way tomb. It is possible that the builders of the site were aware of the future 2012 winter solstice sun and designed the site to mark all winter solstice suns till that date when it was believed the first resurrection of the morning would take place, else why design the passage way tomb to illuminate on that day in the inner chamber? They may not have known the actual 2012 year date but they knew the resurrection would occur on a future winter solstice sun at the end of the age. Ancient Irish mythology says the Tuatha De Danann who first ruled Ireland in ancient times built the site as a tomb for their chief, Dagda Mor and his three sons.

Wait, there is more. Another larger megalithic passage way tomb, near Newgrange is apparently even older and larger than Newgrange. Radio carbon dating places the construction of the site 500 years before the building of Newgrange. It has 134 engraved carvings very similar to those found at Newgrange, a stone phallus at the entrance, and built in a circle. The site is Knowth and the symbolism would have the same meaning as found in Newgrange.

Another nearby megalithic passage way tomb site is Dowth. Unfortunately only half of the original structure is in tact because many of its stones were taken to build a road. Smaller similar megalithic passage way tomb sites of Fourknocks, Loughcrew and Tara, are nearby. In all, there are about sixty or more passage-way tombs in the vicinity that have been identified. Thus, it appears the entire area was one great cemetery; no doubt chosen because of its sacred Life Force energy which was equated to the power of the Holy Ghost whose power will bring forth the resurrection at the appointed time at the end of the age. These sites are all located in the Irish Boyne Valley in the present day county of Meath on the east coast of Ireland.

Below are the two kerb stone back side engravings from the Newgrange site. Picture credits are from the book titled *Newgrange Archaeology, Art and Legend,* authored by Michael J. O'Kelly, published by Thames & Hudson Ltd, London, 1982, with contributions by Claire O'Kelly and others. Please note that the kerb stone engravings are not sketches but rather tracings done by Claire O'Kelly, wife of Michael. She traced all the ornament directly from the stones onto either cellophane or clear polythene, which was then re-traced onto tracing paper and photographically reduced to one-quarter of the actual size. It was from these reductions that the finished pen-and-ink drawings were made. The process was laborious and time-consuming because of the shear size of the stones. For example, the full-size tracing of the entrance stone, which was by no means the largest stone, when laid flat would take up most of the floor space of an average living room. And we note that the back sides of the kerb stones, once in place as found, can no longer be seen. We wish to thank Jim Teeter, a reader, for drawing our attention to the Newgrange site and for submitting the kerb stone pictures to us.

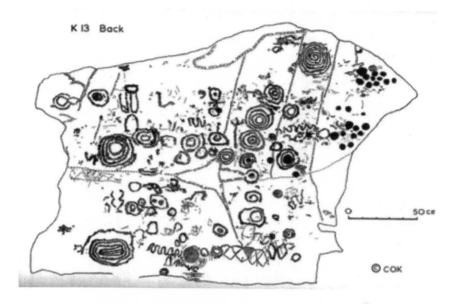

Figure 10: K13 Back side of Kerb Stone 1

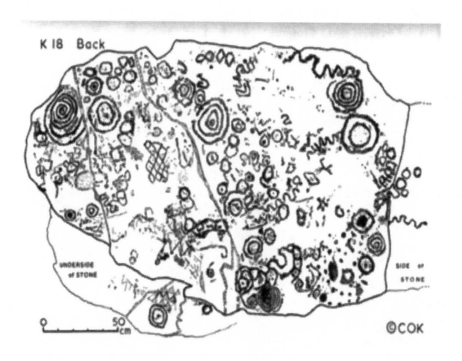

Figure 11: K18 Back, underside and west side of Kerb Stone 2

The Aztec Sun Stone

Volume Two
The Wheel of Time Untime chapter
p. 147 add at end of last paragraph

The Aztec Sun Stone may not be Aztec after all. It could be Toltec. According to the book, *He Walked the Americas*, by L. Taylor Hansen, she states that scientists who have studied the calendars of Mexico now realize the Sun Stone is far beyond the comprehension of the Aztecs. They place it further back to the time of ancient Tula, capitol of Mighty Tollan, and the Toltec Empire. This would most likely be the present day site of Teotihuacán. Ancient Tula (Teotihuacán) may just be an earthly representation of the capitol of Tollan. Tollan is an Aztec word for heaven. From the Aztec point of view, Tula could be compared as the New Jerusalem, capitol of heaven. Hansen notes the "Aztecs had but a fifty-two year ritualistic calendar which is but a degenerate copy of the Toltec masterpiece of astronomical observation." If the above is true, then the Maya inherited much of their calendar knowledge from the Toltecs.

Hansen draws from an ancient legend that says the Toltec Calendar Stone was removed from ancient Tula by the Chichimecas and given to the Aztecs who then placed it in the Aztec temple in Tenochtitlan (Mexico City) where the people could see it.

The legend further says that the white God, Quetzalcoatl made the calendar stone from a dark highly polished boulder, which he caused to be marked forever with the Dawn Star's (Venus) future cycles. He chose this massive boulder because it could survive the times of earthquake and pillage far into the time of the future. This boulder was then placed in the temple at ancient Tula, now called Teotihuacán, as a constant reminder of two future events. The first event was a cycle of time encoded on the Toltec stone which was the year Te-Tec-Patl, the prophesied year of the arrival of Cortez. Quetzalcoatl, in his farewell address, told the people the year of the white mans arrival. Carved upon the top of the stone is the date Thirteenth-Acatl. He warned the people to remember this date always as it is the Day of Retribution. In his final words, He left them with the most fundamental Law of His Father to serve as their guiding life pattern: Always love one another.

It is unmistakable that the Aztec purpose of this stone was to perform human sacrifice upon it. The Aztecs chiseled a channel through the intricate ancient carving to carry off the blood of the sacrificial victim. Hansen further informs us that around the base of the massive stone can be seen the axe marks of the Spanish conquerors, who finally gave up when it broke their instruments and consequently it was buried deep in the mud out of the view of the people who knew the meaning of the carved dates and feared the stone. I suppose the theory "out of sight, out of mind" was the ploy used here by the Aztec rulers to control the people's fears.

Those researchers who do not know this story have wrongfully assumed that Moctezuma's ancestors, who predicted the arrival of the Spanish conquerors, were psychic. They were not psychic but were merely passing down known information taught by Christ who had the date carved on the Sun Stone so that future generations would never forget.

When the first two centuries of the Conquest had passed, the Calendar Stone was again dug up, either by accident or intention, and returned to its present place of honor in the National Museum where it covers most of the great blank wall facing the entrance, so that it is the first sight to greet the visitor. It has been theorized that there was another companion piece that perhaps included more cycles of time.

The meaning of the center panel remains the same. It was chiseled in stone, by the great God Quetzalcoatl, the set time for the *harvest* at the End of the Age; the Toltec Day of Retribution or December 21, 2012. Quetzalcoatl (Christ) taught it to the Toltecs (Nephites) in Tula, during one of his long visits. In fact, the legend says the Plumed Serpent (Quetzalcoatl) rested after his visit to the dead before finally coming to Tula. The same previous ancient legend, referred to earlier, speaks of the heavens opening above the now site of Teotihuacán (Tollan) where the white God Quetzalcoatl walked down as if on the steps of a holy pyramid to the earth and stayed for a long period of time teaching the people many things such as astronomy, science, calendar calculations, writing, music, dance, literature, agriculture, and arts of government to prosper them. He gave them the stone so that they would never forget the far off future date as a reminder for future generations. Later, the Toltecs became corrupt, fell into disbelief and perished in the 385 AD. great battle between the Toltecs (Nephites) and the Nonoalca Maya (Lamanites). Following the Great War, the Chichimec Toltecs, different from Toltecs, rose to power. The surviving Nonoalca Maya and other Maya tribes did remember the Day of Retribution and ended their Long Count Calendar on that date.

The Telleriano-Remensis and Floretino Codices declare Quetzalcoatl created the first human beings in his image, and that only he, and no other god, had a human body. He was the god made flesh; a man embodied with divine spirit.

When I first viewed the ancient stone in Mexico City, I was impressed by the intricate detail and marveled at its complicated precise design. I've always wondered if the ancient Aztecs were capable of such work. It appears that they were not. It would have been all but impossible even for the Toltec artisans to have carved such a masterpiece. Early on, it became quiet evident to me that this stone was not fashioned by mortal hands; it is the handiwork of a God. Do you realize the implications of such a statement? The Toltec Stone is the only known surviving relic on Earth that is said and believed by the Mesoamericans to have been made by the Lord himself. The title of Quetzalcoatl is an Aztec Nahuatl word which meaning translates as Lord or feathered serpent. Remember a feathered serpent is a title bestowed on Lords/gods who were creator gods.

When an onlooker views this stone, one is immediately drawn to the face carved in the center. It is a carved face of God with his tongue shaped like a sword sticking out. It is a symbolic biblical teaching to remind people "Out of his mouth goeth a sharp sword" (Revelation 19:15). Readers are referred to Volume Two, pages 85, 146, and 147, for close-up views of the center of the stone and of the stone itself where it sits in the Museum of Anthrolopology in Mexico City. On each side of the face of God are images of a jaguar eating the hearts of men. Symbolically these images are associating 2012 with death and destruction. What seems pagan to us was clearly a style understood by the Toltec, Aztec, and Maya that was not pagan at all. We have put new meaning to old symbolism incorrectly. Actually this stone is evidence of Christianity existing and being taught in Mesoamerica.

Hansen's book also pointed out "The Aztecs were the first conquerors to burn the ancient books, and what survived the holocaust of the Aztecs was consumed by the Spanish." Christians refer to the *harvest* as the Day of the Lord's Wrath. To the Toltec, it was the Day of Retribution. To the Hopi and Zuni tribes, as well to many other Native American tribes, it was the Day of Purification. To New Agers it is the Day of Renewal. Some refer to this date as the Time of Cleansing. Regardless, every civilization had a name for the *Harvest* time. From whence did it come? Read or review Volume Three.

Golden Plates on Display in Bulgaria

Figure 12: The book dates back to 600 BC., which is roughly the time that Lehi and his family left Jerusalem.

The world's oldest multiple-page book—in the lost Etruscan language—has gone on display in Bulgaria's National History Museum in Sofia. And something about that book has particular interest for Latter Day Saints.

As is evident from the photograph, this book was created on metal plates that are bound together with metal rings which are similar to the original source documents that became the Book of Mormon.

The small manuscript, which is more than two and a half millennia old, was discovered 60 years ago in a tomb uncovered during digging for a canal along the Strouma River in southwestern Bulgaria. It has now been donated to the museum by its finder, on condition of anonymity.

Reports say the unidentified donor is now 87 years old and lives in Macedonia. The authenticity of the book has been confirmed by two experts in Sofia and London, museum director Bojidar Dimitrove said quoted by AFP. The six sheets are believed to be the oldest comprehensive work involving multiple pages, said Elka Penkova, who heads the museum's archaeological department.

There are around 30 similar pages known in the world, Ms Penkova said, "but they are not linked together in a book."

The Etruscans----one of Europe's most mysterious ancient peoples---are believed to have migrated from Lydia, in modern western Turkey, settling in northern and central Italy nearly 3,000 years ago. They were wiped out by the conquering Romans in the fourth century BC., leaving few written records.

The long debated question about bound metal records existing in the Middle East 2,500 years ago as claimed by the Book of Mormon can now be put to rest. Critics should take note and check that item off their list of objections to the authenticity of the Book of Mormon which we, your authors, believe is a Mesoamerican record of the Toltecs (Nephites).

(picture and story used with permission from Ancient America Foundation www.ancientamerica.org copyright 1999-2002) In addition we want to thank Randy Franks, a reader of the Ark trilogy, for bringing our attention to this story.

Pakal

Update to Volume Three
Chapter The Coming Cataclysm of 2012
Page 64 end of first paragraph

Further proof that lends credence to the fact that Pakal was Christianized is that he took upon himself the name of the Maize God (Christ) and emulated him by wearing a corn tassel hair style as pictured in this famous bust pictured below. Pakal's hair was thick and luxuriant which he wore in layered tresses that flopped forward like corn silk surrounded by maize leaves and healthy cobs of corn at the top of his head. His son, Kan B'alam, wore a similar maize corn stalk hair style.

What I present next is really going to blow your mind! There is evidence that suggests Pakal was a Mason. He was buried with a carved jade sphere (symbol of the spiritual creation or Spirit Earth) in his left hand and in his right hand was a carved jade cube (symbol of the physical creation or the Temporal Earth). The circle and the square are ancient Masonic symbols of the Union of the Polarity. This finding leaves no doubt that he was knowledgeable of the Union of the Polarity and of the events to take place in 2012. These findings are unprecedented in known Maya royal burials but do lend further credence to the fact that the Maya were aware of the Union of the Polarity knowledge to the extent that it was at the very core of their religion which will be discussed more at the end of this update.

Figure 13: Pakal's bust.

Ukit Kan Le'k Tok (Snake Gourd) (790-835 AD.), also called Coch-Cal Balam, was a Maya ruler and founder of **Ek'Balam**, a pre- Columbian archaeological site located in the northern Yucatán, about 40 miles north of Chichen Itza. Ek'balam means black jaguar in Yucatec Maya. The city rose to power during the late Classic period

(600-900AD.) after the decline of nearby Coba and was still inhabited during the Spanish conquest. The largest structure at Ek'Balam is called the Acropolis which rises to 105 feet. On the fourth level of this structure, inside the "White Temple" is the location of Ukit Kan's tomb. Entry into the White Temple is through the gaping toothed jaws of a huge jaguar (an Earth symbol). Symbolically, the Earth has swallowed up the king in death. His body returns to the dust of the Earth or has been eaten up by the jaguar. The jaguar was also a symbol of the Underworld and a symbol of the Aztec/Toltec god Tezcatlipoca (Lucifer), ruler of the Underworld and the dead. On the capstone of his tomb (vault 15 of tomb 1) is his portrait as the Maize God wearing the same corn cob hair style. Surrounding the temple walls of his tomb are large statues of winged angels. His earthly remains were found lying on a jaguar skin surrounded with gold and jade funeral offerings. Placed at his feet was a large conch sea shell; a symbol of Quetzalcoatl the Maize God. This is further evidence that most of the Yucatán was Christianized prior to the arrival of the Spanish. The Maize God symbolized the resurrection and eternal life and featured prominently in Maya art during the Classic period (200-900AD.). Eight stone busts of the Maize God (600-800 AD.) were found on the cornice of structure 22 in **Copan** which had been commissioned by 18 Rabbit. One of these busts can be seen in the British Museum.

In February 2010, I visited the archaeological site of Ek'Balam. It is believed that its ancient name was Talol. My English speaking Maya guide was excellent; in fact he was the best guide I have ever had on an archaeological site anywhere. Throughout the years, he worked with US and Mexican archaeologists on various sites; therefore he knew his job well and could answer most of my questions. Not surprising, Ek'Balams king bore the genetic defect of having only three fingers and a thumb on each hand and had only three small toes and a large toe on each foot which proved his divinity and right to rule. Although he was missing digits instead of having extra digits, it proved to me that he carried the same corrupted genetics of the Nephilim Elder Gods as did King Pakal. Archaeologists believe that it was the result of incest but this condition has occurred in lineages without apparent incest such as found in King Pakal's lineage.

Ek'Balam is different from other Maya sites in the area as it was built in a combination or mix of Rio Bec and Chenes architecture style found in a few sites in the central Maya lowlands region of the Yucatán such as Chicanna, Rio Bec, Xpuhil, Balamku, Becan, Hermiguero, and Calakmul. The guide told me that King Ukit Kan Le'k Toks name was found written on a lentil above a doorway; now housed in the British Museum. This finding suggests that the King was a frequent visitor to nearby Chichen Itza, so much he even had his own personal living quarters. Ek'Balam had many wide sacbeobs (white raised roads) (sacbe

127

is the singular) leading to other cities, one of which went to nearby Chichen Itza.

According to the Popol Vuh, every aspiring would be Maya king, whether by inheritance, marks of divinity, or by appointment, had to make a trip to Chichen Itza to receive his investment or authorization to rule from the priests and ruling authority. The future king would receive instruction on ruling and religious duties of a king. Upon completion of the course he would be authorized to rule over a certain city region and would receive his symbol of authority, a stylized K'awill serpent bar scepter. Apparently Ek'Balams first king did just that. After receiving his authority to rule and given his scepter, he was assigned the present day area of Ek'Balam to rule and build his city. Why that particular area when clearly Ukit Kan Le'k Toks came from the Rio Bec area? Most likely a city was needed in that area to protect the viable salt trade routes from which the city derived most of its wealth. Ek'Balam was the salt supplier to the Yucatán and surrounding areas. The city differed from other Maya cities in that it had three walls surrounding the city instead of one. The walls were close together and about five feet high. One wall had round holes on its top that once contained a palisade of tree trunks. Obviously, the walls were for defense against attackers. Although the area was a settlement as early as 400 BC., the stone religious center was not built until the time of Ukit Kan Le'k

Toks ascension to the throne and remained occupied until the arrival of the Spanish.

What I wish to get across to the reader is there is a great deal of evidence to support my findings that much of Mesoamerica was Christianized before the Spanish arrived. Human sacrifice came about through apostasy because they chose to follow Tezcatlipoca instead of Quetzalcoatl.

San Bartolo Murals

Although the pre-classic Maya ceremonial site of San Bartolo, Guatemala, located in the eastern Petén Jungle low-lands near the border of Belize and the Yucatán, was discovered in 1991, the murals found there in the oldest known Maya royal burial ca. 150 BC., were not made public until 2005. The mural on the recently excavated west wall is thirty feet long and three feet high and is a masterpiece of ancient Mayan art. This mural shows the creation of the cosmos and a highly developed hieroglyphic script which has not been fully deciphered as it appears to be a much older style of hieroglyphic writing than the style of the classic Maya. To view this mural, just Google San Bartolo, Guatemala Mural and visit several websites where it is pictured. Accompanying each scene of the mural is an explanation of the meaning given by those working on the project. I do not fully agree with their interpretation and wish to offer mine as follows, noting that I'm working only with online images which do not show the fine details.

On entry to the tomb, appropriately there is an image of the Maize God (Christ). The Maize God is one of the many names the pre-mortal Christ was called by the ancient Olmecs and Maya. His picture on entry to the tomb announces that this king was a believer in Christ and he expects to be resurrected at the last day to eternal life.

The first part of the west wall mural is taken straight out of the creation text of the Popol Vuh. The Creator and the Maker of five worlds is shown before five World Trees or axis munde piercing his penis with a spear using his blood to create. The First World Tree depicts the first stage of creation…water and fish life. The Second World Tree of creation depicts the creation of animals. When the animals could not speak to praise their maker, the animals according to the Popol Vuh, were sacrificed and condemned to be killed and eaten. Thus the symbolism of the sacrificed deer on the mural. Following the failed attempt to make talking animals, the animals were banished to forests and ravines. Several attempts to create man were done in the third stage of world creation without success. According to the Popol Vuh, the third world was destroyed by a flood. On the mural the Third World Tree represents the creation of air as symbolized by the turkey. The Fourth World Tree shows an intertwining trunk rather than being straight as seen in the previous worlds. Now we have all the elements present to make the Fourth World Tree successful. Symbolically, Water and Earth united with Fire and Air as in the Union of the Polarity to create the world we presently live in. **The intertwining trunk represents the two creations, one spiritual and one temporal or simply said; it represents the duality of the creation; one spiritual and one physical.** Bold type emphasis on the statement is important in order for the reader to realize the knowledge of the Union of the

Polarity was known among a few tribes of the first migration from the old world prior to the resurrected Christ opening the sealed Toltec/Nephite record for a later people. The Olmecs and Quiche Maya (Chichimec Maya) came in the first migration and possessed this knowledge. The End Times chapters in this book will clarify that statement. The red flowers surrounding the tree are actually Fire symbols. At the top of the Fourth World Tree is the Bird of Paradise representing the supreme god. The bird is holding onto two fruits of the tree with his talons in preparation of taking the "fruits" of the tree off into the world. This of course would be the plan of salvation knowledge as previously discussed in Volume Three. To the right of the Fourth World Tree is a figure dancing the dance of Life Force energy. Just above and a little to the right of the dancing figure is a large glyph "IK" which represents CHANGE probably in reference to the Fourth World making a transdimensional change into the Fifth World Tree. The Creator and the Maker of the emerging Fifth World Tree which was understood by the ancient Mesoamericans to happen on the last day that translates to December 21, 2012, when the Earth makes a spiritual and transdimensional change into the fourth spiritual dimension. Next is the Maize God crowning himself as ruler over the emerging Fifth World Tree. This of course is the Spirit Earth now in the fourth dimension as discussed in the trilogy books. The Maize

God or Christ is the ruler over the Spirit Earth while it is in the fourth dimension.

The next section of the mural panel depicts the birth of the Maize God or infant on the physical earth into mortality as represented by the turtle-shaped Earth. Here he is shown growing by the power of the Rain God and God of Surface Water. He is likened to a stalk of corn growing. Next he is shown as dying. Next is the Life Force energy spiral symbols and the Flower of Life (ascension symbol) symbol which interprets as, the Maize God was resurrected by the power of the Life Force energy (Holy Ghost) and has ascended…He has arisen and ascended. Next a priest attendant is shown crowning or passing a crown to a man on a scaffold throne. The Tzute headdress worn by the attendant identifies him as a priest. The glyphs identify this man as the dead man in the tomb. His name is identified as "King Tali." The glyphs on the scaffold throne, under the seated King Tali read… Holy Tali; thou (art) a righteous ruler. The glyphs between the priest attendant and King Tali read, "The Governor (ruler or king) desires to be (made) sacred and breathing. He is sanctified." In other words King Tali is receiving a crown of righteousness and eternal life from the priest attendant for being a good ruler while in life. The following continues with the segment of the mural called the North Wall Mural.

At the bottom of the mural there is a fragment showing the Olmec sky band that has the long dragon body of the Life Force creative energy, symbolized by the raised dragon head on one end and the dragon's curled up tail on the opposite end, resting on top of the sky band. The Maya have a name for the Life Force energy. They call it ch'ulel. Other interpreters of this section of the mural call it a boat. It is not a boat but a dragon symbol of the creative energy of the universe. This is a common theme among the ancient Olmecs and Maya which is discussed at length in *The Ark of Millions of Years* trilogy.

Above the sky band and Life Force energy dragon, is Heaven. The Creator and Maker is shown, in heaven, facing a bottle gourd which is spewing out creative blood and four infants with their umbilical cords still attached. This depicts the birth or creation of the four Bacabs which are the four pillars of heaven and the guardians of the four cardinal points on Earth. The four Bacabs are a set of divinities or creator gods who after previous failures represent the successful attempt to construct the present world. Note that the bottle gourd was often used to collect the red sap of the Blood Tree which looked and acted like human blood. The red sap of this tree forms clots when in contact with the inside wall of the bottle gourd. Thus the infant Bacabs were created from "blood clots." Behind the Creator and Maker is another scene of a kneeling woman offering food in a basket to the Creator and Maker. She is seated on the inside curved portion of the tail of the Life Force energy dragon. Next is a dead man with black Olmec features kneeling before the Maize God. The Maize God is presenting him with a gift of the green gourd on a vine. The green gourd comes from the calabash tree which was another representation of the World Tree, the ceiba tree being another. Eating of the fruit of the World Tree represented the power of divinity to bestow new or eternal life to the deceased. Simply said, the Maize God is presenting the deceased kneeling man with eternal life as represented by the receiving of the green gourd. The Maize God was also called the god of the green gourd. One of the calabash subspecies is known as the bottle gourd. Directly behind the Maize God are two other kneeling women with out stretched arms in an act of adoration and worship. On the cheek of one woman is a glyph that states "she is righteous." Other glyphs identify the other woman as a "righteous cult specialist." These are deceased righteous women who are about to receive the gift of eternal life from the Maize God. The three standing attendants behind them are preparing to present them with baskets of "gifts" or further rewards for their righteousness. The little circle chains about the ankles and wrists of some of the figures are cloud symbols indicating that they are indeed in heaven. Also the Maize God in the murals is a bearded figure. Other interpreters of the murals say the mural shows the divine right of kings to rule; their succession is divinely appointed by the gods. This is not true. The Quiche Maya tribes as well as the Toltecs always selected their rulers, governor, or king, from their pool of priests who were the sages. Furthermore, the Maya always understood the concept of the soul. In ancient Maya inscriptions, the human soul was called Sak nik'nal (white flower thing), referring to the white flowers of the Ceiba World Tree or axis munde. They believed the soul came into being as a sacred flower on the branches of the Ceiba World Tree, thence to be clothed with flesh at birth. This ends my interpretation of the San Bartolo Murals. Do view them online as these murals are a masterpiece of Mayan art.

Figure 14: Seated Olmec Lord Maize God ©Dumbarton Oaks, Pre-Columbian Collection, Washington, D.C..

The knowledge and teachings of the Maize God were obviously known among the Olmecs and Chichimec Maya (Quiche Maya) who must have been visited by him in ancient times. Even the earliest Olmec kings were portrayed wearing the regalia of the Maize God. By doing so, they made public that they were the teachers in a dual role as priest/

137

king of the message of the Maize God and it identified their kingdom as Christian followers of this god. The back curving cleft cranium, positioned above the headband, of the Olmec Maize God denotes young, growing maize. A statue of the Maize God was found in a tomb at Monte Alban, an early Olmec site.

Kaminaljuyu

Please Google stele 11 Kaminaljuya for a picture of a Maya stele. This stele is from the site of Kaminaljuyu located in present day Guatemala City. Among most Mormon researchers, this is the proposed site for the City of Nephi. One of the earliest Maya kings is shown dressed as a divine being with a branching headdress that portrays him as the World Tree that unites the layers of the heavens, Earth, and underworld. This stele has been dated to 200-50 BC. The significance is that the Maya at this site knew about the Milky Way World Tree at least 800-1000 years before Pakal's time. The World Tree appears to be the central core and main religious theme of the Olmecs and Maya from earliest times. Most likely, this early knowledge of the World Tree came from their belief that the last world was destroyed by water in 3,114 BC., the date the Long Count calendar was first started. According to the Popol Vuh, it was on this date that Quetzalcoatl raised the collapsed sky by making the World Tree to support this new creation, the fifth world.

Stele 5 from Izapa (see page 80, Volume Three) is most likely of Olmec origin. The Olmecs were the first ones to use the sky band design as shown on Stele 5 and on other stelaes in Izapa (see page 83 in Volume Three), the same sky band design used on Altar 4 in La Venta, an Olmec site. Although the Maya were also present at Izapa, the use of the Olmec sky band shows the Olmec influence upon the

Maya culture and likewise the influence of the Popol Vuh Maya ideas upon the Olmec as found carved on the stelaes in Izapa. Later, the Maya borrowed this design from Olmec influence as used in the San Bartolo tomb site which was also an early Olmec site. The new book covers featured on *The Ark of Millions of Years* trilogy uses the Olmec sky band. We suspect the sky band is Chinese Tartar in origin, however to date, have not found the exact design but did find one very similar in Chinese Tartar cloth weavings.

The Guatemalan Quiche Maya (Chichimec Maya) tribes were always loyal followers of the Maize God, Quetzalcoatl. Their form of Christianity was not exactly like the modern age because at times they did practice human sacrifice unto the Maize God (Quetzalcoatl or Christ). When Quetzalcoatl made his premortal visit to these people, he taught them against this practice. He would only accept offerings of flowers and butterflies.

The Giza Dig

In the Spring of 2010, a night time video was dumped onto the Internet claiming to show a secret archaeological dig near the Sphinx on the Giza Plateau. It was immediately and globally excoriated as being a fabrication and sensational nonsense. Within a few days, an engineer and close friend of Dr. Agnew was on the scene. This friend was able to get close enough to the dig to get daytime pictures very close to the actual shaft.

Just from a surface view you can tell the shaft being excavated now resembles the shafts from the Saitic period due to how wide it is. Although the depth could not be determined, it was wide enough to be perhaps 4 stories deep. Besides that, the area had been excavated an additional four stories deep by clearing away the loose sand to make the opening more stable. Additionally, sandbags were brought in to shore up the slope and prevent sloughing of the sides making it somewhat safer. A short time before this, another shaft was dug by private explorers beneath a home in Cairo. It caved in killing several men. The site was discovered and taken over by the Supreme Minister of Antiquities, Zahi Hawass.

Also something very large was witnessed being brought up out of the shaft, possibly a sarcophagus known to be the ones from the 26th dynasty. Burials were monolithic in size during that age. The only problem with the date or the actual item description it is that the color seemed a little too light, as most of them were of black basalt but they could have draped something over it while they were moving it.

Figure 15: An actual photograph of the opening to the shaft dug near the Sphinx.

When Hawass first proposed installing the pumps around the Sphinx he admitted the reports came back saying the Sphinx was NOT in jeopardy from rising ground water at that time. But that it was a 'good idea' to go ahead and install them for the future. Ask the question...If they were not needed to protect the Sphinx then why has there been so much water being continually pumped?

**Figure 16: The location of the Red Bull
Event staged in front of the Sphinx.**

In Figure 16, the Red Bull Event staging is shown. Why would anyone allow such a huge construction project to be erected so close to one of history's most delicate antiquities? Why would Egypt's notorious minister of antiquities allow the world to see the Sphinx as a mere backdrop to young men riding bicycles in a dangerous manner? The answer might be to cover up the most sought-after archaeological dig in history. The dig to find the Hall of Records under the Sphinx is among the top five prizes in history. Below, you will see the true location of the dig. Notice the red scaffolding erected in the background on the left of the picture. You can clearly see the location of the shaft excavated to the lower section of the right hand side of the photo. You can also see irrefutably that the Giza Shaft has absolutely nothing to do with the Red Bull Event, and that the atmosphere of construction clearly provided cover for the mysterious excavation.

Figure 17: The Giza Shaft located next to the Sphinx.

Hassan having entered caverns and natural tunnels under ground was not a rumor. It came from someone who was actually shown an opening by Hassan and who then entered into it. This person then shared where the entrance was with me. Like you and the others I enjoy exploring but in my case I don't tend to share it publically. And I'm sorry but I won't be sharing its location and how I came to know about it with anyone.

**Figure 18: Crates of antiquities packed
and ready for the warehouse.**

John Van Auken said the event was a 4x4 event, He didn't know it was a Red Bull event, so his source was not as well informed as he believed. The Giza dig and the Red Bull event are two separate things. The night time video is real and not a hoax. No one knows where the antiquities have been hauled, nor if they will ever be fully revealed to the world. The authors predicted that the records would be found. We are dumbfounded that they are being crated away, perhaps transferred from one hiding place to another for very different reasons. The daytime photos are real, they do show a dig taking place directly in front of the Valley temple and the digging has nothing to do with the Red Bull event. What they are looking for and what they may or may not have found will just have to be left to speculation until more information is available.

The Symbol of Tibetan Buddhism

In the seventh century, Tibetan Buddhism was founded. The symbol for this is found all over Tibet, on every place of worship that permeates Tibetan culture. The modern interpretation is that when the doctrine was first introduced to the people, the animals came out of the forest to listen. We found a deeper meaning that brings far more reason to the symbolism. Shown below, you can see the symbol, very similar to that of Nostradamus and to that of the William St. Clair as his tomb logo for the Holy Grail (see pg. 76 *Volume Three*). The symbol is very ancient, having roots dating to the Sumerian and Babylonian periods.

Figure 19: With the Himalayas as a backdrop, the symbol of Tibetan Buddhism rests atop the college at Llasa, Tibet.

The twelve spokes represent the twelve ages radiating from the Yin Yang, which is the symbol of the Union of the Polarity. The dot in the center, containing the Yin Yang symbol, is the central source of the symbol of Precession. The deer shown in the act of looking at the symbol do not represent the animals coming out the forest to hear the Tibetan message, but rather represent Christ as the testament to the message of peace and unity of the spirit of mankind. It was this exact same message of peace He taught while He was on the Earth. This symbol places Christ in the vicinity of the roots of Tibetan Buddhism, offering explanations for the origin of His doctrine he tried to teach the children of Israel. (See *Volume Three* pgs. 309-311)

The End Time Updates

2012 Recapped

2012 is not a hoax and should be taken seriously. Roland Emmerich's 2012 movie pretty much depicts what is to happen only the cause of the cataclysm in the movie is wrong. Will the oceans top the Himalayas as shown in the movie? We don't think it will; but it could. The reason we don't think it will is because God promised to never flood the Earth again, however he was talking about the true Earth or Spirit Earth. Since the two worlds are united as one until the Maya last day, it would be impossible to flood the physical Earth without flooding the spiritual creation. Taking that point into consideration, we feel at least one third of Earth's population will survive to face tribulation as prophesied in Revelation; therefore the water will not top the Himalayas prior to the last day and ascension of Spirit Earth. After the ascension of Spirit Earth anything goes; it will be the survival of the fittest for those one-third left behind.

The Maya were not the only ones who knew about the end time date of December 21, 2012, as most of the ancient world did from 3,000 BC. up till the late 1800s when the knowledge was lost. Washington D.C. was laid out, by our Freemason founding fathers, to reflect 2012 as a reminder to visitors. Monuments carved in stone were left worldwide to warn our generation of 2012. The I Ching prophecy time line comes to an end on that exact date as does the Cherokee calendar. Many cycles of time end on 2012 for a reason. Christ taught about 2012 in the Bible so we were meant to know what to expect. It is not the second coming of Christ as that occurs after tribulation and no man knows the hour of his coming then.

2012 is complicated as a series of events will occur almost simultaneously. It is not the end of the world but it is the end of the true Earth, the original creation, or Spirit Earth in this universe or dimension. If you live in the northern hemisphere, the winter solstice date is December 21, 2012. When this day arrives, it will set off a chain reaction of terrifying cosmic and planetary destructions not seen since the days of Noah's flood. For those living in the southern hemisphere, the winter solstice date is June 21, 2012. It is the Day of the Lord's Wrath spoken of in the Bible when the fiery indignation of the Lord is poured upon the Earth (Zephaniah 3:8)); a day of destruction (Isa. 13:6) (Joel 1:15); a day of gloom and thick darkness (Joel 2:2) (Zephaniah 1:15) (Amos 5:20) where the light of the sun, moon, and stars fade (Joel 3:15); a day of quaking of the Earth and trembling of the heavens (Joel 2:10). It is spoken of as a very dreadful day which will be ushered in with a mighty and terrible universal noise defined as the voice of the Lord; everyone will hear it (Zephaniah 1:14). So terrible will be these events that men's hearts will fail from fear for fear will come upon all people (Doctrine and Covenants 88:90-91) (Qur'an 6914). The Day of the Lord's Wrath is not a 24 hour event but rather will extend past tribulation until Lucifer is defeated and death and hell are destroyed. In other words, God's wrath or vengeance will prevail until Lucifer is finally defeated. Remember a day with God equals 1,000 years of man's time on this planet.

After the movie 2012 was shown around the world, thousands of worried people contacted NASA wanting to know the facts. NASA was flooded with calls so they responded by referring people to their 2012 website where they issued a statement. Their website assured people their fears were unfounded. It was not the end of the world but rather an end to a cycle of time when they expect the Maya to restart their calendar in a new cycle of time. Furthermore they said the sun's ecliptic had crossed the galactic equator of our galaxy at midpoint at least once yearly and nothing happened. That statement is true. What they didn't tell you, and perhaps they don't know, is every time the sun makes a transit over the galactic equator at midpoint, it is advancing closer and closer with each pass until on the 2012 winter solstice it will be positioned in the vaginal opening of the dark rift of the Milky Way. When this occurs, it is the Sign of the Suntelia Aeon which marks the End of the Age. The last time the sun did this was 5,125 years ago or 3,114 BC., the date the Maya started their Long Count calendar. It will have taken about 2,562.5 years for the sun to retreat from the vaginal opening of the dark rift and then about another 2,562.5 years to steadily advance back toward the vaginal opening of the dark rift. It is a circular cycle that takes approximately 5,125 years to complete. The Maya believe the 4th World was destroyed when it last made this transit 5,125 years ago. According to their creation myths, Quetzalcoatl created the present 5th World after the last destruction, thus the basis of the 3,114 BC. date to start reckoning time for the new world in their Long Count calendar.

That one event, the sun being positioned in the vaginal opening of the dark rift, is the big difference from all other transits of the sun at midpoint of the galactic equator and it is the event that triggers the 2012 chain reaction of a series of cataclysmic events. One has only to serf the web to find dozens of other 2012 websites with misinformation and most surprising from people with credible credentials who claim to be Maya experts. The fact remains, they are misinformed. In order to understand 2012, it is necessary to trace the origin of this belief to its roots. Without doing a very comprehensive search, ones focus will be too narrow to grasp the truth. Had proper research been done, it would have become evident that this was a world-wide ancient belief which continued up till the late eighteen hundreds when the knowledge was suddenly and very abruptly lost.

We want to correct some of this misinformation with fact. **First** of all the ancient Maya said they will not restart their calendar again as it will not be necessary because time will be measured differently in the fourth dimension. The ancient Maya expressed this evolutionary period as "The Time of No Time." **Second**, the ancient Maya, as well as most of the ancient world, understood that it was not the end of the world but rather it is the end of the true Earth or original creation in this dimension. It is the ascension of the Spirit Earth into the fourth spiritual dimension by a process that we now call "rapture." Not all will ascend with the Spirit Earth; only those who are righteous. **Third**, it was a worldwide belief that it is the appointed time of the first resurrection of the righteous dead. Your authors have tried to show numerous monuments that reflect this belief. Therefore, to say the Maya only left behind their tradition that their calendar cycle ends is not true as they left behind many stelae and monuments which express their belief of ascension and resurrection. **Fourth**, most of the modern Maya Elders have been schooled into thinking it is only a restart of a new cycle of time. They, as well as many others, have not done their homework concerning this ancient belief. However they are partly correct as it is true that a new cycle of time will restart for those left behind on the physical Earth. Having said the above, let us continue on the mechanics of 2012.

When the 2012 winter solstice sun is positioned in the vaginal opening of the dark rift, it will appear to be rising out of the mouth of the dragon Ouroboros which is best seen from the constellation of Sagittarius. On Earth, it may appear as a collapsed sky as the orientation is such that the Milky Way rims the horizon at all points around. Thus, the Milky Way literally "sits" on the Earth, touching it at all points around, opening up the Ouroboros cosmic sky portal. When this occurs, the physical Earth will be in the center of the Ouroboros. The cardinal constellations will be aligned to form a cross; prophesied as signs in the sky. When this event happens, it is the Sign of the Suntelia Aeon. It marks the End of the Age or the end of a 26,000 year Precession or Great Year which is a minor cycle of time. Many cycles of time end on December 21, 2012. Four Great Years make up a major, sometimes called great, cycle of time called a Sun Year or 104,000 years. The 104,000 Sun Year cycle also ends on 2012. According to ancient belief, each time a major cycle (Sun Year) of time ends, destruction follows. Christians can relate to this as the opening of the Sixth Seal followed with a great destructive earthquake as prophesied in Revelation and in the D&C.

At the moment the Sign of the Suntelia Aeon appears, the Earth will be positioned to start a three day transit probably through a narrow lower portion of the dark rift of the Milky Way. The trump sounds (the universal noise) at the opening of the Sixth Seal which will be accompanied by a great universal earthquake. Then the Earth will lose one of its tetrahedrons as its spiritual counterpart, the original creation or Spirit Earth, will separate from the physical or Temporal Earth by a process called in today's time, the "rapture." The departure of the

Spirit Earth causes the universal earthquake because the eight mighty tetrahedron engines are revved up to launch or separate the worlds. Currently as the end of the age approaches, we are experiencing an increase in the number of big earthquakes, climate change, and global warming because of tetrahedron excitement. Anciently it was called the time of the change, the removal of Earth, the ascension of Earth, the renewal of Earth, the transdimensional change, transfiguration of Earth, and translation of Earth. LDS (Mormons) can relate the transfiguration of Earth to the return of Earth to its terrestrial glory, albeit is the true Earth and not the physical Earth. New Agers and spiritualists call it a rise to a higher level of consciousness, but it involves much more. It is a pre-tribulation rapture of not only the righteous living people, but of the Earth itself; and believed to be the time of the first resurrection of the righteous dead. Christ taught the *Harvest* would happen at the end of the age when his angels will separate the wheat (good people) from the tares (bad people). This separation process is done by rapture or removal into the 4th dimension, 4th universe, or 4th heaven via entry by way of the Ouroboros cosmic portal. Spirit Earth will ascend through the Ouroboros portal. Isaiah prophesied that the Earth will be removed amidst the great shaking of the Earth. Old Testament prophets understood the original creation or true Earth was the Spirit Earth. Most of the time when they reference Earth, they were referring to the Spirit Earth. After the removal of Spirit Earth, the tares are left behind on the physical Earth to face a destruction and tribulation.

After the earthquake and removal of the Spirit Earth, the physical Earth will immediately start a three day transit through the dark rift in darkness as this region is filled with black non luminous clouds that block out the light of the sun, moon, and stars. As previously written, we think the Earth will transit a narrow lower portion of the dark rift which is an upper portion of the vaginal opening. It is what lurks in the dark rift that causes the cataclysm.

In the center of our Milky Way galaxy is a supermassive spinning black hole around which everything in this galaxy rotates. It has two axis; a rotational axis and an electromagnet axis along which flows much of its energy directly into the dark rift. Even though the black hole is about 24,000 light years away, due to its supermassive size, the energy flows down this axis as if it were running down a couple of blocks. At present no one knows the strength of the energy flowing along the electromagnetic axis, but it did destroy a beeper satellite in 1997 when some of this energy strayed nearly thirteen years ago. Bear in mind, thirteen years ago our Earth was much further away from where it is now in relationship to the dark rift. The US military became aware of this over 20 years ago and have made the following statement "A time will come soon when the electromagnetic grid will go down." It is said that plans are now well advanced to deal with this but the public is still being kept totally in the dark. Since the electromagnet axis is spawned by an enormous supermassive spinning black hole, common sense dictates it is super powerful and dangerous. The rotating Earth generates its own electromagnetic force field that envelopes the planet from pole to pole. When the physical Earth transits the dark rift, it will pass through the electromagnet axis of the black hole. A cataclysm will happen on Earth when these two magnetic force fields collide. And it is possible that the two magnetic force fields will have interaction several weeks before our planet actually starts the transit. Terrible electrical storms, deluges of rain, and tidal surges of water inland from gravitational pulls may happen. Even worse, the planet's power grid could be wiped out leaving the planet without any source of electricity. Airports, seaports, radio, television, computers, satellites, cell phones, generators, etc. will be rendered useless. All communication, for the most part, will be impossible. Even ham radio and generators may fail if batteries are drained by this energy; not to mention cars and trucks. Again, it is said that the US military and government have plans well advanced to deal with failure of the power grid. Will the plans be adequate? We don't know but we do know without this back up plan with all the raging terrible tempests and deluges of rain, not even a smoke signal could be sent. In an instant, our planet would be paralyzed by day and paralyzed in total darkness by night. People will quickly sense a feeling of doom such as, the world is coming to an end, followed by panic. Unless you are temporally prepared with some sort of underground well-stocked emergency shelter, you may not survive until the time of the rapture of Spirit Earth.

When Earth passes through the magnetic axis in the dark rift, the external powerful forces of the axis will cause it to shake. Prophecy says the great shaking of Earth will come from above the planet and not beneath the crust. We think Earth will be like a ping pong ball in front of a fan. The great shaking of the Earth will cause tectonic plate movement, earthquakes, volcanic eruptions, island and land masses rising and sinking, and enormous tsunamis. One third of the world's population is prophesied in Revelation to perish. Need we say more? If you are one of those souls who are left behind, your best chance of survival is in an underground shelter located at least 1200 feet above sea level away from coastal areas, islands, earthquake faults and volcanic areas. It is possible that the sea will surge inland to the foot of the Appalachians at a depth of 200 feet or more. Remote viewers have seen the sun's corona being affected by the electromagnetic axis and reported "seeing" great globs of fiery like plasma flying off into space, striking the Earth. Where ever those globs struck, the Earth was burnt. This is the prophesied purification and cleansing of Earth.

After the Earth makes its three day transit, things will slowly simmer down. As the Earth approached the dark rift, so it will be as it departs out of the area. According to ancient belief, this is the fifth and last time planet Earth will make this transit. US Navel astronomer Tom Van Flanders (now deceased) verified Earth will make this transit during a radio talk show interview with Dr. Brooks Agnew on X-Squared Radio. All prophecy and predictions say the transit will be cataclysmic. Shortly after the three day or 72 hour transit, the Seventh Seal in Revelation will be opened.

According to prophecy, this is the last time the physical Earth will make this transit as the events of tribulation will eventually wind down for those left behind, the second coming of Christ will happen following tribulation, and the thousand year millennial reigns will commence on the Spirit Earth and on the physical Earth. The realization that the Second Coming has already begun renders the dogma of man ignominious. Following the millennial reigns, the final great judgment happens before the throne of God, whereby the state of each person's judgment will be revealed. There is no *being* that will suddenly judge a person. That part is already done, and kept current up the moment by your own thoughts and actions. Not even God can change that irrefutable fact. A fox will not suddenly become a swan. Likewise, the dark heart will have an allergic reaction to the light.

Death and hell are destroyed. When death and hell are destroyed, it is destroyed throughout the physical universe. Because death and hell are destroyed, we **now** feel our planet's Spirit Earth is the last of the Spirit Earths to return back into another dimension. We are the last to return. It may be this very reason why most of you are here. You came here to make sure not one soul is lost, least of all your own. And, now you are empowered to go forward without fear. The Christ is within you and only needs the air of your awareness to glow brightly enough to show you that loving yourself, and then your neighbor is the ultimate expression of love for God.

That statement alone revises our statements found on page 202 in the second volume and on page 235 in the third volume. A universal destruction of the physical universe will then occur. It is the end of an eternity, which is one of many eternities. After a long period of rest, another "big bang" will occur and another creative process will take place. The cycles of creation and destruction are eternal endless rounds. Like a circle or a ring, the cycles of creation and destruction have no end or no beginning...just one endless round.

The great *I Am* awareness is the driving energy of existence. It is consciousness that creates time, and thus distance, in a universe that from the perspective of the speed of light is still the singularity from it burst forth. Letting light *be* is the God act of creation. The Union of the Polarity is the act of birth, and the separation of that union is the metamorphosis of the soul. The soul of man, the soul of a planet, and the soul of a Sun, are manifested as bodies only when this Union occurs. The rest, and it is the overwhelming majority of the energy in the universe, is what we call dark matter. Keep in mind that we only call it *dark* because we can't see it. It's there. And the visible portion of the universe is only that which has crossed through the *I Am,* to become physical. All of this will happen before another transit is made through the dark rift by the physical Earth. Therefore prophecy has it right, 2012 is the fifth and last time the physical Earth will transit the dark rift.

In light of these things, it is better to be forewarned and forearmed by both spiritual and temporal preparedness. Y2K came and went without incident but this date is far different; it has been prophesied for five millenniums warning people to prepare for the *Harvest* at the end of the age. Every religion, whether major or minor, non-religious spiritualists, even atheist and agnostics agree something will happen on the end time date of 2012. Those who believe nothing is going to happen; they are asleep at the wheel. We are constantly being asked…..do you really believe this will happen? My reply is…given the world's present situation; don't you think it is time?

After pondering my question for a few moments, almost everyone over 35 nodded their head in agreement. It is our belief and our opinion these things will probably happen on December 21, 2012, as prophesied.

Milky Way "Dark Rift"

My co-author, Dr. Brooks Alexander Agnew PhD., hosts his own radio talk show every Sunday on X-Squared Radio for three hours via internet radio through BBC. He interviewed Tom Van Flanders, a former chief astronomer for the US Naval Observatory and a former NASA astronaut, twice. Tom verified for Dr. Agnew that our Earth will indeed make a transit through the "dark rift" of the Milky Way on December 21-23, 2012 and that the Solar System would pass through the Black Axiom.

He explained that this cataclysmic event was the collision of the planets, asteroids, and the Sun with a cloud or layer of dense, granular matter resulting in a 150 thousand mile an hour rain of small particles. Although short in duration, the evidence that this occurred approximately 25 thousand years ago is there to see, and will happen again in 2012.

We are in agreement that Earth will make a transit through the "dark rift" but believe that the cataclysm is caused by the magnetic axis of the supermassive black hole interacting with the Earth's magnetic force field. Perhaps there is another hidden danger lurking in the dense non-luminous dark clouds that will add to the destructive forces of the black hole magnetic axis identified by Tom as the Black Axion. Most important, we are in agreement that Earth's transit through the "dark rift" will be cataclysmic whether it is caused by the black hole magnetic axis, the Black Axion, or both. Unfortunately, Tom passed away on January 9, 2009, from a short bout with cancer but fortunately for us those two interviews were archived on X-Squared Radio for public listening for a small fee.

As most of you know, NASA scientists are down playing the Maya End Time date of December 21, 2012. They have received thousands of emails from worried citizens that it is the end of the world. They are assuring people that it is not the end of the world but only the re-start of the Maya calendar when it ends at the end of Precession or the Great Year which calculates on the Gregorian calendar to December 21, 2012 or the End of the Age. They further assert that Planet X or Nibiru is non existent, and that no known comets or asteroids pose any threats. On those two subjects, I firmly agree.

There is a hieroglyphic text discovered on Monument 6 in Tortuguero, a classic Maya site near Palanque, which refers explicitly to December 21, 2012. The legible part of the text reads: "At the end of 13 Baktuns, on 4 Ahau 3 Kankin, 13.0.0.0.0; "something" occurs when Bolon Yokte descends." This "something" or verb glyph describing what happens is effaced; therefore unreadable. But Bolon means nine in Maya and should read....the god nine wind, Bolon Yokte, descends. On page 75 in Volume Three is a redrawn image from the Maya Codex Vindobonenis, of the god nine wind (Bolon Yokte) or Quetzalcoatl/

Christ descending down from the "dark rift" portal on his serpent rope to Earth on December 21, 2012. Please read the full account on page 75. Some Maya experts have interpreted this to mean the return of Quetzalcoatl at the end of the age. Perhaps this was fueled by the Books of the Chilam Balam or Books of the Jaguar Priest which date to 1168 AD. and probably was not the original title because it was comprised of sacred books kept by each community that were written and maintained by the high holy order of the Jaguar Priests.

These sacred books were the pre-conquest Bible of the Yucatán. The text of the Chumayel Chilam Balam states the high holy order of the Jaguar Priesthood was established directly by Quetzalcoatl/ Christ in ancient times and makes reference to the white garments worn by the priests of Quetzalcoatl. Not surprising, the ancient Toltec Mesoamerican record known today as the Book of Mormon speaks of this holy high priesthood calling as being after the order of the Son, the only begotten of the Father and that Melchizedek, King of Salem, belonged to this high priesthood calling (Book of Mormon, Alma chapter 13).

Today, The Church of Jesus Christ of Latter-Day Saints, nicknamed the Mormons, calls this same high priesthood calling, the Melchizedek Priesthood, after Melchizedek, the King of Salem whom Abraham paid his tithes. And they wear white priesthood clothing when officiating in the LDS temples just as the Jaguar Priests did when they officiated in Maya temples. Therefore this same high holy priesthood calling dates back to very ancient times, even to Abraham who received it from Jehovah (Book of Abraham page 30, verse 18). Note, Noah may have been the uncle of Melchizedek (Volume One, pages 468-470). Mormon was a great Mesoamerican Nephite/Toltec prophet and a writer of one of the books he named appropriately after himself, *The Book of Mormon,* which is contained collectively in the Book of Mormon. Back to the Chilam Balam.....each book of the Chilam Balam bears the name of the community in the Chilam for identification purposes. Nine manuscripts survive. These are the Chilam Balam of Chumayel, Mani, Tizimin, Kaua, Ixil, and Tusik. What has survived was translated from Yucatec Maya into Latin around the late seventeenth century post conquest. Although much was added to these texts such as a blended mixture of the old faith with Christianity, many passages were originally transcribed from much older hieroglyphic manuscripts that date back to the Eleventh Century. Chilam Balam was the last great Maya Jaguar Priest prophet who appeared among the Itza-Maya who were of Chichimec Toltec descent or related to the Toltec and Toltec Maya. The Maya word Chilam translates as priest and the Maya word Balam translates as jaquar. Therefore the high holy priesthood in Yucatec Maya was called the Chilam Balam or Jaguar Priests. Chilam Balam took upon himself the name of the holy priesthood as a prophet; his true identity unknown.

His dates are uncertain, but it is thought he lived during the last decades of the Fifteenth Century and probably during part of the Sixteenth Century. These Itza Mayas were followers of Quetzalcoatl or Kukulkan as he was known to the Maya in much of the Yucatán.

They were probably descendants of the Chichimec Toltecs who were driven out of Tula with their priest leader Topiltzin Quetzalcoatl who took upon himself the title of Quetzalcoatl being a priest and follower of Quetzalcoatl. This group traveled to the Yucatán and was assimilated into the Maya city of Chichen Itza (Volume Three pages 377-381). In his book of Toltec prophecies Chilam Balam put great emphasis on the return of Quetzalcoatl at the end of the age. The prophetic book speaks of withered fruit, probably from heat, deluges of destructive rain, the ornaments or stars of heaven falling, and the face of the sun extinguished because of the great tempest to happen on December 21, 2012. His book of prophecies associates this date as the day of resurrection and states the union ended, probably in reference to the separation of the two planets or Union of the Polarity. Interestingly enough he identifies the Toltec and Toltec Maya belief of 13 Gods as the Gods of 13 heavens. According to the Toltec/Book of Mormon record, these 13 Gods or 13 shining spiritual beings descended from heaven and traveled over the Earth (1 Nephi 1:9-11) (Volume Three, pages 307-308) (Volume One, pages 478-482) (Volume Two, pages 84, 92, and 150). They were the Shining Ones. Chilam Balam also said the Milky Way World Tree represented the Tree of Life which Adam and Eve partook of its fruit in the Garden of Eden. He said its many branches reached to heaven and poked through its many portals (read *The Gates of Heaven* chapter, Volume One). Back to the Tortuguero text. Our interpretation of Monument 6 is: Christ/Quetzalcoatl will be present at the renewal or ascension of the Spirit Earth into the 4th dimension via the "dark rift" portal or wormhole into the spiritual 4th dimension. It is another carved in stone monument warning of a pre-tribulation rapture at the end of the age.

The ancient Maya said that it would be the end of the world, the true Earth or original creation in this dimension or universe on December 21, 2012, through a process called translation or transfiguration, now called in modern terms "rapture." Their calendar will not re-start because time is measured differently on the true Earth in another dimension or universe; therefore there is no need for it. The physical Earth is not the true Earth however; it will experience a cataclysm as it makes a three day transit through the "dark rift" of the Milky Way which will knock civilization back to the Stone Age. Roland Emmerich's 2012 movie pretty much depicts what is to happen, although the cause of the cataclysm in the movie is wrong. Will a wave of water top the Himalayas as shown in the movie? Probably not, but it could if there is enough tectonic plate movement. The physical earth will survive but one-third of the Earth's population will perish. Christ taught 2012 in the Bible. He called it the Day of the Lords Wrath. John, the revelator, recorded the cataclysm in Revelation. Isaiah saw the true Earth or original creation being removed. For these reasons, 2012 must be taken seriously. Roland Emmerich, unknowingly, did a great public service by the making of his 2012 movie because it has brought about public awareness of 2012.

If Tom Van Flanders, a former NASA astronaut and naval astronomer knew about Earth making a transit through the "dark Rift" in the Milky Way on December 21-23rd, 2012, why don't the other NASA scientists also know this? What one knows, the others should know as information is generally shared. They are giving out a lot of dis-information concerning 2012. However just recently NASA disclosed powerful solar storms in 2012-2013 could knock us off the grid for up to 3 years.

It is true that the suns ecliptic (path) crosses the Galactic Equator at near mid-point yearly without event. What scientists and astronomers fail to disclose is the sun in its path has been steadily advancing toward the "dark Rift" over a 5,125 year time span, until on the Summer and Winter Solstices at the approach of December 21, 2012. When the sun crosses the exact mid-point of the Galactic Equator, it will be positioned in the *vaginal* opening of the "dark rift." That is the difference. Earth will then be positioned to start its three day cataclysmic transit through the upper narrow vaginal portion of the "dark rift." Keep in mind that as this intense gravity is applied, time itself will become relative. Half an hour could be twenty-one years. Don't think for one moment that you only need a 72-hour kit and a good place to hide for three days to survive this.

Do not astronomers and NASA scientists know this? Even I, an amateur astronomer, figured it out over five years ago, when I and Dr. Agnew wrote Volume One of the trilogy, and a noted astronomer Tom Van Flanders verified it. This is pure science and nothing else. Or is it another government cover-up? For what reason? Perhaps it is in preparation for the coming New World Order and the reappearance of the Nephilim before 2012? If so, then NASA is in cahoots with alien off world beings, something other writers and UFO organizations have accused them of for many years. Or....are a few select human beings preparing to board arks built to preserve the human race along with selected animals in anticipation of the coming 2012 global cataclysm? Do you have your ticket to board an ark as Roland Emmerich's 2012 movie portrays? Roland Emmerich's 2012 movie may be right on target with the floating arks.

A Nephilim Presence

In Volumes Two and Three of *The Ark of Millions of Years* we wrote the Nephilim could possibly return as early as 2010 to help the people of this planet survive 2012. We based this theory on the belief that they did so in the past when they helped populations of people survive the cataclysm of 9,500 BC.; the day the Earth nearly died. Tunnels and underground facilities were constructed world wide to save mankind. Some are open to the public to visit. Because history tends to repeat itself we expect their imminent return....or are they here already? Perhaps they never left, but rather went into hiding until they could recruit government or economic leadership greedy enough to trade their knowledge and power for personal wealth. That is the question.

What we present next is taken from a website called Project Camelot and the content is titled *A Letter from a Norwegian Politician*. The website states they have checked the authenticity of the letter, written in 2008, and are certain of their bona fides, but they cannot reveal the name of the writer of the letter without consent. The website added the following disclaimer, " The content of this message, if true, could hardly be more important." Because the letter is long with further correspondence to Project Camelot, we have elected to take excerpts of the most important parts as follows:

"I am a Norwegian politician. I would like to say that difficult things will happen from the year 2008 till the year 2012. "The Norwegian government is building more and more underground bases and bunkers. When asked, they simply say that it is for the protection of the people of Norway. When I enquire when they are due to be finished, they reply "before 2011."

"I have been to several underground bases (number given). We used the railcars to get around. Only a few special people were selected to be shown around. Those that run with the elite know of this.

"The NOAH 12 railcars are transport railcars between the different bases underground. They have a support system of there all around from one base to another. They are mainly used by the military and they control all of them. There are orange triangle symbols in each base and the check-ins are a kind of energy field that everyone has to go through.

"When I was in the military I was in the (name of service given). At one point we were given a task to get something out of a base and deliver it to another base.

"We were told: 'DO NOT ASK ANY QUESTIONS; JUST DO YOUR JOB.' Later, when we landed outside the base, we were taken by trucks to outside the base where there were large doors heavily guarded by other military personnel.

"Or it seemed like they were military, but they had different suits on them; orange and black suits with the orange suits having a golden triangle on them and the black suits having a green triangle.

"We went through the large doors. We then came to a 500 meter long tunnel and there were more of these military personnel waiting with guns and transport for us. We were divided up in groups. My group was asked to come with the black suited guards so they could take us to another location. When we came to the end we were asked to put on some masks "for our own protection."

"We were then asked to step inside a railcar…and this is what I know of the railcars. They are run by some kind of blue crystal energy, I think, or at least that is how it appeared. Then we sat in the cars and I asked one of

171

the guards "What is this?" He replied, "You don't need to know this, sir."

"At the front where the operator sits there was a box with a window just beside him, and just when before powering up you could see the large purple-blue crystals emitting a purple-bluish light...not blinding you but quiet beautiful to watch indeed. I have never ever seen such energy light or crystals anywhere. I was thinking that must be the power source.

"Later on in the base I saw that some people were working on these purple-blue crystals. They were larger than the one I saw in the railcar calculated one meter in length and they were lined up one after the other. They were taking some light through them. They were in fact purple-blue and when the light went inside they turned more blue and had a stronger color—the people had white masks on and goggles standing away from them when the light was going inside the crystals. I was about 20 meters from them and we were quickly rushed along when they said "Move on now."

"I could see that there was a tube-like system and the other railcars were just going so fast you just saw a light going by. I think this was a vacuum tube system where there is no drag. The rail system runs for miles and miles.

"Later on, after I went into politics, I found out what was inside of the rest of the base and what the bases are for, which I have already told you. (Note: he was told that that Planet X is coming). What I found out was that these bases were Arks for the government and some of the people and military to survive inside. There was a threat from outside that was going to be in the year 2012 and that the human species had to survive.

"The Planet X I learned about is from all what I have seen till now. The government knows this and are keeping it from the public. They have been tracking this object for a long time now and were given the first warnings from the USA. If this object goes by, there will be a lot of problems on the surface of the Earth. This is why they go underground. When they know it's safe to surface, they will rebuild again. We were just told that we have to leave before 2012 and that there is something in space that is going to cause much destruction.

"All the major politicians know this in Norway, but few will say it to the people and the public because they are afraid in case they too will be denied access to the NOAH 12 railcars that will take them to the underground ark sites where they will be safe. If they tell anyone, they are dead for sure.

"In 2009 the government of FRP will come into power and Siv Jensen will be elected Prime Minister. This is already known. It's important to understand that. The elections are all fake and the same persons and power elite get elected each time in turn. Look up the political history of Norway, and the people that run the country now.

"I know that 18 bases exist in Norway. These bases have been built over a period of 40 or 50 years. But what I know is that before 2012 the different governments are going to leave for the bases.

"All the sectors and arks are connected with tunnels and have railcars that can take you from one ark to the other. This is so that they can be in contact with each other. Only the large doors separate them so that the sectors are not compromised in any way.

"The plan is that 2,000,000 Norwegians are going to be safe, and the rest will die.

"The marks of the alien presence are also there, and I often see the Norwegian elite politicians are not what they say they are. It's like they are controlled in every thought, and what they have to say is just as they are told to do things in such manners. It is clear for me who they are, and who they are not. You can see it in their eyes and in their minds.

"When we came outside we were given goggles and asked to go through a security check by going through an energy field. At the energy field check-in there was a screen, which I mentioned before with a weird language on the screen. The only thing I could read was HUMAN---NOT HUMAN---PURE---NOT PURE.

"I can say that I have already said too much; I am just telling what I have seen and nothing more." (letter signed by politician)

End of Letter

The Project Camelot website states they were told by Henry Deacon (and this has also been widely reported by others) that the South Pole Telescope has been built to track what Henry called the 'second sun'. They urge readers to do their own research.

As for us, your authors, we contend there is no Planet X lurking in the shadows. If governments are buying this, it is a diversionary tactic of the Nephilim presence to gain control and allegiance of governments to the upcoming New World Order following 2012. The Norwegian politician did say that many other governments were building these underground facilities only naming the USA and Israel. We can understand why Israel would build shelters underground to survive a nuclear attack from her enemies. Nuclear fallout shelters are a different thing. On the other hand, deep underground bases may not be the safest place during tectonic plate movement unless the Nephilim know where and how to construct underground arks to withstand a global cataclysm affecting the Earth's crust. Is the letter genuine? Maybe yes and maybe no but it does raise the possibility that there is already an alien Nephilim presence here helping governments and small populations of elite people, such as scientists, doctors, physicists, engineers, computer experts etc., to survive 2012 unbeknown to the general public. Saving the technically advanced elites will aid in the rebuilding of civilization to usher in the New World Order. Roland Emmerich's 2012 movie played out this same scenario as a few thousand selected government elites and their families were given tickets to board survival arks waiting for them high in the Himalayas. When the oceans rose violently to the peaks of these mountains, the arks floated safely away with people and animals to repopulate the Earth much like Noah's Ark. Makes for a good story but highly improbable that arks are waiting there. Your best ark is the Spirit Earth.

There is more. Bill Gates, along with the Rockefeller Foundation, Monsanto Corporation, Syngenta Foundation, and the Government of Norway, among others, has invested millions of his own money in an Ark in the Rock or Doomsday Seed Vault in Norway. Its official name is the Svalbard Global Seed Vault located on the Norwegian island of Spitsbergan near the town of Longyearbyen in the remote Arctic Svalbard archipelago, about 810 miles from the North Pole. Construction of the seed vault was funded entirely by the Government of Norway. Operational costs will be paid by Norway and the UN supported Global Crop Diversity Trust (GCDT). The primary funding of the Trust came from the Bill & Melinda Gates Foundation, United Kingdom, Norway, Australia, Switzerland, Sweden, Brazil, Columbia, Ethiopia, and India.

The seed bank is constructed inside a sandstone mountain. Its site was considered ideal due to its lack of tectonic activity and its permafrost, which will aid preservation. The location is 430 feet above sea level that will ensure the site remains dry even if the icecaps melt.

It was designed to withstand even nuclear strikes. A study determined that the vault could preserve seeds from most major food crops for hundreds of years and possibly thousands of years for important grains. The seed vault opened officially on February 26, 2008.

The Svalbard Global Seed Vault's mission is to provide a safety net against accidental loss of diversity in traditional genebanks due to mismanagement, accident, natural disasters, wars, civil strife, equipment failures, funding cuts and climate change. These events occur with some regularity. Case in point, in recent years, two national genebanks have already been destroyed by war and civil strife. The seed vault functions like a safety deposit box in a bank. The bank owns the building and the depositor owns the contents of his or her box. This means the Government of Norway owns the facility and the depositing genebanks own the seed they send. Ownership remains with the depositor, who has the sole right of access to those materials in the seed vault. No one has access to anyone else's seeds from the seed vault. Storage of seeds in the vault is free of charge. There are about 1,400 seed banks in the world who store seeds in this vault in case their deposits are lost. Approximately 400,000 seed samples thus far are in storage. Each sample contains about 500 seeds so the total number of seeds presently being stored is approximately 250 million individual seeds. It is estimated the facility now houses at least one-third of the world's crop seeds.

We ask "Is it by coincidence that Norway was chosen as the site of the Ark in the Rock or do they know more than what they are telling?" Does 2012 have anything to do with the construction of a super safe seed bank? If the letter from a Norwegian politician is genuine; there is a connection. We urge our readers to be aware of what could be taking place in a sublime manner. Perhaps Henry Kissenger said it best when he said "Who controls the food supply controls the people; who controls the energy can control whole continents; who controls money can control the world." It appears the world is preparing for the New World Order to be ushered in after 2012 under the auspice of the Nephilim.

2012 in the Toltec Record/Book of Mormon

Alma 26:5-7

Verse 5 Behold, the field was ripe, and blessed are ye, for ye did thrust in the sickle, and did reap with your might, yea, all the day long did ye labor; and behold the number of your sheaves! And they shall be gathered into the garners, that they are not wasted.

Verse 6 Yea, they shall not be beaten down by the storm at the last day; yea, neither shall they be harrowed up by the whirlwinds; but when the storm cometh they shall be gathered together in their place, that the storm cannot penetrate to them; yea, neither shall they be driven with fierce winds whithersoever the enemy listeth to carry them.

Verse 7 But behold, they are in the hands of the Lord of the harvest, and they are his; and he will raise them up at the last day.

Here in verse 5, we see Ammon talking about the Lamanites who have been converted by their labor in the mission field. Verse 4, not quoted, states there were thousands of Lamanites who were converted while Ammon and his brothers served in the mission field. Continuing on in verse 5, Ammon compares the converted Lamanites to harvested sheaves that are gathered into the garners for safe keeping which means that even after death they are gathered together in their place for safe keeping which is in the hands of the Lord. This of course is the spirit world where they are not lost or wasted. In verse 6, we see they are gathered and protected from the fierce winds and storms that cannot penetrate to them in the spirit world which will occur on the last day. In the spirit world the enemy, being Satan, has no power over them; they are safe in the hands of the Lord. The Maya understand to this present day that the *last day* calculates in the Gregorian calendar to Dec. 21, 2012, when their calendar ends at the End of the Age. They even have a symbol for it which is the Omega sign (Omega means end) or upside down U which is pictured on all three of the trilogy book covers. The symbol has always meant the *last day* or 2012. Verse 7 then says the Lord of the Harvest will raise them up at the *last day*. The *Harvest* of course is an archaic word which means the translation, transfiguration, ascension, renewal, refreshing, change, or transdimensional change of the Earth and living righteous people, that we now call in more modern terms, the *rapture*. The Lord of the Harvest separates the wheat from the tares by a process called translation, transfiguration, or *rapture*. It was also believed by the Maya and the ancient world, on both sides of the continents, to be the time of the first resurrection of the righteous dead. Later Book of Mormon doctrine calls this the first resurrection of the morning (Mormon Doctrine by Bruce R. McConkie) when the righteous dead are resurrected.

These verses in Alma support a pre-tribulation rapture and in turn supports my theory that the Book of Mormon people were habitants

181

of Mesoamerica because the Maya and other tribes of Mesoamerica who used the Maya Long Count calendar during Book of Mormon times and up to present time were the only people on this continent who believed Dec. 21, 2012, is the *last day*, that is until the Freemasons arrived and founded America.. Washington D.C. was designed and built to reflect the End Time knowledge of the Union of the Polarity and 2012 by the Freemason founding fathers as a reminder to visitors. In other words, until the Freemasons arrived on this continent, the End Time date was known only to Mesoamerican tribes who used the Long-Count calendar. They, users of the Long Count calendar, also were the only early people, on this continent, who used the term...*the last day* in connection with their calendar End Time date. Therefore we can conclude that Ammon had to be one of those Mesoamericans who used the Long Count calendar because he used that term in Alma 26:7.

It was not possible to fully understand these verses until the publishing of *The Ark of Millions of Years* book trilogy unless of course LDS church leaders and their prophet have recently received it by revelation.

The Maya Creation Panel

Recently while in Playa Del Carmen I, E.J., found a large Maya carved wooden panel on display in the lobby of the Illusion Hotel. It perhaps is about 25 years old. I recognized the style of the artist because he carved two tables and an eight foot mahogany library door that has a five foot tall Maya priest carved in relief on it for my home. The Maya artist lives in Orange Walk, Belize. The carved wooden panel expresses the Maya belief of the creation and of the last day of Spirit Earth in this dimension on December 21, 2012. When I first saw the panel, I could read the glyphs and understand its message, pictured and explained below.

The first picture below shows the entire panel. The panel shows two jaguar priests dancing the Dance of Life (Life Force energy) which symbolically means the universe is ever moving and ever changing. Each priest is dancing on the back of a dual or two headed jaguar. One jaguar represents the spiritual creation and the other jaguar represents the physical or temporal creation. Each jaguar is standing on the back of the turtle earths resting on the Maya three stones of creation. The Maya believe that this present creation (the physical world) was created from three stones.

Figure 20: Maya Creation Panel

Figure 21: Jaguar priest dancing on the Maya Creation Panel

At the bottom of the panel are glyphs that read to the effect.... History of the Earth or Creation of the Earth. The glyphs read the same for each side of the panel. One side of the panel is referring to the spiritual creation and the other side is referring to the physical creation.

Figure 22: Bottom edge of Maya Creation Panel

The glyphs pictured below at the top of the panels really tell it all. Starting on the outer left and right sides of each panel are triangles or tetrahedrons that represent each creation or Earth; one spiritual and one physical. The next two glyphs show a fist with a yin yang sign of the palm of the hand. They symbolically read….the two worlds are firmly knitted together (as in the Union of the Polarity). Next to the fist glyphs are two glyphs showing three circles in a row or the three stones of creation now formed together as an Earth. Above and a little to the side is a dot within a circle which is a precession sign marking the time of the End of the Age or Dec. 21, 2012. The last glyph shows one stone of creation (circle) above the S shaped yin yang Union of the Polarity sign. Below the Union of the

Polarity sign are the two remaining stones of creation (two circles). The artist is symbolically telling us that on December 21, 2012, the top stone of creation (the spiritual Earth) is leaving behind the two stones of creation or the physical Earth at the end of precession or the last day.

Figure 23: The top edge of the Maya Creation Panel

The old Maya still believe December 21, 2012, is the last day however when talking to the younger present generation (15-30 year olds), most do not believe their parents as they are products of a modern education that does not mix science with religion. None of the younger generation that I interviewed knew anything about precession however they were aware of the End Time date of December 21, 2012, even if they didn't believe it was the last day.

The Latter Day End Time Books

When Joseph Smith lived in Nauvoo, he had Jewish friends who taught him to read and speak archaic Hebrew. Together they would meet, 2-3 times a week, and study the ancient manuscripts of the *Zohar*, a record preserved by the Jews, which I document from very heavily in *The Ark of Millions of Years* trilogy; books I wrote with a co- author. It is from the *Zohar* that I learned of the missing "key" of creation, which the *Zohar* calls the "one mystery" that I in turn named the Union of the Polarity. It is from the *Zohar* that Joseph Smith learned of and gave the teaching that when the Earth is glorified, "it will be rolled back into the presence of God and be crowned with celestial glory." Later, Brigham Young in a sermon stated "when man sinned, the Earth was hurled millions of miles away from its first position." He apparently had learned this from Joseph Smith in one of their many discussions on the creation, because this knowledge is found in the *Zohar*. Brigham Young was a brilliant man but not quiet the scholar that Joseph Smith was as is evident by the fact that he did not learn to read or speak Hebrew and study the *Zohar* as did Joseph Smith. We can therefore conclude with certainty that he learned of this knowledge from Joseph Smith.

It is evident that Joseph Smith and Brigham Young understood the concept of the Union of the Polarity because the Nauvoo Temple, **Salt Lake Temple** and many other Mormon temples are designed with the sacred number of the Union of the Polarity, which is the Hebrew word Vau or the number six, incorporated into their building design as was done in Solomon's Temple and in later Jewish temples. The little **Assembly Hall**, located near the Tabernacle, on Temple Square in Salt Lake City, even has four small round stained glass windows, on each side of the building, with the Star of David on it; just a Star of David and nothing else. Surrounding these windows are a modern day version of serpent bars with a center peak denoting or representing the end of the age or December 21, 2012, when the worlds separate by process of translation, transfiguration, or rapture. The Star of David is the symbol of the Union of the Polarity. Below the Star of David windows are many long narrow windows with serpent bars over them. These windows symbolize the fall of the spiritual world into the physical world. The Salt Lake Temple has six spires as do many other Mormon temples. The **Nauvoo Temple** has a large six pointed star on its balustrade and many round windows with five pointed pentagram stars set above the cornice sky band which represents the many feminine gendered Earths in the spiritual creations. The upright five pointed stars on the temple represent the telestial glory as the theme of the sun, moon, and stars, which represent the degrees of glory, are incorporated into this temple's design. There are also six columns topped with six sun stones across the front façade and the top spire is a layered octagon having eight angles that represent a dual star tetrahedron or a three dimensional Star of David. The long narrow windows on both temples represent the fall of the spiritual creation into the temporal creation. In Masonry, the circle represents the spiritual creation and the square or rectangle represents the temporal creation. The Salt Lake Temple has the squared circle repeated on its front doors symbolizing the union of heaven and earth. The Nauvoo and Salt Lake Temples are resplendent with round windows built into rectangular buildings which symbolize the union of the two creations that I named and call the Union of the Polarity.

LDS temples are heavily encrypted with much symbolic meaning. A symbol could mean several different things depending on the context you are seeking. There is Freemasonry symbolism, cosmic symbolism, spiritual symbolism, and gospel symbolism encoded in them. An example would be the six spires on the Salt Lake Temple. As written above, the number six in Freemasonry symbolism represents the Union of the Polarity. In gospel symbolism, Brigham Young said they represent the priesthood. Both are correct because they have multiple meaning. The interpretations given above on the temple symbols are taken solely from the Freemason standpoint.

It is known that Joseph Smith was a 33rd degreed Freemason, a later re-organization of the Knight Templars. The Knight Templars discovered the knowledge of the Union of the Polarity in manuscripts found hidden in the bronze columns of Solomon's Temple which was preserved in their organization. This is the reason the bronze columns of Solomon's Temple have always been held in high regard, if not sacred regard, in Masonry (pictured on front cover of this book). This knowledge was subsequently preserved in later off shoot organizations from the Knight Templars. This is proven in *The Ark of Millions of Years* trilogy as the Rosicrucians, an offshoot branch of Freemasons, even have a picture of the Spirit Earth uniting with this planet (pictured in Volume Three, page 340) in one of their lodges.

As a Freemason, Joseph Smith also knew of the End Time date of December 21, 2012, as this knowledge was also preserved in their organization and proven in Volume Three because the Freemason City of Washington D.C. was laid out to reflect this End Time knowledge as a reminder to its many visitors and habitants of the upcoming events associated with 2012. I went to Washington D.C. and got the pictures to prove it, now published in Volume Three. Brigham Young also knew the End Time date of 2012 as his home in Salt Lake City has a beehive symbol on its front entry. His Salt Lake home is referred to as the Beehive House. In Freemasonry the beehive was the arcane symbol of the astrological sign of Cancer. The sun will be in the house of Cancer on December 21, 2012, thus the beehive is another symbol for the End Time date of 2012. This beehive symbol is found on many Freemason ceremonial aprons. Brigham Young was initiated as a Freemason in the

Nauvoo Lodge on April 7, 1842. In fact, the first five presidents of the LDS Church were Freemasons.

Joseph Smith also knew of the prophecy found in the *Zohar* which says **that in the destined time of the renewal of the Earth,** which is the "rapture, translation of Earth, the removal of Earth, the ascension of Earth, the change of Earth, or Harvest at the End of the Age," **the knowledge of the "one mystery,"** which is the Union of the Polarity, **would be restored back to the Earth right before the imminent return of the Savior.**

So, if Joseph Smith knew about the Union of the Polarity and the End Time date, why didn't he give the LDS church the doctrine to prepare them? It is because of the *Zohar* prophecy itself which was cast by another unknown prophet many thousands of years ago. The prophecy says right before the imminent return of the Savior (the End Times) for the renewal of the Earth (the rapture, the refreshing of Earth, Harvest, ascension, or translation of Earth at the End of the Age due to happen on December 21, 2012), the knowledge of the "one mystery" (the Union of the Polarity) would be restored. Joseph Smith, knowing of the End Time date, knew he wasn't the one to give the doctrine because he was born on December 23, 1805, which is approximately 200 years from December 21, 2012. The knowledge of the restoration of the Union of the Polarity was to be given by someone else other than him; one who lived in the End Time generation right before 2012. Joseph Smith also knew the writings of the apostles Peter and John, who wrote of a coming "restitution of all things" (Acts 3:19-21). Again, why didn't he give the LDS church the doctrine? It is because a prophet always honors the words of another prophet and never over steps or supersedes another prophet's prophecy. He could not give the doctrine until the first *Zohar* prophecy was fulfilled which was cast by another prophet several thousands of years ago. Even God honors the words of his holy prophets. Joseph Smith knew the *Zohar* prophecy would be fulfilled in the form of records (books) in the latter days or End Times. Many records, both secular and non-secular, have been kept and preserved throughout the world for the era that we live in, which is the dispensation of the fullness of times, when all things in Christ will be gathered together (Ephesians 1:9-10) (D&C 9:2). Consequently, the future Freemason prophets of the LDS Church, including all future non-Freemason prophets of the church, are obliged to honor the *Zohar* prophecy as did Joseph Smith until that prophecy is fulfilled in the End Times. Simply stated, church prophets will not be inspired to give the doctrine on the Union of the Polarity until the *Zohar* prophecy is fulfilled.

The trilogy of books called, *The Ark of Millions of Years*, fulfills that prophecy found in the *Zohar*, because that is what the books are all about, the restoration of the knowledge of the "one mystery" I named and call the Union of the Polarity. Interestingly enough, the *Zohar*, the *Sefer Yetzirah*, the *Bahir*, and the *Book of Jasher*, are ancient records preserved by the Jews that have recently come forth for the world through translation into several languages. The Jews consider these books sacred. Another book, *The Secrets of Enoch*, was thought lost but was revealed to the world in 1892. It was known only to a few people in Russia. This book was referred to by Origen and used by the Church Father, Irenaeus. These records qualify to be some of the records of the lost ten tribes mentioned in the *Book of Mormon* which have come forth in the "due time of the Lord" (BOM 1 Nephi 14:26). We are the only authors in the world who have written on the subject of the Union of the Polarity which knowledge pertaining to the creation was found in many ancient records kept by the Jews but primarily the *Zohar*. The Ark books have also been identified, by the authors, as *The End Time Books*, which identity is written in the text and on the back cover of Volume Three of the trilogy. We can therefore conclude with certainty these are some of the inspired books (writings) prophesied to come forth in the latter days (End Times) which restore ancient knowledge pertaining to the Earth, as to its creation and destiny (commonly called by the LDS Church as *The End Time Books*). In addition they restore some of the plain and precious parts of our biblical books that were altered or removed. Not only does the trilogy fulfill the *Zohar* prophecy but they are part of the fulfillment of Bible prophecy found in Ephesians 1:9-12, in the D&C 27:13, and Book of Mormon prophecy concerning the records of the lost ten tribes (1Nephi 14:26). Last but not lest, the still small voice inspired us throughout the entire writing of the trilogy (D&C 76:5-10).

Figure 24: Temple Square Assembly Hall round Star of David window with peaked serpent bar above it. Long narrow windows below with serpent bars that symbolize the fall of the spiritual world into the physical world.

The Sealed Plates of the Book of Mormon

In doing my Mesoamerican research, I noticed that the knowledge of the Union of the Polarity and the knowledge of the last day of Spirit Earth in this dimension which was believed by most Mesoamerican tribes, especially the Maya, to occur on December 21, 2012, was prevalent through out most of ancient Mexico. That is the date the Maya Long Count Calendar ends. If my findings are indeed true and the Mesoamericans are indeed Book of Mormon peoples, then why isn't more to be found in the Book of Mormon concerning the Union of the Polarity and 2012, other than a few short verses found in Alma 26:5-8? After all, this knowledge appears to be at the very heart and core of their religious belief. I believe that it is in the Book of Mormon. It is contained in the sealed portion.

What do we know about the sealed portion? The following is excerpted from the Neal A. Maxwell Institute for Religious Scholarship website. "The sealed portion of the plates was first mentioned by Nephi (Nephi 27:6-10). When the plates were delivered to Joseph Smith, he was told not to translate the sealed portion. Both Nephi and Moroni commented on the contents of the sealed part and gave similar testimonies that supplement each other. Nephi, quoting Isaiah 29:11-12, and in *Inspired Version* Isa. 29: 11-16, said it contained 'a revelation from God, from the beginning of the world to the ending thereof' (2 Nephi 27:7; see v. 10). Moroni described the sealed portion more specifically, saying it contained the vision shown unto the brother of Jared of 'all the inhabitants of the earth which had been, and also all that would be....unto the ends of the earth.' The Lord commanded the brother of Jared to write the things he had seen and to seal them up until the Lord's own time, 'until after that he should be lifted up upon the cross;....that they should not come unto the world until after Christ should show himself unto his people' (Ether 3:25-27; 4:1). After the Lord's people had all dwindled in unbelief and there were none left but Lamanites who had rejected the gospel, Moroni was to seal up the plates again (Ether 4:3-5).

Moroni told us that the sealed part should not go forth unto the Gentiles until they had repented 'of their iniquity, and become clean before the Lord.' He wrote further that when 'they shall exercise faith in me (the Lord), saith the Lord, even as the brother of Jared did, that they may become sanctified in me, then will I manifest unto them the things which the brother of Jared saw, even to the unfolding unto them all my revelations, saith Jesus Christ, the Son of God, the Father of the heavens and of the earth, and all things that in them are' (Ether 4:6-7).

Nephi, through Isaiah, commented further on when the sealed plates will be revealed. 'And the day cometh that the words of the book which were sealed shall be read upon the house tops; and they shall be read by the power of Christ; and all things shall be revealed unto the children of men which ever have been among the children of men, and which ever will be even unto the end of the earth' (2 Nephi 27:11). How these words will be read from the housetops by the power of Christ is not specified, but with today's miracles of radio, television, satellite, and the Internet, it is easy to see how it might happen (compare D&C 88:5-13). Nephi, through Isaiah, further testified that these things would 'not be delivered in the day of the wickedness and abomination of the people' (2Nephi 27:8). He gave instructions to the translator (Joseph Smith) to 'touch not the things which are sealed, for I (the Lord) will bring them forth in mine own due time' (2 Nephi 27:21)". (Excerpt from website finished).

From the information above, we learn that the plates which contained the sealed portion of the Book of Mormon were unsealed to the Nephites (Toltecs) after Christ made his appearance to them following his crucifixion and resurrection, which was about 34 AD., and then resealed sometime in Moroni's time before the last great battle between the Nephites and Lamanites in 385 AD. Therefore, we can conclude that the knowledge of the creation from the beginning to the end was known for approximately 351 years during Book of Mormon times.

I believe that even after the battle of 385 AD., this knowledge didn't die out immediately, but continued to be spread and taught by word of mouth among the Lamanites until the arrival of the Spanish, as documented in *The Ark of Millions of Years* trilogy. There is evidence that suggests that the pre-mortal Christ and his 12 shining ones even taught of his advent into mortality, resurrection, plan of salvation, and the last day (2012), in Mesoamerica, before the sealed portion was unsealed to the Nephites (Toltecs) after he made his appearance following crucifixion because the Olmecs (Jaredites) and Chichimec Maya (Quiche Maya) certainly possessed this knowledge. If the Lord did so, it would not be contradictory to the Book of Mormon because he can do as he pleases in his own due time. However, for the Nephites (Toltecs), the record would be unsealed for their knowledge after he made his appearance to them. Only a remnant of the Olmecs (Jaredites) remained during Nephite (Toltec) times because most perished as the result of some sort of calamity in 240 BC. as written in Volume One, pages 361-362.

My research indicates that this same knowledge was known among the Sumerians, Babylonians, Assyrians, Egyptians, Chinese, in Ireland, England, the Pacific Islands, and in parts of northern South America in ancient Old World times. This knowledge was taught by the pre-mortal Christ and his shining ones who traveled over the earth teaching his plan of salvation, coming advent into mortality, crucifixion, resurrection (atonement for mankind), and *Harvest* at the End of the Age (2012). Legends speak of their appearance to the Chinese, Tibetans, Peruvians, and Tahitians. Christ taught it to his apostles while in mortality. The knowledge repeatedly came and disappeared through out time however, one organization, the Knight Templars, preserved and passed on the knowledge to their off shoot branches, namely the Freemasons (now Masons), the Knights of Columbus, and the Rosicrucians, who preserved it in their rituals performed in their temples and lodges. Over time, some of the knowledge and true meaning was further lost but the symbolism remained the same. Washington D.C., a Freemason city, was laid out to reflect the End Time *Harvest* of 2012. Around the late 1800's, the knowledge had all but vanished. Why? Mostly because it was never written down but rather taught, passed, and understood by word of mouth. The true meaning of many ancient symbols, over time, gave way to new interpretation. Some knowledge was also lost through mistranslation of the KJV of the Bible. The Jaredites and Nephites had a great advantage in having written records that were full and complete concerning the creation from its beginning to its end, in spite of being sealed up from time to time. These records were unsealed only when the people exercised great faith in the Lord and were righteous following his appearance. When they lost faith and became unrighteous, the records were once again sealed up.

An ancient record preserved by the Jews, the *Zohar*, contains some of the creation history pertaining to the Union of the Polarity and the End Times. Joseph Smith studied these records in Hebrew; therefore, he knew it but could not give his church the doctrine until the *Zohar* prophecy was fulfilled in the End Times. The books, *The Ark of Millions of Years* trilogy fulfilled the *Zohar* prophecy. These books contain the story of the creation from the beginning to the end, which story was taken from the *Zohar* text when they were translated into English about 18 years ago. We now have the story but not the complete written record that the Nephites enjoyed during the times of their great faith and righteousness. My approach is that some new enlightenment pertaining to the creation is better than none until the prophet of the LDS church receives the sealed plates from the Lord. This of course, is determined by our faith and righteousness, at the Lord's pleasure in his own due time. As everyone knows, our times are filled with unbelief and unrighteousness however; the LDS church membership continues to grow world wide as well as other Christian denominations. Our faith is being tried, church membership and Christian belief is growing world wide but much of the world still remains in spiritual darkness and unrighteousness. Religions of Earth are once again reaching that historical crescendo of war. Oppression and tyranny are facing an ever-awakened populace and are turning the sights on their own people in an attempt to retain sole access to the people's bank account. Perhaps the knowledge of the creation from the beginning to the end as taken from the *Zohar* and rewritten in *The Ark of Millions of Years*, is all that we can get under today's circumstances. We can obtain the knowledge but not the full written record at this present time.

There can only be one history of the world from its beginning to its end. At the writing of this book, the Islamic countries are revolting as the people protest the dark, wet blanket of ignorance and domination by the leaders of their countries. The knowledge of this truth is making its way through cell phones, laptop computers, and web-casted communications to every corner of the Earth. The *Zohar* knowledge, as re-written in *The Ark of Millions of Years* trilogy, contains an account of the creation as pertaining to the Union of the Polarity and the End Times, noting that the record is not complete. If you compare what is known to be contained in the sealed plates and lost or destroyed records of the prophets to what is written in the above trilogy, they are markedly similar. The Source is the same. Truth is truth as surely as the Golden Proportion supports the existence of all matter from chaos. It is the Word. The Word is, and can only be hidden if people will not see it.

First, the sealed portion contains a history of the world from its beginning to its end. So does The Ark trilogy.

Second, Nephi commented that the day would come when the words of the sealed portion would be read upon the house tops and all things shall be revealed even unto the end of the Earth. He didn't say that the sealed portion would be unsealed, only that the **words** pertaining to the creation, meaning all things, should be revealed even to the end of the Earth. We have the words, taken from the *Zohar*, but not the full written Nephite record dictated by Christ. By comparison, The Ark trilogy is doing just that. These books are being electronically transmitted via the internet and satellite transmission from house top to house top as audio down loads and E books. Also the knowledge is being spread or advertised by radio, in published books, and social networking. Hopefully, the books will attract national television in the near future and perhaps attract a traditional publisher who will publish them into foreign languages.

Third, the Lord told Moroni when the sealed portion comes forth, the revelations written by John would be understood. By comparison, The Ark trilogy makes it possible for the words of John to finally be more understood in his revelations as pertaining to the creation as well as the words of Isaiah. With what information we now have as written in The Ark trilogy, it is now possible to understand John's revelations and Isaiah's words pertaining to the creation, even though the record is not complete.

Fourth, The Ark trilogy does not add to or take away from the doctrine and messages of the Revelation of John or of other scriptures. The English version we have is only a shadow of what John saw and recorded. The artistic license taken in innumerable interpretations of his enigmatic and archetypal visions is enough to confuse anyone. That's the design of the perpetrators of these stories. The Ark trilogy makes clear and plain the picture of the universe and our place in it. The *Zohar* record pertaining to the creation as rewritten in The Ark trilogy restores some of the plain and precious parts of our biblical books that have been altered and antiseptically expunged from the record. In our opinions, the *Zohar* record is part of the record of the ten tribes which was handed down to them from Noah, who had them before the ten tribes were even conceived as a single child.

At least five different sets of records—all of which we expect to come forth—are identified in the Nephite account. The record of the lost ten tribes is the fourth set of records that are identified in the Nephite account. The Jews preserved the ancient *Zohar* record. They teach many of its doctrines today. In ancient times, scribed copies were given to each tribe and it was recited orally, by memory, for generations until re-scribed in later times in Hebrew and finally translated into English about 18 years ago. The *Zohar* record qualifies to be part of the records of the ten lost tribes, but be clear in the knowledge that even they inherited the record from an even more ancient people. Nevertheless, it does contain a history of the Earth from beginning to end, although not the complete written record of the Nephites. Nephi had been taught in all the learning of his Fathers, but chose not to share that knowledge with his people in the new world. There had already been enough bloodshed and corruption, in his own words, and he wanted to start fresh with the pure word as it came to him.

If we had the sealed records today and compared it to the *Zohar* record as pertaining to the creation history, from beginning to end, I feel they would be one and the same record; the main difference being the Nephites had the complete record in its fullness dictated by Christ. Some of the fullness was not recorded, as the people at Bountiful in III Nephi chapter 11 testify, and some of it was sealed with metal bands to come forth when the world was ready for the knowledge. Until that time, the mystery of the mortal journey would be the destination of mankind. When enough souls came to Earth at the same time, just before the end of the *age*, the knowledge would be revealed. There are nearly seven billion of us here now, alive and conscious at the same time. Those that accept it will cease their dark thinkings and doings like trading in an old car. Those that do not accept it, will be found sitting with a bowl full of pride and envy along the road in a broken down old car.

The *Zohar* record is not complete as it is a hodgepodge of unorganized verses however, the history of the creation from its beginning to its end can be found in spite of unorganized and fragmented verses. Therefore, it is not unreasonable to conclude that the ten lost tribes also possessed this same knowledge besides the Jaredites and Nephites; just from another source or record. The *Zohar* record pertaining to the creation, from beginning to end, has been rewritten in *The Ark of Millions of Years* trilogy.

In conclusion, I would like to make a few comments about the plates containing the sealed portion. Moroni said that the sealed part should not go forth unto the Gentiles until they had repented 'of their iniquity, and become clean before the Lord.' The Lord has made it clear that the sealed portion would remain sealed until the people exercised more faith and righteousness. For the LDS, in my opinion,this is best accomplished by doubling the number of LDS church members holding temple recommends because in order to obtain a temple recommend, one is certainly exercising faith in God and in Jesus Christ as well as living righteously, being repentant and clean before the Lord. Increased temple attendance certainly would help as well because temple work sanctifies the person doing the ordinances. For the non-LDS Christians, increased church attendance, payment of tithes, keeping the commandments, and righteous living certainly would help. It is expedient that both groups practice charity by loving and helping their fellow men. The same is to be said about Muslims, Buddhists, and Jews. Honor God by righteous living, keep the commandments, treat others as you want to be treated, and practice charity.

The two commandments upon which all the laws and prophets hang, when recited in correct order, are the plainest and most beautiful truths in the universe. Love yourself; for if you do not you can love nothing, and in doing so you are empowered and commanded to love your neighbor. Directing these two perfect expressions of energy is the act of loving God with all your heart, mind, and strength. God is within you, and you are never separated from Him. Look for the good in everyone, and help it to grow a little every day. And before long, you will have saved the planet. It begins with you.

If this is done by all, then the Lord may take notice and reveal the whereabouts of the other four End Time records mentioned in Nephi as well as delivering the sealed plates to its proper authority, namely the LDS prophet, who in turn would prepare the world for the *Harvest* at the End of the Age.

Unveiling the Sealed Plates

As previously written, if the Lord unsealed the Jaredite record to the righteous Nephites shortly after his appearance to them following his resurrection as prophesied by Ether, an ancient Mesoamerican prophet, and if Mesoamerica is the land of the Book of Mormon, then one would expect to find some evidence of these teachings because the knowledge was known for 350 years before Moroni resealed the record until a more righteous generation would come.

We believe there is plenty of evidence but it has been misread by Maya experts and archaeologists. First, in order to find the evidence, you have to know just what are you looking for. Second, you have to know the time frame to correlate the findings to the Book of Mormon time periods.

So, what are we looking for? We are looking for evidence of teachings of the sealed portion contained in the Book of Mormon to the Mesoamerican people. What is contained in the sealed portion? The Mesoamerican prophets, Nephi and Moroni, both commented that the sealed record contained a history of the world, from its creation to its end written in the words of Christ. When did the Mesoamerican prophet, Ether, prophesied the Jaredite (Olmec) record would be unsealed? He said when the resurrected Christ made his appearance to the righteous Nephites, the record would be unsealed. Approximately what time period would this be? Sometime around 34 AD. Therefore we will be looking for the evidences of the sealed portion from 34 AD. until the time the record was once again sealed by Moroni around 384-385 AD. It is the **first phase** of our search. Now we can start looking for the evidence.

The Aztec Sun Stone is the first piece of evidence. Review the update in this book titled appropriately enough, *The Aztec Sun Stone.* It is said that the resurrected Christ or Quetzalcoatl caused this masterpiece to be made, interpreted as fashioned by his own hands, for the Toltecs (Nephites) so they would always remember him and his teachings. His appearance was around 34-35 AD., so the time frame is correct. The stone was made big and strong enough, over 20 tons, to endure time, war, and natural disasters. He carved two dates on the stone for the Toltecs (Nephites) to never forget. One date was 1519, the arrival of the Spanish; the other date was December 21, 2012 when the World (Spirit Earth) ended and the 5th World (physical Earth) would be destroyed by earthquakes. Quetzalcoatl called December 21, 2012, the Day of Retribution. In the Bible this day is called the Day of the Lord's Wrath. Certainly the Toltecs (Nephites) understood the concept of the Union of the Polarity, knowledge later lost through apostasy. Centuries later, the Chichimec Toltecs gave the stone to the Aztecs who used it for human sacrifice. Today this stone is the centerpiece of the Museum of

Anthropology in Mexico City. It is the first thing seen on entry to the museum.

Stele 5 in Izapa is the second piece of evidence. The Stelae on this site were carved around 100-200 AD., so the time frame is correct. Please review pages 80-83 in Volume Three for a picture and description. This particular monument is clearly teaching about 2012 and the coming resurrection of the righteous to eternal life. A high ranking priest, scribe, or prophet is instructing seated listeners. This knowledge could only come from the teachings of the sealed portion.

On the north side of the ball court in Izapa is found the third piece of evidence which is an image of Christ or Quetzalcoatl standing in a boat. With outstretched arms, he appears to be teaching about the end of the age when the events associated with 2012 will take place. This indicates that Christ is the one giving the teaching. The time frame would be the same as above, approximately 100-200 AD. To see picture and 2012 story description, readers are referred to Volume Two, pp.78-79.

On the Maya calendar is to be found the fourth piece of evidence. Readers are referred to Volume Three p.74, for a picture of the Maya Day Glyph called **Ix.** This day glyph commemorates the day that heaven and Earth embraced by the union of the Spirit Earth with the Temporal Earth.; a process we named the Union of the Polarity. We don't know when this glyph was added to their calendar but we surmise it was when Quetzalcoatl helped the Toltec and Toltec Maya perfect their Long Count calendar with several calendar adjustments. Surprisingly, it appears that the date of Calendar Round 1 Ben 6 Mak marks the origin on **one** of the Mixtec calendars on what calculates to Thursday, 6 April 1 BC., the birthday of Quetzalcoatl. Most biblical scholars now agree 6 April 1 BC. is the probable date for Christ's birth. According to the record of 3 Nephi 2:7-8, the Nephites developed a new calendar that began to reckon their time from the coming of Christ. In other words, the Nephite revised calendar started their New Year on the date of Christ's birth. Therefore it seems likely that the Mixtec and Nephite calendars are one and the same which also means that Quetzalcoatl and Christ are the same deity! In the year 46 AD., the Mesoamerica calendar was again adjusted, which changed the beginning of the New Year to correspond with July 26. Perhaps that is why Mormon, who wrote in the 4th Century, and whose calendar New Year would now begin with July 26, said "I will show you that in the ending of the 34th year" the Savior appeared. It has been theorized that this New Year change probably came about because of the visit of Christ to the Nephites. (Warren and Ferguson 1987:50) Note, the Toltec (Nephites) lived in the land northward and the Toltec Maya (Nephites) lived in the land southward. Because the knowledge of the Union of the Polarity deals with the early creation history of Earth and 2012 events, this knowledge, along with calendar adjustments, most likely came from the sealed portion which was opened and taught by Christ/Quetzalcoatl.

These calendar adjustments were probably made during the 100 BC.-200 AD. time frame during the Savior's many appearances and prolonged visits to various Mesoamerican tribes as recorded in *Mosiah* 27: 6-7, in the Toltec Mesoamerican record known today as the Book of Mormon. Some of these visits were made by the pre-mortal Lord and later as the resurrected Savior. In 3 Nephi, chapters 11 through 17, the Book of Mormon recorded one of those visits. We should not suppose that all of Christ's visits were confined to the land Bountiful as there are other accounts of his visits to other Mesoamerican areas. One such visit was to Teotitlan in the valley of Oaxaca, the land of Desolation, on day Flint in the ritual calendar. (Shearer, Tony, *Beneath the Moon and under the Sun,* Albuquerque Sun Publishing Company, 1975, p.72) This event is depicted in the *Codex Gomez de Orozco* from northern Oaxaca, Mexico, that shows a picture of the footsteps of Quetzalcoatl descending from the multilayered heavens in the year 982 AD. Another visit was to the ancient city of Tula, theorized to be Teotihuacán, as told in the update *The Aztec Sun Stone.* The Book of Mormon is silent about these other visits, other than a brief two verse mention of them in Mosiah, but the Mesoamerican record is not.

In Volume Two, p. 213, is a picture of a ball game marker found on the Teotihuacán site; now located in the Museum of Anthropology in Mexico City. It is the fifth piece of evidence. This marker depicts the wormhole opening above the earth and the phases of the elements. It is a reminder of 2012 upcoming events. The round sphere beneath the swirling wormhole represents the earth. One correction to the text beneath the picture… the text should read…Water represents the *Temporal Earth* and fire represents the *Spirit Earth*. If ever Volume One's front cover is redone, the Temporal Earth flaming tetrahedron would be colored blue. It is the triangle pointing up part of the Star of David. Therefore it affirms the ancient belief that fire and water united as in the Union of the Polarity which is part of the creation story. Volume One restores this information back to the world as prophesied in the *Zohar.* And the time frame is correct.

It is more difficult to find evidence of knowledge of the sealed part in the 34 AD. to 200 AD. time frame because of looting and destruction of sites by the Spanish. After the destruction of the Toltecs (Nephites), Moroni sealed up the record once more however, the knowledge had already spread and was continued to be believed by the Maya Lamanites up till the arrival of the Spanish. It is easier to find evidence of the sealed part after 200 AD. to the year 1519 AD. when the Spanish arrived. This is the **second phase** of our search.

Let us begin with the archaeological site of Palenque, Mexico. Please review pages 51-70 in Volume Three. On page 53 of Volume Three is a picture of Pakal's tomb lid. The message being conveyed to onlookers of his tomb lid is, "when the path of the sun (ecliptic) crosses the exact midpoint (galactic equator) of the Milky Way, I expect to be resurrected." The Maya portrayed the ecliptic in their artwork as a double headed serpent therefore there is no mistake in the meaning carved on Pakal's tomb lid nor on the Palanque crosses discussed below. It was understood by the Maya that when the sun conjoined the galactic equator at the center of the Milky Way, it would be positioned in the vaginal opening of the dark rift marking the time of the End of the Age and the appointed Day of Resurrection. This knowledge could have only originated from the sealed part of the Toltec/ Nephite record. It is the sixth piece of evidence.

There is more to be found in Palenque. These are the Palenque crosses pictured on pages 54, 55, 66, and 67, in Volume Three. We again suggest readers to review the text on Palenque. Cross symbolism was used by Quetzalcoatl/Christ to teach the plan of salvation and events associated with 2012. The time period is 603-683 AD. It is the seventh piece of evidence.

The same elements and themes from Palenque are found in the Maya ruins of Copan, Honduras, a few years later from 695-738 AD. time period. This suggests the knowledge was spreading. Again please review pages 70-71 in Volume Three. On page 71 in Volume Three is a picture of ruler 18 Rabbit in Copan dressed as a World Tree and holding a serpent bar. He like Pakal, is expressing the same belief of events associated with 2012 and the resurrection to occur on that day. It is the eighth piece of evidence.

On page 72 in Volume Three is a drawing made from a panel found on the Pyramid of the Niches in the Maya ruins of El Tajin. It is El Tajin's version of the Axis Mundi which shows the wormhole with many dimensional fringes listed around it. On 2012 it opens; knowledge originating from the sealed record. The time period is 600-1150 AD. It is the ninth piece of evidence.

In Volume Three, page 75, is pictured a redrawn image from the Mayan Codex, Vindobonensis. Pictured is a star gate wormhole in the center of the Milky Way with serpent bar passing over it, denoting the 2012 End of the Age. Descending from the star gate wormhole is the serpent rope (ladder) carrying the god Nine Wind (Quetzalcoatl/ Christ) to this universe or dimension.; information from the sealed record pertaining to the end of the spiritual world in this dimension and coming resurrection. The Vindobonensis Mayan Codex is a pre-Hispanic record so the time period is correct. It is the tenth piece of evidence.

New research on World Trees indicates the picture found on page 318 in Volume Three is not an Olmec World Tree but rather a Mixtec World tree. The picture is also found in the Vindobonensis Mixtec Codex. The End of the Age events associated with 2012 is definitely encoded in the Mixtec World Tree. As previously stated the

Vindobonesis (Vindobona) Mixtec Codex is pre-Hispanic making the time period correct. It is the eleventh piece of evidence found.

Two-headed dragons, different from two-headed serpents, were common in Mayan art. Pictured on page 252 in Volume One is a similar carving found on an inscribed cliff at the Maya archaeological site of Piedras Negras. The dragon is the classic symbol of creation. Note we are talking about dragons and not serpents. They are two different things and have different meanings. The double or two- headed dragon is a powerful symbol of the Union of the Polarity; knowledge that could only come from the sealed record. As the classic glyph indicates the creation force of the two worlds, the dragon symbol used by this particular artist kept the people aware and reverent of this event. This Maya city site was already of some importance by 400 AD., but the most impressive period of sculpture and architecture dates from 608-810 AD.; therefore the time period is correct. It is the twelfth piece of evidence.

Pictured in Volume One, page 277, is the coronation of Pakal seated on a two- headed jaguar throne. Another two- headed jaguar throne is found in the center of the Maya archaeological site of Uxmal. Two-headed jaguar thrones, like the two- headed dragon symbol, were a way of expressing knowledge of the two united creations. Only kings sat on them. The legends of ancient Mexico demonstrate that the worlds of matter and spirit are coexistent and each has something which the other needs; knowledge that could only originate from the sealed record for this group of people. Uxmal dates to 1000 AD. and Palenque to 603-683 AD., so the time period is correct. It is the thirteenth piece of evidence.

Although not pictured in any of the trilogy books, ear spools or large backed earrings have been found in Uxmal with the Star of David image on them. These ear spools were so large that they almost covered each half of a face cheek.. Also on the same site another Star of David was found with a feathered or pennated tail. It is shown in Volume One on page 250. A Star of David was found in the Maya ruins of Kaminaljuyu, the site of present day Guatemala City which many Book of Mormon scholars believe is the City of Nephi. Kaminaljuyu dates from 1500 BC. to 1200 AD. Again, the Star of David is an ancient symbol of the creation event we named the Union of the Polarity; knowledge contained in the sealed record. As written previously, Uxmal dates to 1000 AD., and Kaminaljuyu dates to 1200 AD., therefore the time period is correct. It is the fourteenth, fifteenth, and sixteenth pieces of evidences found.

As written in the trilogy, cross symbolism was used to represent the Union of the Polarity but in addition it had several meanings, depending how it was used. In Volume One, page 251, are found two Maya examples of the knitting together of the spiritual and temporal worlds. One example is found at the archaeological site of Piedras

Negras and the other is found in the archaeological site of El Cayo. The subtitles under each picture are self explanatory. El Cayo is located on the banks of the Usumacinta River. It dates to 600-800 AD. and Piedras Negras from 600-810 AD.; all in the correct time period. It is the seventeenth piece of evidence.

Mayan art on temple wall friezes symbolized the knowledge of the Union of the Polarity. In Volume One, page 279, are found some illustrations that express this knowledge. Art work such as this are all in the correct time period and are found at various sites. It was a popular design on wall friezes and even painted on pottery. It is the eighteenth piece of evidence.

The Maya understood the resurrection of the dead would occur on the winter solstice of December 21, 2012. They knew the Sign of the Suntelia Aion would herald this event and that it would occur on the winter solstice of 2012. To keep track of the solstices, they designed the winter solstice light to fall on certain markers. These markers served a dual purpose. Besides marking the solstices as a reminder of 2012, it marked the time of the seasons of when to plant. The shows are very impressive. At Tikal, there are markers in the main plaza where the light strikes for 10 minutes marking the summer and winter solstices. In this same plaza are two great funerary temples built facing each other. The kings buried there are awaiting the resurrection day. During the Monte Alban Period 111, a tomb of a high ranking person was discovered that had a hole in the roof of the chamber that illuminates with a shaft of light on each winter solstice for about 10 minutes. Why else illuminate a tomb except to await the day of resurrection? At Tulum, a small temple arch just frames the rising sun on the winter solstice. This knowledge came from nowhere else than the sealed record. Most of the biggest, grandest, and impressive temple buildings at Tikal date to 400 AD. Tulum dates to 900 AD. and the Period 111 at Monte Alban dates to 350-750 AD. Of course the most impressive and famous light show is at Chichen Itza where the great God, Quetzalcoatl, descends the pyramid of Kukulcan as a serpent on the spring and fall equinoxes. It is a reminder that he is Lord of the spring plantings and Lord of the Harvest of the End Times. It is a reminder that he will come on a future winter solstice at the End of the Age or December 21, 2012. All are within the correct time period. It is the nineteenth piece of evidence.

In the Maya ruins of Lamanai, located in the jungles of Belize, another symbol of the Union of the Polarity is found at the entrance to the city. It is a stone seat fashioned as a yin yang symbol. This symbol has two meanings; the Union of the Polarity and a representative of the dual creative forces of the cosmos. Even though the symbol has two meanings, the dual creative forces are part of the Union of the Polarity; knowledge learned from the sealed record. It is the twentieth piece of evidence.

Not to be overlooked, but known to a few archaeologists, King Pakal was buried with a polished stone sphere in his left hand and a polished stone cube in his right hand; the circle and the square of Masonry which are Masonic symbols of the Union of the Polarity. These symbols represent the Spirit Earth (sphere or circle) and the cube represents the physical Earth. This is conclusive proof of his knowledge of the two creations; knowledge which came from the sealed Nephite (Toltec) record. Though nothing is ever said about the stone symbols in his hands, it is the twenty-first piece of evidence within the correct time frame.

More evidence not to be overlooked are the prophecies found in the Books of Chilam Balam or Book of the Jaguar Priest which has been previously discussed in the chapter, *Milky Way "Dark Rift."* Chilam Balam, a holder of the high order of the Jaguar Priesthood, was merely teaching passed down information that was contained in the sealed plates of the Toltec/Book of Mormon record. His writings are eleventh century so the time frame is correct. It is the twenty-second piece of evidence.

If we could explore the many other lesser known Mesoamerican ruins, I'm sure more evidence could be found. Some sites are newly opened and some sites are simply inaccessible. However, the most compelling piece of evidence rests with the all the hype about the 2012 Maya end time date itself. Unless you have been living under a rock, you know numerous books have been written about it (you are reading one) and Roland Emmerich made a highly successful movie about it. Everyone wants to know from whence did the Maya get this knowledge? It is the twenty-third and last piece of evidence we will discuss. The answer is …..

The current knowledge of the Maya end time date is all that is left of the sealed record. It is a passed down remembered remnant of that now sealed record.

Christ taught about 2012 in the Old World as recorded in the New Testament and Christ taught about 2012 in the New World when he opened the sealed record for the Nephites (Toltecs). Websites and various Maya experts don't even have it fully correct when they say "it is not the end of the world but merely a restart of cycles of time." According to the evidences presented, the ancient Mesoamericans understood the End of the Age or December 21, 2012, is the end of the spiritual creation in this universe. It will ascend by a process we now call "rapture" into the 4th dimension. They end their Long Count calendar on that day because time will be calculated differently there therefore; their calendar will no longer be needed. The ancient Maya said they will not restart their calendar. It was also believed to be the day of the first resurrection of the righteous. This no doubt was in the sealed record but is also found in the current Toltec/Book of Mormon record where it says, "...I know that I shall be lifted up at the last day" (Mormon 2:19) (3 Nephi 27:22) (Alma 37:37). The "last day" was understood by the Maya to mean December 21, 2012, and the term "lifted up" meant to be resurrected on that date. Rather than repeating the lengthy date of December 21, 2012 over and over again, the Maya shortened it by using the term "the last day." We have offered sufficient proof in the Ark books to show the "last day" in Maya understanding has always meant December 21, 2012. In fact sufficient proof has been presented in the Ark books to demonstrate this was not only believed by the ancient Maya but by the entire ancient world as well. Bare in mind language meaning has changed somewhat which has created problems in the understanding of true intent of ancient scripture. We came to this conclusion only after doing a very thorough comprehensive search world wide on the end time date. Without doing a world wide comprehensive search on the end time date, one cannot possibly arrive to the correct conclusion; it is impossible to do so. Therefore, if you are one of those unfortunate souls left behind on the physical Earth, the Gregorian calendar will continue but the ancient Tzolk'in and Long Count calendar will not. The Maya Long Count calendar has not been in use since the adoption of the Gregorian calendar but its tracking of time ends on that date. Readers are referred to Volume Two, p.178 for more on the Maya Tzolk'in calendar predictions.

As it turns out, the fifteenth century Catholic Jesuit priest from the Ribera family of Italy, who tried to convince the Catholic Church that a pre-tribulation "rapture" was due to take place at the End of the Age or December 21, 2012, was sent to New Spain (Mexico). There he changed his name to Bernardino de Sahagun (ca. 1499-1591). He was without a doubt one of the outstanding scholars of the Spanish priests of the sixteenth century in Mexico. Besides carrying out his appointed duties in the Church, he also spent his time preaching to and teaching the natives in religion and languages—Spanish, Nahuatl, and Latin. He became interested in the history of the Aztecs and in their language and customs. Sahagun, wanting to preserve the history, customs, and beliefs of the Aztecs, spent his time compiling and writing twelve volumes of works which include the Florentine Codex. His writings are filled with notes and are well illustrated, with the art having been done by Aztec artists. As a historian and a scholar, he is considered the greatest authority on the sixteenth century Aztecs. It is while he was studying the native beliefs that he was taught by the natives their belief of the end of the world in 2012. Apparently the sealed record knowledge was still being passed down, taught and believed by many tribes in the sixteenth century. Sahagun became convinced that a pre-tribulation "rapture" would take place on that date and tried to convince the Catholic Church to reconsider their doctrine. Of course, it was to no avail. Readers are referred to Volume Three, page 168, for the full account. Sahagun was a man not easily indoctrinated with new religious ideas, especially from uneducated natives. So in order for him to believe the native teachings, the message had to be powerful. It was powerful enough that he tried to convince the Catholic Church of the doctrine, which was immediately rejected. As stated in Volume Three, the doctrine of a pre-tribulation rapture is not a new doctrine, but is one of the oldest doctrines in the world. Sahagun (Ribera) accidently ran into the ancient doctrine, believed it, and tried to resurrect it.

Readers are now referred to the chapter, The Maya Creation Panel, in this book. At the end of that chapter, several pictures show a carved screen made of two connecting panels. These panels retell the 2012 Maya end time story in pictorial form. Although the screen is only about 25 years old, it does show the end time knowledge is still known among some Maya living in isolated areas. Most important, we feel sufficient evidence has been presented in this chapter to prove the Book of Mormon lands were indeed ancient Mesoamerica.

Since you have now learned the Maya end time date derives from knowledge taken from the sealed plates of the Book of Mormon, does that change your perspective on the authenticity of the Book of Mormon and on things to come? Combined with the teachings of Christ in the Bible concerning events associated with the End of the Age, we now have the complete picture of 2012. A good detailed review of 2012 is the chapter, *The End Times*, found in Volume Two. Now is the time to prepare both spiritually and temporally for this great event. It is two minutes till midnight. When the clock strikes twelve, where will you be? Left behind or on the Spirit Earth? Each soul chooses his own destiny by the way he lives as defined by the Golden Rule.

The Golden Rule

Christianity

Do unto others as you would have them do unto you.

Judaism

What is hateful to you do not do to your neighbor.
That is the entire Torah. The rest is commentary. Go and Learn.

Islam

No one is a believer until you desire for another
that which you desire for yourself.

Bahai

Blessed are those who prefer others before themselves.

Zoroastrianism

Human nature is good only when it does not do unto
another whatever is not good for its own self.

Sikhism

Be not estranged from one another for God dwells in every heart.

Janism

In happiness and suffering, in joy and grief…

regard all creatures as you would your own self.

Buddhism

Hurt not others in ways that you yourself find hurtful.

Just found this piece of information and thought it was too good to not make some mention of it. Christ was known by many different names to the Mesoamericans. In Peru he was known as Amaru, which name has an identical meaning of the Feathered or Plumed Serpent. From the Peruvian name for Christ comes Amaruca, out of which some scholars now believe the name America resulted. Certainly this derivation appears to be more plausible than the one currently believed. It is astounding the impact that Christ had upon the Promised Land….. the Americas.

Another update has just surfaced that offers more proof that Mesoamerica was indeed knowledgeable of information pertaining to the *last day* or December 21, 2012; information that was taught by Quetzalcoatl. As written previously in the Etowah Mound update, the Chontal Indians migrated from central Mexico eventually making their way to what is now Macon, Georgia. There they built their first city, Ocmulgee, which was patterned after the city site of Xochitecatl in Mexico, from where they last left to migrate northward. Ocmulgee, meaning "where they sat down," has seven mounds and associated plazas. One mound is a funeral mound built in at least seven stages for the village leaders. Over 100 burials have been found in the mound. Near-by is an earthlodge built very similar to the Newgrange passageway tomb. It is a round dirt covered lodge with one entrance. Inside the lodge is a fire pit with seating for fifty people located around the interior wall. Every seat is progressively higher than the one before it like a theater. It is obvious this lodge was for ceremonial purposes.

On the winter solstice the earthlodge is designed to allow the solstice sun to shine through the entrance and illuminate the interior of the lodge for about 17 minutes. Why? Two reasons, one to mark the seasons and one to prepare for the resurrection at the *last day* which they believed to be December 21, 2012. Not having a calendar, this solstice marker served as a calendar. These Indians having migrated from out of Mexico obviously knew the passed down teachings of the sealed record. Ocmulgee was inhabited for about 200 years, and then the Chontal Indians abandoned the site, went northward and built the Etowah mounds. Both sites had a large temple mound dedicated to Quetzalcoatl. Both temple sites had a perpetual fire. It is said that Quetzalcoatl came to the Etowah temple site, gave the dedication speech, and lit its eternal flame as he often did whenever a temple was dedicated to him. It is likely he did the same at the dedication of the Ocmulgee Temple, 200 years earlier. During that visit, Quetzalcoatl reaffirmed the sealed record teachings about the creation and the *last day*.

The Chontal, later known as the Muskogean Indians, were Christians during that early time period. There is evidence to suggest that followers of Quetzalcoatl were being persecuted around 750 AD. in Teotihuacán which later spilled over into Xochitecatl. Maybe this is the reason a branch of the Chontal tribe, along with three other tribes, chose to migrate northward; to escape persecution. Today the Muskogeans are known as the Creek Indians. The Ocmulgee and Etowah mound sites are open to the public.

In closing, we hope you have enjoyed all these Updates as much as we have enjoyed the writing of them. 2012 is the most intriguing date in the history of the world. The Ark trilogy books, in fulfillment of prophecy, have solved the great mystery associated with this date. We have taken the birth of the Earth to its 2012 destiny and beyond. The biggest surprise of all was to find the Maya End Time date derives from teachings found in a very remarkable Mesoamerican record of the Toltecs/Nephites known today as the Book of Mormon. Who would have ever thought that the Book of Mormon would play such a big role in the Maya 2012 End Time date? Will wonders never cease? The second biggest surprise was to learn that we, the authors of The

Ark trilogy, share a common thread with Joseph Smith, Columbus, Nostradamus, Freemasons, Knights of Columbus, Rosicrucian's, the Knight Templars, the mystery schools of Egypt and Babylon, King Solomon, King David, Moses, Abraham, Isaiah, other Biblical Old Testament prophets, and Noah. Just what is this one common thread that links us all together? Answer...... **We all received our esoteric end time knowledge from the same source, namely the Zohar manuscripts!** That indeed is remarkable and what is even more remarkable, The Ark books, all four of them, prove it! To date, we have written more on 2012 than any others authors in the world and the only authors in the world who have written about the Union of the Polarity. In fact, without the knowledge of the Union of the Polarity, it is impossible to fully understand 2012; therefore we have the 2012 chain of events correct. And we might add that The Ark trilogy books are the most comprehensive books ever written thus far on 2012. They are based on well documented facts and not myths. We have presented the truths, unaltered, as we discovered them. In doing so, we hope your "third eye" of wisdom has been awakened enabling you to take a giant leap forward spiritually. The World wants to know the truth about 2012; we have delivered it.

Readers of the Ark trilogy have been awarded 4 important keys. Volume One gave you the Key to the Creation. Volume Two gave you the Key to the Maya Calendar. Volume Three gave you the Key to

2012. Volume Four gives you the Key to the Universe. Treasure these 4 keys. Lucifer has sought to destroy the 4 keys of knowledge since he was banished from heaven. From time immortal every generation has tried to find these keys. Men have fought over this knowledge; others have paid the ultimate price for them. Some have managed to find one key, others were fortunate enough to locate two keys, but you are among the lucky few who possess all 4 of them. Therefore you are now entitled to be called a Lord of the Keys. Guard them well like the Lord of the Rings. It is the same story with a different twist.

The ancient Maya have had it right all along; it is literally carved in stone. Therefore, it appears this thing is going to happen so please get prepared and warn your neighbor. You, the reader, can help us get the word out by telling your friends about these books through Facebook, MySpace, Twitter, Google Talk, Chat, Aim, and other social net working media. What better way to warn your neighbor? We, as authors of The Ark books, have done our part by solving the 2012 great mystery. Now, we are asking you to do your part by helping us get the message out to the world through social net working. Ask your friends to message their friends, who in turn will message their friends etc. Using social net working, the message could travel around the world in a matter of days as opposed to the much slower traditional ways. Because time is short and because of the urgency in this matter, we personally thank-you for any assistance you can give to promote the message in these books. We are available for media interviews and as guest program lecturers. Please feel free to contact us through the email address on front book cover.

May God be with us through 2012 and beyond.…..**Amen.**

The Chosen People

As written in Volumes One and Two, the Jews are descendants from Noah who came to this planet by virtue of the *Genesis* fall of mankind when the flood of Noah was upon the spiritual creation. The spiritual creation literally fell through time and dimensions from the highest heaven or universe to arrive to the physical or temporal universe and merge with this planet we now call Earth. The *Zohar* expressed this union as fire uniting with water; a sacred marriage or union of the two planets.

Anciently this sacred union of two planets was called "the one mystery"; we renamed it the Union of the Polarity. It is the first "key" to the correct understanding of the creation. Originally this key piece of knowledge was contained in *Genesis* but was mostly removed by Constantine's hired scriptural henchmen called the correctors. Only traces of it remain in *Genesis* today. Once you thoroughly understand this missing "key" piece of information pertaining to the creation, the biblical accounts literally open up to lost truths which mankind has so diligently searched in his quest for answers. The loss of this "key" piece of information has caused a great chasm between creationists and evolutionists. Volume One of *The Ark* trilogy restores the missing "key" back to the world in fulfillment of an ancient Jewish prophecy found in the *Zohar* that melts the chasm between the creationists and evolutions and brings new understanding to the creation.

When the spiritual creation united with the physical creation the two realities became a co-dimensional planet. This event occurred when the flood of Noah was upon the spiritual creation. When the spiritual waters of the flood dried up, Noah and his entourage became fully mortal. All those aboard Noah's ark, including the animals, were alien off worlders. Close examination of the *Genesis* account informs us there were two creations; one spiritual and one physical. There was an upper Adam and a lower Adam. The spiritual creation was created by God in the highest heaven or universe. It is the original creation or true Earth. When *Old Testament* prophets spoke of Earth, in most cases they were referring to the original creation, the true or Spirit Earth and not the physical planet. The physical or temporal creation was created by the son of God in a lower universe. From the ancient viewpoint the spiritual creation was always thought of as our heaven or as heaven united with Earth and believed that we live in two worlds at the same time.

Noah's family and all others who were on his ark were descendants from the upper Adam. They were called the Adamic race. Human beings on the physical or temporal creation, created by the son of God, are descendants of the lower Adam and are rightfully called the Hu'man race. The Adamic race of men were an older advanced race of men who were sent to this planet, following the great cataclysm of 9,500 BC., to teach survivors of the Hu'man race the arts of civilization, about the true God of heaven, and to counter the teachings of the Nephilim who had enslaved and corrupted the Hu'man race. Leaders of the Hu'man race very quickly recognized the superiority of the Adamic race and referred to them as Gods from another world, the heavenly spiritual world. Thereafter they were called the Divine Seed or Holy Seed because they were descendants of the upper Adam created by the supreme God. In time the term "Divine Seed or Holy Seed" gave way and evolved into "God's chosen people." It is more correct to say they were created and not chosen by God but by the same token in biblical times, even to this day, the Adamic race has had tender mercies extended to them from God because they were his creation by the work of his hands. By virtue of their divine DNA, the Adamic race lived to great age as attested to in *Genesis* and by this one fact were declared to be Gods by the Hu'man race and treated as such.

After arrival to this planet, Noah and his family migrated and finally settled in the plains of Shinar/Shumer/Sumer, or ancient Sumeria which was called Chaldea (Volume One, page.465). They were the people of the Shem who were known as the Sumerians (Volume Two, page 52). The sons of Noah paired off into tribes and were scattered over the entire region but remained in relative close proximity to each other. They remained thus until the confusing of languages at the building of the Tower of Babel which then scattered them into distant lands of other tribes of the Hu'man race (Volume Two chapter, *The Tower of Babel*, pages 49-70) (Volume One, pages 472-475). When the sons of Noah scattered into distant lands of other Hu'man race tribes, they fulfilled their divine mission to establish the arts of civilization and to teach them about the one true God.

Noah and some of his descendants remained in Chaldea and built the city of Sumer, one of the earliest civilizations on earth. Noah's people restored civilization to the earth following the great cataclysm of 9, 500 BC. defined later as the flood of Ogyges. It is incorrect to say that Noah's people, the Sumerians, invented or developed some of their technology; correctly stated they brought this advanced technology and knowledge with them. They had already formulated all the attributes of civilization when they arrived on the scene. Everything we have today in our society can be directly attributed to Noah and his descendants.

They brought with them advanced technology in farming, tools, construction, metallurgy, and writing. For example, Noah introduced new grains, such as barley and wheat, to farming. New farming techniques were employed such as irrigation and the use of the plow. The use of wheeled vehicles, the sailboat, and the potter's wheel were all of Sumerian origin. Sumerian architects made use of the arch, dome, and vault which was later adopted by the Greeks and Romans.

The Sumerians introduced a system of cuneiform script and pictograph writing and devised a decimal system which probably was a prototype of the Hindu-Arabic decimal system currently in use today. They formulated the earliest concepts of algebra and geometry. They were the first to pave roads, the first to have a postal system, the first to have public libraries, the first to found a public university, the first to have public schools, the first to write literature (poetry, epics, hymnals, medical texts), and the first to make a magnifying glass. Thomas Crapper was not the first to invent the flushing toilet; the Sumerians were, although Crapper has gotten the credit for the invention. The Sumerians were the first however to devise a complex sewer system complete with flushing toilets.

They even mapped the heavens and had scale maps of our solar system; knowledge that we didn't have until the 20th century. They had electric batteries and probably had electric lights. They had the knowledge to electroplate gold which knowledge the Egyptians may have learned from contact with Noah's people. They brought with them legal and ethical concepts with moral ideals which enabled them to spell out in writing law codes so that no misunderstanding could happen. These laws became the foundation for their central government and future governments throughout the world. In commerce, they employed a system of weights and measures which was used until the Roman period. Last but not least, they were the first to brew beer.

The descendants of the sons of Noah were assimilated into the Hu'man race tribes and became as "one blood" as written in the Table of Nations in *Genesis* with the exception of the tribe of Judah who eventually became known simply as the Jews. When Noah and Abraham learned from God the lineage of the coming of the Savior, they forbade outside marriage in order to keep the lineage pure and uncorrupted. The Savior had to be born of the pure bloodlines of the divine Adamic race. That brings us down to today's times.

Even though the tribe of Judah did have outside marriages and still continue to do so, they remain for the most part the most pure of all bloodlines. Even after six thousand years, their genetic make-up still retains much of their divine portion inherited from Noah.

When the nation of Israel was formed in 1948, many Jews returned to their homeland which produced a high concentration of "divine DNA" that has enabled Israel to make remarkable technological advances. Call it a superior intellect or a superior insight or as I call it, a divine portion, wherever Jews go they generally succeed in the business world and wind up controlling the wealth of a country. Face it; historically they have a knack for it.

Before the world boycotts, abandons, and writes off Israel as hopeless in making peace treaties in the Middle East, perhaps we should examine the facts of this remarkable race of people. Israel is one of the smallest countries on Earth with one one-thousandth of the world's population. In proportion to its population they have earned more PhD's per capita than any other country.

They have been awarded more Nobel Prizes per capita than any other country in the world. They have more laureate awards in real numbers than China, Mexico, and Spain. They have produced more scientific papers per capita than any other country. They lead the world in medical equipment patents. Two in particular come to mind, the Babysense 11, a monitor designed to protect from sudden infant death syndrome, and a radiation free computerized mammogram diagnostic machine named Mirabel. They rank second in the world in space sciences.

Ninety-three percent of the country uses solar powered hot water heaters; the highest percentage in the world. They rank first in the world in usage of solar plants having invented much of the technology. They have invested more in electric and hybrid car technology than any other country in the world They rank number one in tree replacement in a mostly desert country. In proportion to its population, Israel ranks number one in business startup companies next to the U.S. They have the highest number of female entrepreneurs of any country in the world. Next to the United States, they rank second in listing of NASDAQ companies. Israel ranks third in the world in scientific institutions. Israel is ranked number two in the world for venture capital funds right behind the U.S. In fact, Israel has the highest concentration of hi-tech companies in the world—apart from the Silicon Valley, U.S.

In medicine, they invented the hand held computerization of doctor written prescriptions eliminating much error from hand written prescriptions that are often difficult to read. Cardiac stints and medical devices that directly help the heart pump blood and which can diagnose the heart's mechanical operations through a sophisticated system of sensors in the heart are their inventions. Camera endoscopy pills that are swallowed by patients to video their intestinal systems from the inside are another one of their inventions as are the defibrillator and the cardiac pacemaker. They have developed drugs to combat multiple sclerosis and invented a Clear Light system to treat acne.

They invented the water saving drip irrigational systems, the ultra violet filter protector to decontaminate fish farms, and the floating tsunami warning systems which they donate to countries free of charge. The eye dropper, Levi Strauss jeans, lipstick, contraceptives, ball point pens, holography, instant photography, video tapes, and the television remote control are some of their many inventions.

They invented the Intel microchip, most of the Windows NP and XP operating systems in Microsoft-Israel, both the Pentium-4 microprocessor and the Centrino microprocessor, all laptop computers made in the twentieth century, and voice mail. The technology for the AOL Instant Messenger ICQ was developed in 1996 by four young

Israeli computer programmers in Tel Aviv. ICQ is a firm founded by these same four young computer programmers. Within six months it claimed the title of world's largest online communication network. Cell phones and camera phones are Israeli inventions. Added to this list of inventions are the Microsoft Office latest version of fire wall protection and the latest version of Microsoft Office.

They invented the USB flash drive and the Quicktionary Electronic dictionary.. In fact, Jews dominate computer software for corporate databases and in the computer world itself. The co-founder of Google is Jewish. The founder of Dell Computers, Michael Dell, is a Jew. Larry Ellison, the founder of Oracle, is a Jew. Not surprising Israel has the highest percentage of home computers in the world per capita. The country leads the world in the number of scientists and technicians in the workforce. Israelis designed the airline industry's most impenetrable flight security.

In agriculture, Israeli date trees now produce 400 pounds per year per tree and are now short enough to be harvested from the ground. They developed the cherry tomato and improved the pomegranate. For the last three years, Israeli film companies have won in the category of Best Foreign Film. Jews also dominate the Hollywood film industry. Jack Benny, Sid Caesar, Milton Berle, Jerry Lewis, and Bob Hope were famous Jewish Hollywood actor/comedians. A few well known Jewish Hollywood stars and television personalities include Tom

Cruise, Elizabeth Taylor, Brad Pitt, John Travolta, Leonardo DiCaprio, Jack Nicholson, Jim Carrey, Mel Gibson, Nicholas Cage, Tim Allen, George Clooney, Tom Hanks, Johnny Depp, Anthony Hopkins, Alec Baldwin, Kirk Douglas, Lisa Kudrow, Suzie Orman, Judge Wapner, Sharon Osbourne, Sarah Jessica Parker, Richard Gere, Adam Sandler, Kevin Costner, Harrison Ford and Barbara Streisand. Film Moguls of Paramount Pictures, Universal Pictures, Fox Film Corporation, Warner Brothers Studio, Metro- Goldwyn-Mayer, and Columbia Pictures, are all Jews. Jewish music composers include George Gershwin, Leonard Bernstein, Irving Berlin, and Victor Borge. Mike Wallace, a well known journalist, is a Jew.   Sport broadcaster of Monday Night Football and sports journalist, Howard Cosell, was Jewish. A few famous Jewish athletes include 1972 Olympic Champion swimmer Mark Spitz, Olympic Champion ice skater Sarah Hughes, Dodger baseball player Sandy Koufax, Olympic gymnast Kerri Strug, NBA basketball player Ernie Grunfeld who was inducted into the National Jewish Hall of Fame in 1993, NFL football player Lyle Alzado, Baltimore Oriole pitcher Steve Stone who is one of the best Jewish pitchers in major league history, and Hank Greenburg who was the first Jewish baseball superstar. He earned two AL MVP awards; one in 1935 and another in 1940.

Immigrant Jews who came to America in the 1920's invented American ready-to-wear clothing which replaced homemade and

241

tailor made apparel. Jews have risen to management and ownership, thus achieving exclusive control of the entire apparel industry. They are masters of merchandising, business insight, and are keen at beating the competition. A few of Jewish apparel companies include Liz Claiborne, Jordache, Ralph Lauren, Levi Strauss, Calvin Klein, Ann Klein, Guess, Donna Karen, DNKY, Tommy Hilfiger, Banana Republic, Big and Tall Company, Eddie Bauer, The Gap, Cloth World, Jo Ann Fabrics, Gottex Swimwear, Cole, Diana Von Furstenberg, Gitano, Yves Saint Laurent, Puritan Fashions, London Fog, and Maiden Form Brassiere Company. The modern bra is a Jewish invention. What invention could possibly surpass the bra? There is one.....the Jewish inventor of Coca- Cola, John Pemberton.

Revlon, Helena Rubenstein, Estee Lauder, Arpel, and Max Factor are Jewish owned cosmetic companies. Cartier, Perrin, and Christian Dior, are Jewish owned jewelry companies. Albert Einstein, Nostradamus, and Christ were Jews. In general Jews excel in almost anything they do simply because of their inherited divine portion, a trait most of them possess unaware.

On the other side of the coin, having inherited this divine portion in high concentrations may not be so good in the temporal world ruled by Lucifer (Satan). The Adamic race, particularly the tribe of Judah descendants, is not welcome here on this physical planet or in this universe. They are a marked race by the mere fact of possessing the

242

divine portion which sets them apart from the Hu'man race. Lucifer can "see" they are descendants of Noah who came from another world and are descendants of the upper Adam created by God; a God whom he hates. In revenge for being cast out of the highest heaven or universe by God, he stirs up nations, leaders, and people against them for he desires to exterminate them off the face of this planet. Thus the main reason for their many persecutions (Volume One, page 473) (Volume Three, pages 217-218). The good news is that the righteous portion of them is given divine protection until the end of the world.

For military use, Israel developed the Arrow anti-ballistic Missile, the IMI Uzi submachine gun, the Merkava tank, and the IMI Lavi jet fighter aircraft. They developed a laser for military use, and developed an effective solution for countering surface-to-air heat seeking missiles. The MagnoShocker taser gun is another one of their inventions. Add to that list, the atomic bomb and the thermonuclear bomb. Their list of achievements goes on and on; the surface has hardly been scratched.

Israel may have just out done itself recently in achievements and in doing so may have fulfilled another prophecy. As previously written in this book, we stated that Israel is already standing alone and that we felt an attack from Israel was imminent toward Iran to take out Iran's nuclear plants. This attack may have already happened; the battlefield being cyberspace. It was first reported on September 26, 2010, that a highly sophisticated computer worm, named Stuxnet, has infected

Iran's first nuclear station and has spread to the personal computers of staff workers. It was reported that the rate of infection in Iran was "off the wall" with 60,000 computers being affected. Computers in India and Indonesia were also infected but at a much lower rate. About 2% of U.S. computers were infected.

Stuxnet is a self-replicating malworm computer program. It uses a computer network to send copies of itself to other computers with a specific designated target to inflict damage to computers. The worm hides inside the computer unbeknown to the operator and can cause systems to malfunction. It appears the Stuxnet worm was designed specifically to target nuclear power plants. This worm can lie dormant until certain conditions are met in the machine. What conditions the worm waits for are unclear. What is clear is that the worm targets industrial software made by Munich based Siemens AG. Siemens has been actively creating software to remove the worm but it could take several months. No new cases of Stuxnet have been reported since the end of August and Siemens was not able to determine the worms country of origin.

It has been estimated the building of the worm cost at least 3 million and required a team of as many as 10 skilled programmers working for at least 6 months to develop the technology. This narrows the country of origin to the U.S., Israel, the UK, France, or Germany. We put our money on Israel because they are masters of computer technology, having invented much of the technology. We think this may be the first of many of worms to be created to take out Iran's nuclear plants without firing one single missile. The Stuxnet worm may be a test worm to find weakness's in the system. Future worms will be much more lethal and undetectable using stealth technology; technology that is well financed by a government.

Biblical revelation states that Russia will be dragged into the conflict by a "hook in the jaw." The "hook in the jaw" is that Russia built Iran's nuclear plants and probably supplied them with the computer technology to operate the plants. When enough worms continue to come and infect Iran's nuclear power plant systems rendering them useless, Russia and Iran may team up and attack Israel. Sit tight as the cyberspace conflict is probably just beginning.

Some of the Hu'man race that the sons of Noah assimilated into when they were scattered passed their DNA divine portion on into a mixed multitude of both races. Although highly diluted, it pops up from time to time and creates geniuses and people of high intellect and ability. Ordinary parents of geniuses often wonder how they produced such an extraordinary child. It really is all in the genes that were inherited from the Adamic race. Most of the Hu'man race carries some Adamic race DNA because we are now of "one blood" but not in the concentrations possessed by the descendants of the tribe of Judah (Volume One, pages 472-473). Non Jews do produce and invent great things as well but evidence confirms that the divine portion found in Jews gives them an intellectual edge and ability to excel in all fields including the arts of civilization. Practically everything we have in today's society, whether it is medical or high-tech technology, or in the arts of civilization, is the result of Noah's race and his descendants. The knowledge of the Adamic race has made life much easier and enjoyable for the Hu'man race, now a mixed one- blood multitude except for the descendants of the tribe of Judah who still remain a people apart with the most pure of all bloodlines. To destroy the Jews or the nation of Israel is to kill the goose that laid the golden eggs. I wonder what they will invent, achieve, or develop next. I can hardly wait!

What Killed The Dinosaurs?

The Ark trilogy has solved many of the Earth's great mysteries with the exception of what killed the dinosaurs. Many theories abound as to why these behemoths disappeared. We would like to offer ours.

Scientists theorize the dinosaurs disappeared around 65 million years ago at the end of the Cretaceous/Tertiary Period. At that period of time, the Earth was a much different place. Tropical rain forests covered much of the planet because the Earth sat vertical on its axis. Even the Polar Regions were tropical. These tropical rain forests were no ordinary rain forests. Giant tropical trees and giant ferns grew a hundred to two hundred feet high because of the abundance of rain, sun, and rich deep humus soil; the result of millions of years of decay and accumulation. In return, the giant tropical forests produced higher levels of oxygen in the atmosphere, maybe as high as 70-75 percent. Scientists know the oxygen levels were much higher than today's level of 20 percent. Over many thousands of years, the behemoth dinosaurs evolved with bodies designed to roam and forage the giant forests. For example, many species of dinosaurs had very long necks to reach the tops of the giant trees and ferns where food was the most abundant. There were other giant animals as well but the large dinosaurs were the largest land animals in their day. Due to their enormous body size, the dinosaurs had huge lungs that required higher levels of oxygen to oxygenate their bodies in order to survive.

All was well until the seven and one half mile wide Chicxulub Meteorite struck the Caribbean near the Yucatán Peninsula 65 million years ago at the end of the Cretaceous Period. Satellite imaging has located the approximate center of the ancient crater near the town of Chicxulub, named for the crater in Mexico. The crater is over 110 miles/180 kilometers in diameter, forming one of the largest impact craters in the world, which was equal to a billion atomic bombs. This event triggered a planetary cataclysm. Many of the dinosaurs were killed instantly by the shock wave in North America but world wide others were unaffected for awhile unaware their world was coming to an end.

It is estimated the Chicxulub impact was the most powerful impact ever on this planet creating mega tsunamis all over the Earth. Ejected material into the atmosphere from the impact by explosion would have heated to become red-hot that itself would have re-entered Earth's atmosphere, burning and causing fires overall. In the meantime enormous shock waves caused earthquakes and volcanic eruptions globally; maybe even tectonic plate movement. The Chicxulub theory is not a new theory however it is the theory most agreed upon by scientists. But scientists fail to take the theory far enough. We take it further as follows.....

If the Indian Ocean earthquake of December 2004, delivered a blow to our planet sufficient to shake the Earth's entire surface and caused ground movement of as much as 0.4 inch everywhere, accelerated the Earth's rotation which shortened days by a fraction of a second, and even caused the planet to tilt an inch more on its axis, think what the largest impact caused by the Chicxulub Meteorite was capable of doing to the planet. The Indian Ocean earthquake pales by comparison.

We theorize the impact caused Earth to tilt on its axis, perhaps 12-15 degrees, which is enough to cause instant climate change. The Polar Regions began to form ice. A winter effect was then created by the emission of impact dust and volcanic ash into Earth's atmosphere that thickly blanketed the entire surface of the planet for several years, possibly a decade, which blocked out the light of the sun. It became intensely cold in a short period of time. Subsequently the photosynthesis of plants was interrupted. With no sun, the giant tropical forests began to die. When it rained, the rain contained sulfuric acid from the dust and ash clouds which hastened the destruction of the tropical forests. With no giant tropical plants to produce the high levels of oxygen, the levels of oxygen began to drop below levels required by large dinosaurs to survive; maybe to present day levels of 20 percent. Those giant dinosaurs who survived the initial impact of shock waves and fires of North America by virtue of living in other parts of the world, they slowly starved and suffocated to death. With climate change came widespread extinctions. Fossil evidence shows that 70 percent of species living on Earth at the time became extinct. Those animal species that survived had smaller bodies and lungs that could adapt to lower oxygen levels and survive on less food. This would include small species of dinosaurs. Their extinction would come later.

Eventually the dust and ash clouds began to clear from the Earth's atmosphere. Then the sun warmed the planets surface once more. Good rain brought forth smaller trees and vegetation designed to live and grow in 20 percent oxygen levels in different climatic conditions because the tilt of the Earth now caused seasons; winter, spring, summer, and fall.

When the Steven Spielburg 1990 science fiction movie, Jurassic Park, came out, it stimulated interest in perhaps re-creating the huge dinosaurs again by extracting DNA from dinosaur eggs and then genetically clone them. It was a novel idea that was hashed around a bit, but in theory would most likely never work with present technology. Even if babies could be hatched, in a short amount of time they would die because their bodies are equipped with huge lungs that require high levels of oxygen to grow and survive. Therefore the age of the giant dinosaurs is forever gone.

That is our expanded theory on what caused the extinction of the large dinosaurs which is based on the Chicxulub impact theory.

Recent Updates

Another research trip to the Yucatán in January 2011 has resulted in more information worthy of mentioning as Updates to the trilogy. In our opinion, they are significant finds.

The first find will be the twenty-fourth piece of evidence to be added to the chapter *Unveiling the Sealed Plates* in this book. Sayil is the name of a Maya ruin in the Yucatán. It flourished between 800 and 1000 AD. On its grounds is a tall stone stela carved in the shape of an upright standing phallus, which is a symbol of the union of the spiritual and physical worlds; knowledge passed down from the sealed record. The years are in the correct time frame. As late as 1000 AD., the knowledge of the Union of the Polarity was still being taught in the Yucatán.

The second find is the fact that the Yucatec Mayan language is one of the five oldest languages in the world, dating back to 3,000 BC. in the Yucatán. It appears to have its roots in ancient China, perhaps the Tartary region. When the Maya speak it, it has a musical Chinese "sound." From Yucatec Maya has sprung some thirty to thirty-four Mayan dialects which are spoken today by approximately ten million Maya in Mexico, Belize, Guatemala, and Honduras. Because of the antiquity of the language in the Yucatán, we believe that Yucatec Maya was a fourth language brought here by the Jaredite expedition. On page

181, Volume Three, chapter *The Oldest City in the Americas*, we identified three languages that came with the settlers around 2700 BC. Those languages spoken by the 24 families have been identified as Nahuatl, U-Mam, and the pure Adamic language which we believe is archaic Sumerian. Now, we would like to add a fourth language to that list; Yucatec Maya.

The third find came after closer examination of the stucco frieze surrounding the entrance to the tomb of Ukit Kan Le'K Toc in Ek'Balam, Yucatán, Mexico. Please refer to the chapter *Pakal*, pp. 112-113 in this book. The winged angel figures guarding Ukit Kan Le'K Toc's tomb are definitely winged angels because they are standing above the sky band located above the door entrance to the tomb which denotes that these are angelic beings in heaven. Above the sky band of heaven are two human figures. One is standing and the other is actually sitting astride one of the bands. Perhaps the one sitting on a sky band is a figure of Ukit Kan Le'K Toc which indicates that he is now in heaven. On either side of the door entrance to the tomb is an identical stylized cosmic sacred Ceiba tree of Life supporting the sky band. The stylized cosmic Ceiba tree of Life has a stylized feathered serpent wrapped around its trunk. These feathered serpents represent Quetzalcoatl or Kukulcan as he was known to the Maya because according to Maya belief, he raised the sacred tree to lift the collapsed sky after the last world destruction. It was He who created this last world age. The sacred trees each rest on the Earth above the underworld domain which is carved beneath the tomb door entrance. This stucco frieze proves that Ukit Kan Le'K Toc was indeed a Christian.

The fourth find was to discover that the Temple of Kukulcan in Chichen Itza was laid out in the form of a true cross. The cross can only be fully seen and appreciated from an aerial view. The same holds true for a few other temples, for example as in Monte Alban, Dzibilchaltun, and Caral located in Peru, but not all Mesoamerican temples. There may be more but just don't have the information due to inaccessibility. It also holds true for most Christian cathedrals and King Solomon's Temple. The cross as proven in the Ark trilogy is a symbol of the Union of the Polarity. As with all temples dedicated to Kukulcan (Christ or Quetzalcoatl) there was a sacred fire burning at the top of the pyramid. It is said that Christ usually made an appearance to dedicate all temples built for him and then would light the sacred fire. Perhaps he did so at Chichen Itza.. The sacred fire was maintained by the priests around the clock. It was only extinguished at the end of a 52- year Calendar Round. When the sacred fire was extinguished, all home hearth fires in the city were extinguished at the same time. A Calendar Round takes 52 years for the same week day, month day, and haab day, to realign together (18,980 Kin). It was a time of great foreboding that the world could possibly end. The sacred ritual ball game was played to ensure that the Earth would pass through the hoop Ouroboros safely should the world end. There is no doubt as to the meaning of the ball passing through the stone hoop at Chichen Itza because the stone hoop even has the celestial serpent body carved in relief around the rim of the stone hoop indicating the center hole is an Ouroboros opening where the ball representing the Earth must pass into the fourth dimension. Only the king and priests were allowed to observe this particular ball game. But there was a little problem as the ball rarely made it through the hoop. We therefore believe if the ball failed to pass through the hoop, a human sacrifice was made of one of the players to ensure the Earth would ascend safely should the world end. It was a sacrificial act for the safety of the world to appease the supreme God, and an honor to do so. We want to mention that all users of the Long Count calendar played the sacred ritual ball game throughout Mesoamerica and parts of the southwest in North America. That fact alone proves the knowledge of the 2012 end time events was understood in all of Mesoamerica and not just solely by the Maya. All large city complexes had a ball court with the exception of Teotihuacán, Tikal, and Matacapan, who were under Teotihuacano influence. How often the sacred ball game was played remains unanswered but certainly at the end of a 52- year Calendar Round. Also there were other types of ball games played that didn't require human sacrifice, such as handball. Some of these games were played by the kings and elites, some were played by captive warriors (consider them gladiators), and other games were played by commoners. If the sun arose the following morning, following the end of a 52-year Calendar Round, then Earth had not ascended into the fourth dimension and things would resume back to normal until the end of the next Calendar Round. There would be a big celebration then the king would then light the sacred New Fire again with fire drilling sticks he carried in a bundle for such purpose only. Everyone in the city would then light their home hearth fires from the New Fire kindled by the king. December 21, 2012 is the end of the next 52-year Calendar Round. Unfortunately the ancient Maya cities have long been abandoned and the sacred fires long extinguished. The last time the Maya observed the 52-year cycle was shortly before the Spanish conquest. Chichen Itza however is still considered a sacred place by the modern Maya and by hoards of tourist. It is said that the Life Force energy is really strong around the great plaza surrounding the Temple of Kukulcan but the many hoards of people visiting the site daily absorb the energy. However if one comes early enough in the morning hours, between seven and eight am, before the masses of people arrive, the Life Force energy can be readily felt

The fifth update is not a find but rather another Maya end time date researcher by the name of Carl Callemen who contends the date of December 21, 2012 is not the correct end time date but rather the correct date occurs 420 days sooner than traditionally accepted. This places the end time date on October 28, 2011 which he says is the official end of the creation cycle. His theory is long and controversial; too long to describe here so just Google his name and read his theory. But in a nutshell, his conceptual view is one of which the "cyclical nature" of time was a pre- eminent one that was concerned with the completion and re-occurrences of various energy cycles. The current accepted 2012 end time date was not a completed cycle according to Maya ideology but the 2011 date was. He believes the Maya would not end their Long Count calendar mid cycle. Regardless, we don't support his theory because the Maya didn't calculate their end time date from any of their calendars but in truth were tracking Precession to determine the time of the end of the age to know when the Day of Retribution would occur. The fact that the Maya were tracking Precession is confirmed by epigraphers Michael Grofe and Barbara Macleod by independent research, and of course by us as we have written about it in the Ark trilogy many times. How then did the Mesoamericans know to end their Long Count calendar at the end of the 13th B'ak'tun, written by the Maya as 13.0.0.0.0, which date calculates to December 21, 2012 on the Gregorian calendar? Answer...Because Quetzalcoatl told them so in his many visits to Mesoamerican cities. It was recorded in the now sealed portion of the Toltec record known today as the Book of Mormon. After the record was resealed, the teachings continued on for centuries until the arrival of the Spanish. The end time date is carved on the Aztec Sun Stone. Christ even taught his apostles in the

New Testament that he was coming for the Harvest at the end of the age. His "other sheep not of this fold" were the Mesoamericans. It is apparent that Christ wanted everyone to know when he was coming for the Harvest and separation of the wheat from the tares. The end of the age is December 21, 2012 when the Great Year, Platonic Year, or Precession finishes a 26,000 year cycle. The Maya express their Great Year cycle of time as a period of 13 B'ak'tuns or "Great Cycle" of the Long Count. It is 5,128 years long (in 360-day years) or 3, 114 BC. when the Maya started their Long Count calendar. The current Great Cycle ends on December 21, 2012 (winter solstice). In addition, Quetzalcoatl helped the Maya to perfect their Long Count calendar by use of the 52-year Calendar Round cycle which by tracking the Calendar Rounds would eventually coincide with the end of the age. A Calendar Round was just an aid to tracking Precession. Venus cycles, moon cycles, tracking eclipses etc. were other aids of time measurement. Today we rely on supercomputers to keep track of these events which are used in conjunction with the Gregorian calendar. However, the Maya's meshed or interlocking calendars were an early computer of sorts which were highly accurate but not as technically advanced.

The sixth update is in response to a History Channel television documentary called Apocalypse Island that aired on January 4, 2010, part of the "Armageddon" series. Jim Turner, a Canadian explorer, accidently stumbled upon what he believes to be a 150 foot badly eroded Maya monument on a remote island in the middle of the Pacific Ocean.

As it turns out, the island is named Robinson Crusoe Island which is one of three islands in the Juan Fernandez Archipelago located about 100 miles off the coast of Chile. It stretches the imagination to envision a carved standing statue of the Mayan sun god Kinich Ahau gazing toward the sky. Behind him was another rock formation suggesting the shape of a couching jaguar? Turner said it is the only place in the western hemisphere where you will be able to see the planet Venus eclipse the sun in 2011. He questions if the ancient Maya were capable of sea travel to the island and questions how did they know this was the only place to witness such an event in the western hemisphere? In response to his questions: First the Maya were capable of sea travel and did so. Second, the stone formations were probably just that... natural eroded stone spires and nothing more. We base our opinion on what astronomers say about the matter..... The Venus eclipse of the sun cannot be seen from that island in the western hemisphere in 2011.

The seventh update is the motif of the Descending or Diving God found in four archaeology sites in the Yucatán; these being Sayil, Chichen Itza, Coba, and Tulum. Note, there may be more sites not yet identified. The Descending God figure appears more often in Tulum than anywhere else but most prominently in the Temple of the Descending God which was devoted to the teachings and worship of the Descending God who we believe was Christ. The Tulum Temple of the Descending God was built in alignment with both the morning star (planet Venus) and the sun so as to mark April 6th as the birthday of the Descending God. On that day Venus can be seen rising into the night sky directly over the door of the Temple and the day sunlight then forms a brilliant star directly over the door that can be seen only on that day. Remember Quetzalcoatl/Christ was born on April 6, thus the identity of the Descending God which is proven in the chapter *Unveiling the Sealed Plates* in this book. The Great Castillo has three large niches over the three doorways into the Temple. The Descending God is in the middle niche above the middle doorway. On his right hand, in the first niche, stands his father, Hunab-Ku, the supreme God, and the third niche to his left hand is for the Holy Ghost who has no body, physical shape or form, therefore the niche is empty. Inside the Temple of the Descending God are murals or scenes (in bad need of restoration) of heaven, Earth, and perhaps creation. One scene in particular, in the Temple of the Frescoes, shows a woman (Mary) kneeling at the feet of a God who is presenting her with a baby Descending God (baby Jesus) who is identified as the creator of man. Because many images of the Descending God are found on the site, it is evident that Tulum was built in honor of Christ. On the corners of the Temple of Frescoes are large masks of the god Itzamna, another Maya name for Quetzalcoatl. Not with standing, archaeologists believe the name of the Descending

God is Ah Muu Zen Caab, the Bee God who was associated with the planet Venus; a bringer of light and honey.

In the Temple of Inscriptions is a mural that tells the story of three men. The three men are portrayed as seers, who appear to be living in a physical state between life and death. The Toltec/Book of Mormon Mesoamerican record tells a similar story of three men, two of them brothers, who were Disciples of Christ and who traveled and attended to Christ during his many visits in Mesoamerica. According to the record they were seers who were granted power by Christ to live without tasting of death until his second coming in a translated state.

In Tulum we see the red hands image on a wall which was associated directly with the Descending God. This image is found at various sites throughout Mesoamerica. The 17th century Spanish historian Lizana recorded that the Maya represented the Great God of heaven by symbol of the hand. Red was the color the Maya gave to the direction East. It is the direction Christ will come when he returns and the direction from which he came if had he visited them.

Tulum means walled city but its original ancient name was Zama which means City of the Dawn. Joseph Smith, the Mormon prophet, identified the ancient name of the city of Zion as being Zama which is identical as Tulum's ancient name. In 1831, when Joseph Smith identified Zama as the name of the city of Zion, Tulum had not yet been uncovered. Tulum was founded in 1200 AD. and definitely was influenced by the political and religious capital of the Yucatán, Chichen Itza.

Two hundred years earlier the city of Coba was founded and built. At the summit of its largest pyramid Temple, Nohoch Mul, is a partially restored Temple which the visitor can enter and see figures carved into the stone which indicate this was a Temple to the Descending God.

In Chichen Itza the Temple of the Descending God stands to the right of the Temple of Kukulcan. A staircase leads up to the Temple which has a single chamber and a bottle-shaped vault. Over the doorway, there is a niche with a painted stucco figure of the winged God descending from the sky.

Sayil "place of the ants" is located about 33 miles southeast of Uxmal. The city, built in Puuc style, was settled around 800 AD. and reached its peak of splendor around 950 AD. On the second floor of The Great Palace are mosaics depicting the Descending God similar to those found in Tulum.

Uxmal has the detailed feathered serpent decoration on the West Building in the Nunnery Quadrangle. A large circular pyramid temple is dedicated to Quetzalcoatl. As previously written in the trilogy, all circular temples were dedicated to Quetzalcoatl because he was also called the God of the Wind; another one of his manifestations. Archaeologists have named the circular temple, the Temple of the Magicians. Quetzalcoatl's image is found on the East Building in the

Nunnery Quadrangle. He is pictured as a bearded white man. The small human figure is placed against a background of symbols that allude to the four Ages as found on the center of the Aztec Sun Stone. Symbolically it means he is coming at the end of this Age. Although the image of the Descending god has not been found here (so far), the entire Uxmal site is dedicated to Quetzalcoatl.

In the Toltec/Book of Mormon Mesoamerican record it states in Mosiah 27:6-7 that when the people began to be very numerous, they began to scatter upon the face of the earth in all directions building large cities and villages in all quarters of the land. Verse seven says the Lord (Quetzalcoatl translates as Lord) did visit them and prosper them and they became a large and wealthy people. If Christ had visited the people in Mesoamerica as the Toltec record states, he would have come in great glory descending from heaven. The event would have been recorded. Temples were built and dedicated to him. Pyramid Temples are The Mountain of the "House of God." This is the evidence we see with the Descending God.

The eighth update is the Maya Book of the Chilam Balam text of Mani where it describes how the last Age ended in world destruction from water. The text states "Fire seized the heavens and fire rained down....the heavens were seized and split asunder....the heavens shook back and forth (shaking of Earth)...the sky fell down and dry land sank....a sudden rush of water flooded the world." We believe this text is a descriptive remembrance of when the Earth made its last transit through the "dark rift" of the Milky Way, 5, 128 years ago or 3, 114 BC. Following the collapsed sky, the Maya believe that Quetzalcoatl raised the Milky Way World Tree and created this world age. They started their Long Count calendar, to mark the beginning of a new world creation, on the 3,114 BC. date. We have previously described these same catastrophic events in The Ark trilogy to repeat itself soon in December 2012. The process has already begun with climate change, increase in earthquakes, wild weather swings of heat and cold, droughts, high winds, increase in hurricanes and tsunamis, tornadoes, wild fires, and flooding. Tetrahedron excitement is causing some of the natural disasters (see chapter *The Tetrahedron* Volume Three) which will be intensified as we approach the "dark rift's" electromagnetic axis that will start to interact with the electromagnetic force field of Earth.

The ninth update is our explanation of the long nosed Chac masks found on buildings in the Yucatán. They are distinctive elements of Puuc architecture, though they are found at Rio Bec and Chenes. Usually they are identified with the rain god Chac but it is probable that they also represent different aspects of a deity such as Ataman/Quetzalcoatl in his manifestations as the Celestial Feathered Serpent, Earth Monster, Maize God, Wind God, and Rain God. Their long noses were often thought to be a sort of elephant like trunk but were in fact extensions of the face of a feathered serpent. Archaeologists are puzzled as to why some of the trunk like noses curve upward and some curve downward in an upside down U. The following is what we believe. There are two distinctive types of Chacs who probably represent the rain gods. The Maya rain god Chac had his long nose curved upward. The Toltec rain god Thaloc had his nose curved in an upside down U shape. Thaloc was another manifestation of Quetzalcoatl/Itzamna. In Aztec books Thaloc is the Plumbed Serpent's nagual companion (spirit guide). He strides ahead of the Plumbed Serpent waving an incensory. Thaloc's robe is marked with the sign of the cross. Uxmal has the best example of the upside down U shaped nose on the corners of the building of the Nunnery Quadrangle. The mask there is a representation of Itzamna as a feathered serpent; the feathers being stylized. The long upside down U shape nose is an Omega sign; meaning the end of the age or Great Cycle which is the Maya end time date of December 21, 2012. Symbolically the message in stone is stating that Itzamna is coming at the end of the age. It was a reminder to the people to get prepared for the upcoming event. It is the twenty-fifth and last piece of evidence found to be added to the chapter *Unveiling the Sealed Plates* in this book. Uxmal dates to 700 AD. so the time line is correct.

The tenth and final update is on the chapter *San Barolo Murals* in this book. On page 119 the meaning of the glyphs is given. According to archaeologists working on the project, the glyphs are of those of an earlier Maya form of writing. Only one glyph to date has been deciphered by them. We used the decipherment of the glyphs by Clyde A. Winters PHD, author of *Atlantis in Mexico*. He believes the origin of the Guatemalan tomb writing is Olmec and that the Maya built another pyramid over the original Olmec pyramid which was common practice to do so. We agree. According to Winters, the glyphs have not been deciphered because the glyphs are not Maya writing but are written in Olmec which glyphs do not have the common day signs associated with Maya inscriptions. He points out on his website that the Tikal and Rio Azul Inscriptions share many signs that have similar meaning. It is known that the Olmec and Maya cultures intermingled and influenced each other.

It is obvious that the Olmec and Maya cultures influenced each other on this particular site because the San Bartolo Murals are scenes taken from the Mayan bible, the Popol Vuh. This further validates our writings in the chapter *The Twin Feathered Serpents* in this book as the Olmecas and the Quiche Maya of Guatemala shared the same religious views on Quetzalcoatl. We do disagree with Winters that the Olmecas were a black race. There are descendants of the Olmecas, still living in the Veracruz regions, and they are not black but rather brown skinned Polynesian looking in the face with down turned lips, round heads, and flat noses. They are a large people, not tall, built like wide Samo wrestlers. Been there and seen them.

We hold to our belief that the Late Classic and Terminal Classic Periods: Peak and Collapse (600-900 to 1000AD.) and later periods up till the arrival of the Spanish, the Yucatán and much of the surrounding areas (Guatemala, Belize, Honduras) were Christianized prior to the arrival of the Spaniards. We maintain that the archaeological sites have been misinterpreted because archaeologists usually specialize in just one field of study. Unless you do a very comprehensive world study, in many different fields, as demonstrated in The Ark trilogy, you will miss the mark and true meaning. These areas, in particular, became Christianized because of the many visits of Quetzalcoatl to the region and because of the Sealed Portion teachings of Quetzalcoatl/Lord in the Toltec/Book of Mormon Mesoamerican record that continued on for approximately one thousand one hundred thirty five years even after the record was resealed in 385 AD. The Popol Vuh, the Books of the Chilam Balam, the surviving Maya codices, and the Toltec/Book of Mormon Mesoamerican records all attest to this. The evidence is carved in stone for all to see at the archaeological sites.

Remember Tulum was built by the Alux dwarfs who were said to be favored by Quetzalcoatl because of their righteousness and devotion to him.

Great Serpent Mound End Time Update

The Great Serpent Mound archaeological site is located on a plateau of the Serpent Mound crater along Ohio Brush Creek in Adams County, Ohio near Hillsboro. Based on latest technology, including carbon dating, researchers now believe the members of the Fort Ancient Culture built it about 1070 A.D., instead of the Adena Culture. However, the Fort Ancient Culture was influenced by the Mississippian Culture.

Serpent Mound is the largest and most famous serpent effigy in the world being constructed as a 1,370 foot-long raised three to five foot earthen effigy that conforms to the curve of the land on which it rests. Scotland and Ontario have similar serpent effigies.

The serpent winds back and forth for more than eight hundred feet and seven coils that end in a triple-coiled tail. The serpent head has an open mouth extending around the east end of a 120-foot long hollow oval feature with a dot in the center. The most popular belief is the oval symbolizes an egg about to be swallowed up by the serpent. Native Americans regard this site as sacred and did not use it as a burial site, but it is surrounded by other mounds that were. Archaeologists and researchers are perplexed as to what it was created for. Unable to answer that question, the site has remained a mystery until this writing. We will unveil the mystery as follows:

The serpent represents the Life Force energy. It was constructed there because the site is a strong vortex filled with Life Force energy. In other words, the serpent marks the site as a powerful vortex. At the end of this chapter is an illustration of the site. The oval or egg feature in the serpent's mouth represents creation or the Earth and has dual meaning.

If one looks closely at the oval circle in the serpent's mouth, it has a dot in the center. A dot in a circle (in this case an oval but nearly a circle) represents Precession. This is an End of the Age symbol and is telling us by symbolism about the Earth and 2012.

The head of the serpent is aligned to the summer solstice sunset and the coils point to the winter solstice sunrise; therefore there is no error in what the site means. The spiraling triple coil tail also identifies the site as a powerful vortex (spiraling Life Force vortex). Burial mounds surround the site nearby, because the Life Force energy was equated to the power of the Holy Ghost whose power resurrects the dead at the End of the Age or December 21, 2012.

The site was a marker to time the solstices until a future End of the Age winter solstice sunrise alignment was reached in lieu of a calendar. They were tracking the time of the coming resurrection of the dead and the translation or end of the world in this dimension as was done in the Newgrange Ireland site, Stonehenge, Ocmulgee, and Etowah Mound sites. They knew these events would occur at the end of Precession at the End of the Age on a winter solstice. All Ancient Fort Culture serpent effigies, found at two other sites, are linked to the Great Serpent Mound. All three structures contain features which align to the winter and summer solstices. The builders of these sites most likely migrated out of Mexico or were descendants of tribes out of Mexico who knew the passed down teachings of the now sealed Toltec/ Book of Mormon Mesoamerican record or perhaps they were visited and taught by Christ himself as Christ did walk the Americas in times past. Ere else how did they know?

On the winter solstice of every year, the Ohio Historical Society has a "Lighting of the Serpent" ceremony that is open to the public. Everyone lights their candle from a single candle flame and from that single lighting more than 800 candles are lit around the mound that outline the serpent. Prayers are sent out while candles are being lit which celebrate the final long night of winter. It is a sight unlike any other.

Serpent Mound State Memorial is currently being operated on behalf of the Ohio Historical Society by the Arc of Appalachia Preserve system, a non-profit organization specializing in the preservation and protection of prehistoric aboriginal sites in southern Ohio. It is open to the public. There is a museum near the site, walk ways, and viewing tower.

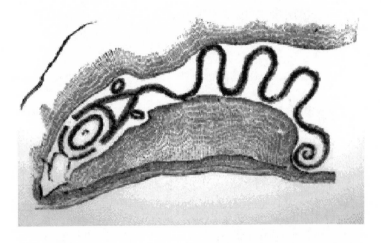

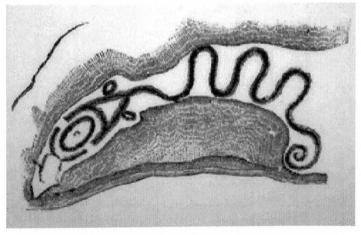

Figure 25 Great Serpent Mound

Masonic Signs and Tokens

According to the Apocryphal books of Adam and Eve and the *Zohar,* Adam and Eve on the Spirit Earth received the priesthood directly from God and wore priesthood garments that were indestructible. These garments had symbols on them. Latter-Day Saint teachings say this priesthood was called the Priesthood of Christ. After Adam and Eve died, Adams garments were passed down and worn by other prophets till they were received and worn by Noah.

After Noah arrived here on the Temporal Earth, Noah received the Melchizedek Priesthood. An account of Melchizedek is given in Volume One of *The Ark of Millions of Years*, pages 468-471. His son, Ham, stole Noah's priesthood garments while he slept off the effects of drinking too much wine. The Bible says that Ham uncovered his father's nakedness but those scriptures meant that Ham stole his father's priesthood garments while he slept or removed Noah's garments from him while he slept. When Noah awoke and realized what had happened, Noah cursed the descendants of Ham that they could not hold the priesthood. Ham's descendants were the Egyptians and the black race; the result of intermarriage with the Hu'man Race. The Egyptians, especially the Pharaohs, wanted to hold the priesthood authority but could not which vexed them somewhat so they instituted unauthorized priesthood ceremonies and copied much of what was passed down through Ham's descendants concerning rituals, tokens, and symbolism. Some of the priesthood ceremonies were done in the Great Giza Pyramid and in Egyptian temples. King Tut had many Masonic items etc. buried with him in his tomb which indicated that he was a Mason. Masonry was taught in the "mystery schools" of Egypt using the same symbols, tokens, and rituals, used today.

Moses was an Egyptian prince who was schooled in the Egyptian ways which included the "mystery schools" so he was familiar with the signs, symbols, and tokens. Later, he received the Melchizedek priesthood, with authority, from his father-in-law, Jethro. Moses wore the Melchizedek priesthood garments and understood the symbolism on the garments and understood the symbolism used in rituals including vows of silence.

According to the *Zohar* and the Apocryphal books of Adam and Eve, Noah's garment made its way to the giant King Nimrod who wore them. Many believed his strength came from wearing the priesthood garment of Noah. He was slain by Jacob's son, Esau, who then took the garment. From there the garment is lost in history.

Abraham also wore the priesthood garments. He received the Melchizedek priesthood from Shem, son of Noah. From him the priesthood knowledge was passed down eventually to King David and King Solomon who also held the Melchizedek priesthood and wore priesthood garments, as did their high priests. Priesthood ceremonies were held in Solomon's temple using the same symbols, tokens, and rituals. All the priesthood knowledge was passed down through the Divine Book of Wisdom or Adam's Book (Adam's Book was carried aboard the ark by Noah, see page 214, Volume One of *The Ark of Millions of Years*), sometimes referred to as the "flying scrolls". These sacred scrolls were sealed or hidden in the bronze columns of Solomon's temple.

Later, the Knight Templars, who were looking for the "flying scrolls" because they were reputed to contain the alchemical formula for turning base metals into gold, found the scrolls concealed in the hollow bronze columns in the ruins of Solomon's Temple. Not only did they find the formula but found the priesthood knowledge of symbols, tokens, and rituals, used for conferring the Priesthood of Christ, renamed later the Melchizedek priesthood, after Melchizedek, from these scrolls. They very quickly adopted a Masonic ritual for themselves, not fully understanding the significance of priesthood authority but nevertheless used it in their temple rites to obtain or build an incorruptible body in preparation for eternal life....exactly as the ancient Egyptians once did.

In Volume One of *The Ark of Millions of Years* (pages 310-320), the Knight Templars sailed out of France on October 12, 1307, with many Templar treasures on board. There were several trunk loads of scrolls that were, as we now know, taken to Scotland and stored in William St.

Clair's home (a Templar) while he built Rosslyn Chapel. Unfortunately, he died before the chapel was completed. These trunks full of scrolls from Solomon's temple then made their way to America via the Templars, later re-organized as Freemasons, which helped our founding Freemason fathers of this great nation establish a free democratic nation to be ruled by the people and for the people with liberty and justice under God. These principles were found in the Constitutional Scrolls which were part of the Divine Book of Wisdom scrolls. It is said that Thomas Jefferson drafted the Declaration of Independence over night without a single scratched out change because he used the knowledge found in the Divine Book of Wisdom Constitutional Scrolls to guide him to found the New Jerusalem and "New World Order" of America. America came to be because of the Freemasons. The Phoenix or Fire Bird, rising out of the ashes, was first chosen to become this nation's symbol for the New Jerusalem. At that time, the old Jerusalem was lying in ruins and burnt ashes. So, the Fire Bird was a fitting symbol for the New Jerusalem. The ancients believed that the Fire Bird emanated from the Solar Spirit or Life Force. It is our personal opinion that these scrolls or at least scribed copies of the scrolls still exist and are housed somewhere in Washington D.C....perhaps in an underground vault at the House of the Temple Masonic headquarters in that city. The House of the Temple in D.C. contains by far the most extensive library collection of books on Freemasonry in the US. We also believe that higher-ups in Masonry have access to this knowledge especially here in American lodges, perhaps though scribed copies of the original scrolls. Ere how else did Thomas Jefferson, a mason, access these scrolls?

Many centuries later, following the times of the Knight Templars, along comes Joseph Smith who not only was a 3rd degree master mason but a student of the *Zohar*. He recognized the sacred significance of the signs, tokens, and symbols. Note: In our personal opinions, we believe that Joseph Smith had access to scribed copies of the scrolls, maybe during some of his trips to Washington D.C., where he may have met with other higher up masons, at their headquarters, who had access to the scrolls. History says that Joseph made several trips to D.C. for political reasons. While there, he most certainly would have made time to visit the Masonic headquarters to study or better yet, have copies of the scribed scrolls given to him? It was probably through the *Zohar* (note the *Zohar* is part of the Divine Book of Wisdom) and the other scribed scrolls of the Divine Book of Wisdom that Joseph learned of the ancient and sacred nature of the signs, symbols, and tokens, that were being used in Masonic temple rituals. In the early years of Freemasonry, the tokens, signs, and symbols, were suitably called "The Mysterious Force." When the time came to build a temple unto the Lord...Joseph Smith restored the ancient knowledge back to temple worship with authority, using the same signs, tokens, and symbolism, used in Masonic rituals as was decreed in the ancient texts. This action met the approval of the Lord. The Freemasons had preserved this information through their rituals until the appointed time came to restore it back to LDS (The Church of Jesus Christ of Latter Day Saints) temple worship unto the Lord. It is interesting to note that these same signs, tokens, and symbols, were always used in temple worship and rites as in the Temple of Solomon, the Egyptian temples, the Masonic temples, and finally in the LDS temples. Although we're not completely sure, they may have been used in some of the Mesoamerican temples, especially in the temple Nephi built in 570 BC. They were always considered sacred, therefore, those endowed with this knowledge took vows of secrecy to protect the knowledge from being desecrated and misused. The Priesthood certainly existed as Quetzalcoatl established it in ancient Mexico.

Remember the Star Wars movie trilogy where the phrase "May the Force be with you" was often used when the leading stars were departing each other or when the stars were trying to learn to use the power of the "Force" for the good of the universe? The writers of the movie scripts were referring to "The Mysterious Force" or priesthood knowledge and power to defeat the forces of evil whose leader was Darth Vader, a representative of Lucifer. How many Star War fans picked up on that allegorical scenario?

As written in Volume Three, the forces of evil attacked and destroyed the plan of salvation in ancient times whenever it re-appeared on Earth. The same evil forces tried to destroy the Knight Templars because they possessed the sacred scrolls of Adam which contained the tokens, signs, and symbols, of the holy priesthood of God who administer the plan of salvation with authority and power. One is not without the other. It is ongoing spiritual warfare between good and evil forces described as the sons of light against the sons of darkness. The forces of evil are trying to defeat God's plan of salvation and gain control of this planet. Today, Masons still protect those sacred tokens, signs, and symbols, as do the LDS temples and church members who receive that knowledge. These institutions continue to be heavily persecuted because of reasons stated above and because the vows of secrecy have been misunderstood by the world. However, it does seem that the forces of evil have regrouped and are following a newer strategy to accomplish that purpose because Masonry and the LDS are not being persecuted as heavily as they have been in the past. The newest strategy to accomplish their goal is warfare through the use of radical Islamic terrorism, coupled with the global economic recession defined in this book as the Fall of Babylon the Great. In more simple terms the newest strategy is to bring the world to its knees. The world is being prepared for the New World Order which will follow the events of 2012, as defined and previously written in Volumes Two and Three of The Ark trilogy..

As you can now see, the tokens, signs, and symbols, are neither of Masonic origin nor of Egyptian origin. Their origins date back to the time of Adam and Eve when they first received the Priesthood of Christ ordinances directly from God on the Spirit Earth. The Divine Book of Wisdom scrolls (the handbook of God) were given to Adam in the Garden of Eden (see Volume One of *The Ark of Millions of Years* p.161). The ordinances of priesthood, signs, tokens, and symbols, are written in them. When Joseph Smith restored the ancient signs, symbols, and tokens, to the LDS temple endowment ceremonies, the restoration of the fullness of the everlasting gospel was complete in this last dispensation of time. As did Adam and Eve, those LDS who receive the sacred ordinances in their Temples, wear the holy priesthood garments.

Latest Effects of the Galactic Plane

In view of what has recently happened in Japan, we feel compelled to warn that nuclear reactors will be affected world wide when the magnetic axis of the spinning black hole begins to interact with the magnetic force field of the Temporal Earth toward the end of the 2012 year. As the solar system enters the galactic plane, the Sun resonates with the energy. There is no doubt by any astrophysical authority that this resonance will take place.

Even the doubts that encapsulated high-frequency regions exist outside our heliosphere have been recently dispelled by the arrival of the Voyager crafts beyond the edge of the solar system. Barely discussed beyond the paranormal display tables at hundreds of conventions and conferences every year, the idea that the solar wind found competition with a galactic wind is stunning. Science is being rewritten as we write this book, and solid scientific history is being shelved in the space next to fables of the flat Earth.

Bodies sympathetically resonate with any energy that is present. Standing twenty rows back from the stage of a rock concert, one will feel the music. Not only will the body vibrate from the sound pressure pumped out by the speakers, but the souls within resonates with the overall message of the music. The sound, rhythm, and harmonies in the music pluck the emotions like a pick hitting a guitar string.

Likewise, when the source is a large choir, or an orchestra swelling with violins and French horns—a la John Williams taking a sci-fi flick and transforming it into a spiritual experience with nothing but his soundtrack—the soul will oscillate between tears and dancing with the inspiration of the artist himself.

The Sun is the largest physical body in our region of space. It is the most energetic. It is balanced between exploding like a giant fusion bomb, and collapsing into itself with the presence of too much matter in the same place. In this delicate and creative balance, which we see as stars all over the heavens, any outside influence will have its effects. Magnetic pimples, like broken sores in the chaotic surface of the Sun, form and explode. These explosions have been watched for millennia by the beings that live on the surface of Earth. Coronal Mass Ejections (CME) lash out into space like a flaming multi-strand wire snapping at one end. The energy released with this event is enough to destroy all life on the surface of a planet. It does exactly that on planets like Mars and various moons that have no way to protect themselves from the full spectrum of energy blasted out into space by the Sun.

The last major solar tsunami stuck the Earth in 1859. The energy that struck the Earth poured so much energy onto the telegraph lines that workers were electrocuted, stations caught on fire, and communications were down for days. The telegraph lines themselves became the antennae that collected the energy. All solar experts agree that Solar Cycle 24 haltingly began and had unprecedented periods of sunspot absence. The activity of the Sun is currently observed closely with the Solar Dynamic Observatory (SDO). The observations are in color stereo and can be broadcasted to Earth days ahead of the effects of a solar blast. Still, two days warning that the entire digital world will plunge into darkness is hardly comforting. Everything from GPS to cell phones, to computer trading services will disappear for as long as a year.

The first thing to go will be the Temporal Earth's electrical grid. Besides the fact that large step-transformer cores would melt from 100,000 volts per meter being loaded onto the lines, the nuclear facilities would be disrupted. With no electricity to pump water onto the nuclear fuel rods to cool them, they will start to overheat. Back-up generators most likely will not work either nor anything motorized. Of course, designing the plant with the generators located in the basement did nothing to protect them from the tsunami's sea water. They never had a chance to save the Japanese power plant. How many similarly poor designs are out there?

Nuclear meltdowns will contribute to the woes of those left behind. The Japan tragedy has made us aware of this possibility and is something we wanted to pass along. Please note that earthquakes in divers' places are now happening in greater frequency and in some places in greater magnitude. These are undersea off shore earthquakes. Richard Gross, a geophysicist at the Jet Propulsion Laboratory in La Canada Flintridge, reported the Japan quake of 9.0 magnitude (the strongest ever recorded in Japan's history) shifted the position of Earth's axis about 6.5 inches and shortened the length of the day by about 1.8 microseconds. Will Alaska or California be next along the Ring of Fire? Scientists say it is possible that a 9.0 magnitude could occur in Alaska along the Aleutian Fault or along the Cascadia subduction zone just off the U.S. northwestern coast that stretches from the northern top of California up to Canada. Both places are capable of producing huge tsunamis and have done so repeatedly throughout the centuries. The San Andreas Fault however is not capable of generating a 9.0 magnitude quake, but rather one of 8.0 or under magnitude. It is something to think about in these *last days*.

The Yucatán Stingless Honey Bee

In the Toltec/Book of Mormon record is found an account in the Book of Ether of a people called the Jaredites and of other peoples identified as their friends who were instructed by the Lord to build eight barges to cross the sea to the Land of Promise which was choice above all other lands, which the Lord God had preserved for a righteous people (Ether 2:3, 7).

They were instructed to bring male and female of every kind of their flocks, food for their flocks and for their families. In addition they were to bring seeds of the earth of every kind. The account says they did carry with them Deseret, which by interpretation is a honey bee; and thus they did carry with them swarms of bees. In fact, the Hebrew word for honey is Deseret. The bees were not active in the darkness inside their barges and fed upon their honey reserves that sustained them during the long ocean crossing.

Whenever these verses are studied in Gospel Doctrine classes or Sunday school, invariably the question arises......"How in the world did these people manage to travel across the ocean in water tight barges with swarms of bees?" The answer is the bees were a tiny non-aggressive stingless variety of honeybees. Stingless is not quiet accurate as they do have stingers but the bees are so tiny their sting is like that of a mosquito bite.

When the Jaredites, later called the Olmecas, arrived in the Promised Land with their friends approximately 2,600 B.C., they immediately began beekeeping with their friends. After the demise of the Jaredite {Olmeca} civilization in 240 B.C., the Chichimec Maya continued beekeeping. The Royal Lady stingless bee variety was the favorite variety brought to the new world and today is only found on this continent in the Yucatán. However about eight hundred species of the stingless bees are found throughout tropical regions of the world and several varieties of stingless bees are found in South East Asia from whence the Jaredites {Olmecas} came.

Please review the chapter, The Oldest City in the Americas, in Volume Three of The Ark of Millions of Years, pages 173-184, for a more detailed account of the Jaredite/Olmeca migration.

The best documented use of honey from stingless bees comes from the Mayan civilization in the Yucatán peninsula. There the bee is called "Xunancab" and beekeeping of this species {Melipona Beecheii} originated independent of hive beekeeping with honey bees in the old world. It was thought that bees in Mesoamerica were unknown until another larger European variety {Apis Mellifera} was imported by the Spanish. Not so, the stingless bees were there for at least eleven hundred years prior to the arrival of the Spanish.

The Maya used their honey in rituals, as a food sweetener, in folk medicine and when fermented produced their alcoholic drink called "balche." The best tasting honey comes from the Royal Lady stingless bee variety. This tiny variety of stingless bees are not aggressive and are kept as "pets" in many places and can often be tended to by children. The stingless bees do not store their honey in honey combs in hives as do their larger European counterparts. Instead they make many small round spongy bees' wax "honey pots" usually inside a hollow log. Traditionally, honey from stingless bees is harvested by squeezing the honey pots with bare hands and collecting the honey as it pours out of the nest. Stingless bee honey is more liquid than the well known honey bee honey because it has higher water content. The honey is light gold in color and mild in taste. It is sweeter, has a delightful distinct floral taste and it never crystallizes. It truly is "liquid gold." Once one has eaten this honey over a stack of pan cakes or slathered on a biscuit, regular honey will quickly take a back seat. It is an OMG give me some more experience! A good hive of honey pots will produce four to five hundred milliliters after a full year due to the bee's tiny size. By comparison the standard European honey bee hives will produce fifty liters or more in a full year because these bees are much larger.

Yet, stingless honey bees are important because they are pickier than their European counterparts about what flowers they visit, making them important for keeping certain tropical forests healthy. As previously mentioned, Apis Mellifera is a species of honey bees native to Europe, Western Asia and Africa; Melipona Beecheii is a genus of tiny stingless bees. In Mexico, the vanilla orchid plant only blooms one morning per year and only the Melipona bee knows how to pollinate the vanilla flower. Without the Melipona bee, there would not be vanilla beans. These two were made for each other. Without vanilla beans to make pure vanilla extract, artificial vanilla extract would be the only source for this cooking flavoring. Artificial vanilla flavoring is made from castoreum or beaver "butt pudding" that is collected from anal glands of beavers and marketed as "natural flavoring." Yummy! Small wonder the more expensive pure vanilla extract outsells the cheaper artificial stuff. Chefs will only use pure vanilla extract made from the vanilla bean as they claim the pure vanilla brings better flavor; now we know why. The Maya people of the Yucatán peninsula have cultivated the Melipona Royal Lady honey for two thousand years. This honey often sells for ten times the price of European bee honey. Xunancab in the Maya civilization was only second in importance to maize {corn} for food and rituals.

But times have changed. Today the tradition of keeping stingless bees has largely been abandoned in favor of larger imported honey bees which yield more honey and profits. In this case less is much better than more because delicious flavor is being sacrificed for greater profits. Sadly, the Maya beekeeping tradition is in serious danger of dying out because of deforestation and failure to pass the tradition to younger generations as they move to cities in search of excitement, more modern living conditions and better paying jobs. The Yucatán is rapidly changing as almost all of the Maya have cell phones, even in remote jungles.

Xcaret, a well known Yucatán ecological theme park is dedicated to breeding Melipona queen bees. These bees are propagated and protected in special areas in this park. Visitors get to look at the hollow log hives lined with honey pots and get to meet the stingless bees, so beloved by the Maya, up close. This honey can be purchased in the Xcaret gift shop area and in the many souvenir shops and markets throughout the Yucatán. It is the honey of choice and definitely worth the trip to the Yucatán to purchase a suitcase full and bring back home or better yet, another reason to make regular trips to the Yucatán paradise. While you are down there, buy some vanilla beans and pure vanilla extract too. At least you will know it's the real thing, made from vanilla beans and not "beaver butt pudding" because beavers are not found in the Yucatán where the vanilla beans are grown in a tropical rain forest environment to make the pure vanilla extract.

Update, Additions and Correction

Tulum Update

On pages 230-231 in this volume, we wrote about this marvelous archeological site. Since that writing, much more information has come forth that will enlighten our understanding and purpose of the site in the Yucatán Mexico.

In Jerusalem, the Temple of Solomon was constructed around three courtyards with a central altar. In Tulum the temple complex was constructed with three temples and a central altar.

There were no steps to climb to enter the first courtyard of Solomon's temple. The same is true to enter the first temple in Tulum known as the Temple of the Inscriptions or Temple of the Initial Series.

To enter the second courtyard of Solomon's temple, one had to climb twelve steps representing the twelve tribes of Israel. In Tulum it is the same. To enter the second Temple of the Descending God, one must climb twelve steps.

In Solomon's temple, one had to climb an additional fifteen steps or twenty-seven steps total to reach the innermost courtyard. In Tulum it is the same. In order to enter the Great Castillo, one must climb twenty seven steps. This numbering system has been used in many temple complexes associated with Christ throughout the Mayan World.

In addition Solomon's temple was built to mark the equinoxes and solstices. The same with the Tulum temple complex and it marks one additional day as well, the April 6th birthday of the descending God known to us as Christ but known to the Alux Maya as Itszamna and Kukulcan.

On one of the buildings, in the complex, is a faint imprint of red hands which are associated with the descending God. Red is the color of the East which is the direction Christ will come in accordance with New Testament scripture and it is the direction he would have come from had he visited them. Like the fish symbol, it is another symbol of believers.

Located to the North of El Castillo, the Kukulcan Group, the most outstanding structure in this group is the Templo del Dios del Viento (Temple of the God of Wind) named after its round base. The God of the wind, Ehecatl, or Huracan is associated with Quetzalcoatl, Kukulcan, or Itzamna which are simply other Aztec and Maya names for Christ. All round temples were dedicated to him, round being associated with wind. The two watchtowers, located on the west facing wall, hold religious altars.

Tulum was built by the Alux dwarfs therefore the complex is small or miniature by comparison to other archeological sites in the Yucatán. It appears that the entire complex was dedicated to the worship of Christ. It is evident that the Alux dwarfs had access to records that we do not possess or were taught by Christ during many of his visits to various cities in the area as recorded in the Toltec/Book of Mormon and Mexican records; perhaps both. Else how did they know how Solomon's temple complex was constructed?

It also was an important port of trade because near the beach was a break in the reef that permitted trading canoes to land on the beach located adjacent to the building site. The tallest building, El Castillo, also called the lighthouse, is located on a cliff overlooking the sea. High atop this building were two torches that served as beacons at night to guide canoes safely through the reef. Land trading routes from other prehispanic cities in what is now Central and South America all converged at this port. This trading port and city complex remained in use for about seventy-five years after the arrival of the Spanish [1200 A.D.-abt.1600 A.D.].

Tulum means walled city but its most ancient name was Zama which means City of Zion.

Muyil Addition

Muyil Maya ruins is about a twenty minute drive by car from Akumal past Tulum. This is a small site embedded in a moss covered wetland jungle. The structures are not as large as found in other major sites but it is free of busy tourist crowds. Muyil, also known as Chunyaxche, means in Maya "wide ceiba trunk." This is a reference to the sacred Maya tree, the Ceiba, which is an example of the tree of life. The site is located on the northwestern edge of the Sian Ka'an bioreserve. This site is much older than Tulum, coming to prominence during the pre-classic era from about 300 B.C. to 800 A.D.

After you enter the gate at the site entrance, follow the wide path to the first temple which is about seventy-five feet high. There is a brass plate sign next to it that says this temple celebrates the place where Heaven and Earth united. The Union of the Polarity is echoed throughout *The Ark of Millions of Years* series. It is an ancient doctrine and belief that is supported by this temple. The origin of this doctrine came from *The Divine Book of Wisdom*. Fragments of the doctrine can be found in the *Zohar*.

Behind this temple is a board walk that wanders through mangrove wetlands and ends on the edge of the Chunyaxache Lagoon. Here tourists may hire Maya guides to take them across the lagoon in boats to the ancient Maya trade canals, which the Maya have maintained for centuries. Chunyaxache Lagoon is a large fresh water lagoon fed by underground streams and springs. The water is crystal clear with a white sand bottom. Nearby is an island reported to be home to alligators but they only come out at night. If one crosses the lagoon on a blue sky day, the sky and water become as one. It is virtually impossible to see where the water ends and the sky begins. One has the sensation of sailing up into Heaven in a motor boat. Muyil really does mark this place as where Heaven and Earth united! It is an illusion the ancient Maya noticed as they traversed the lagoon to enter into their trading canals that lead to a port. At the port is a small ancient Maya building where the trading canoes stated their trade purposes to the port master who then collected port fees before trading began. This place was so sacred the Maya erected a temple on the lagoon's edge celebrating the Union of the Polarity; the place where Heaven and Earth united.

Itzamna Addition

Itzamna is a name of an Itza Maya ceremonial complex taken from the name of the Itza Maya God Itzamna {Christ} and is considered as one of the oldest ceremonial centers of the Maya, populated by the Itzaes group. These Itza Maya were descendants of the 2,600 B.C. Jaredite migration to the New World Promised Land. Their history in the New World is well documented in the *Popol Vuh*, the sacred scriptures of the Maya. It appears that they were always believers or followers of Christ, even before they left the Old World. Truly, these were descendants of some of the friends of Jared spoken of in the Toltec/Book of Mormon record prior to their departure from the port city of Pa Tulan, Pa Civan, ancient Babylonia to the Land of Promise, the Americas. The ceremonial center dates from 200 B.C. to approximately 1000 A.D. when it was partially abandoned from the rising of Chichen Itza. The old section of Chichen Itza was built by the Itza Maya and for years became the new, more centrally located, religious center of the Yucatán where it rose to become the "Rome" of the New World. Anciently the Itzamna religious center was probably the large ceremonial city of the karst plains to the north of the Yucatán. This area has the best and deepest soil for cultivation, although it is often rocky. At one time on entrance through the city gate, a great stucco mask of Itzamna greeted all who entered the city to worship him {Christ}. In 1840 a picture of the stucco mask, mounted on a stone wall entry, was hand drawn by Frederick Catherwood which sketch was later published by John Lloyd Stephens. The image now only exists in this hand drawn sketch.

After the 16th century conquest of the Yucatán by the Spaniards, the Spanish began construction of a city, which began upon the existing abandoned Itzamna Itza Maya ceremonial complex. They probably chose this site because of the rich soil for cultivation and the easy availability of Stones from the Mayan temple ruins to construct Spanish colonial style buildings. Some of the largest pre-Columbian Maya temple structures were spared mid these Spanish colonial houses and Spanish mission style churches. Today the city is fused with more modern structures but the ancient Maya monuments still rise in the center of town amid houses of the colonial time. The mixing of the old structures with the new Spanish style structures is impressive. This ancient religious ceremonial city, named for Christ, is older than 2,000 years and well worth a visit. It was probably the first place where the Spanish introduced a new form of Christianity in the Yucatán.

Olmec Addition

In this book in chapter *The Twin Feathered Serpents*, pages 66-69, we wrote of the Olmec myth that the Olmec were a race of giants who were created by the mating of a woman and a jaguar. Some of our readers thought we were a little "far out" but this clay figurine pictured below was found in Olmec country depicting such a union that validates what we wrote. The giant Quinames were the spawn of Lucifer who took the form of a jaguar. The figurine most likely is in a museum in Olmec territory.

Figure 26 Jaguar copulating with Olmec Woman

(Picture from article by Gene D. Matlock, Fabled Sunken Trikuta: The Real Atlantis? Picture permission by Gary Vey viewzone.com/ Lanka22html)

Figure 27 Carved Stone Picture of Mulekite/Xicalanca Man

Pictured above is a carved image of what we believe is a Mulekite/ Xicalanca man now on display in LaVenta Olmec Park in Villa Hermosa in state of Tabasco, Mexico. This carving was found in Olmec territory. Clearly the man has a beard, Hebrew nose, and slender which is unlike the Olmec/Quinames; however there is historical evidence that the two races of men lived together and were influenced by one another. The three symbols to the right may be either Olmec or Mulekite writing?

To date it has not been translated. He is carrying some sort of banner or flag, not a meat cleaver. Again due to copyright laws and unable to get permission to use the actual photo picture, we had to redraw, by hand, the image from another image. To see the original actual image carved on a large basalt stone, just Google Jim and Carole's Mexico Adventure...the Olmecs. Then scroll down about 13 images to see the original stone carving titled "the walker."

Correction

On page 114 in this book, second paragraph, we wish to clarify a statement as follows: King UKit Kan Le'k Tok's name was found written on a lentil above a doorway in the old section of Chichen Itza. This suggests the Maya king of Ek' Balam frequented Chichen Itza so often that he had his own personal living quarters. He may or may not have been an Itza Maya, but he was Maya. No doubt he was receiving religious instruction pertaining to Christianity when there in order to rule his religious temple complex righteously. The lentil with his name on it is now housed in the British Museum in London, England.

The Origin of the Cherokee

Jesse Brock, son of Aaron Brock, was the first settler on Wallens Creek in Harlan County, Kentucky. He was born December 8, 1751 in Cumberland County, Virginia and died October 13, 1843, at age 91, in Harlan County, Kentucky. He was a Revolutionary War soldier serving in the North Carolina Militia, pension #30887. Jesse married Rebecca Howard who was born March 15, 1756 in Cumberland County, Virginia, the daughter of Samuel Howard and Francis Dryden Howard who were also early Harlan County settlers. She died 1841 in Harlan County, Kentucky. Jesse and his wife had eleven children.

For his service in the Revolutionary War, Jesse was given a new suit of clothes and a land grant. After the war, he moved around several times but eventually he came to Knox County, Kentucky and received his land grant of 206 acres of land, lying on the Cumberland River to include the mouth of Wallens Creek, certificate #147. That part of Knox County, Kentucky became part of Harlan County, Kentucky when it was formed in 1819. Jesse and his wife are buried in the old Mason's Cemetery, sometimes called the Old Wallens Creek Cemetery close to his farm in Harlan County, Kentucky.

Cherokee people, as well as African Americans, who served in the Revolutionary War were permitted to be land owners and were encouraged by the newly formed American government to merge and adapt into American society as civilized people.

Jesse Brock was the son of Aaron Brock, his English name, otherwise known as Cherokee Tsakagi Ugvwiyuhi Totsu'hwa Brock AKA Chief Red Bird. Chief Red Bird was born December 8, 1721 in Overhills, Great Tellico, Tennessee and died February 10, 1797 in Clay County, Kentucky. He married Cherokee Susanna Christian Priber in 1748 in Overhills, Great Tellico, Tennessee. He was the son of Great Eagle Cherokee Willenawah and mother Cherokee An-Wadi. Great Eagle was the son of Cherokee Chief Moytoy 11, born abt. 1687 and died 1741 in Overhills, Great Tellico, Tennessee. The Moytoy Cherokee bloodlines are well documented.

Red Bird River, located in south eastern Kentucky, is named after Chief Red Bird. The boundary between Clay and Leslie county Kentucky follows part of the Red Bird River. A small town, Red Bird, in south eastern Kentucky was also named after Chief Red Bird however its name was changed a few years ago to Beverly, Kentucky. For more information on Chief Red Bird, just Google his name.

In Volume 14, Issue Number 86 Special Edition of the *Ancient American* magazine publication is an article on the front cover of the magazine titled *DNA And The Cherokee In North America.* Turning to the article in the magazine, it is given another title: *Central Band of Cherokee/Brock Cherokee DNA Projects,* written by Donald Yates, PhD.

Donald N. Yates is an American genealogist, author and historian. He holds a PhD. in classical studies from the University of North Carolina at Chapel Hill and has written scholarly works in cultural and ethnic studies, history and population genetics. Yates is one-quarter blood Cherokee descendant. He is the owner and principal investigator at DNA Consultants, a DNA lab, in Phoenix Arizona, that offers ancestry tests, paternity tests, forensic tests and relationship tests. Two specialties are autosomal DNA ancestry and ethnic admixture (www. Linkedin.com/in/donaldnyates).

A Brock male, claiming descent from Aaron Brock, submitted his DNA for testing of the Y chromosome. His test results caused quiet a stir as his DNA was the same as Old Testament Hebrew priests. The following is excerpted material from Yates article: "Aaron Brock/Chief Red Bird's father {Great Eagle?} preserved an ancient male lineage identified in today's literature as the Cohen gene of Old Testament Jewish priests in the Cherokee hierarchy because:

Bennett Greenspan and the scientists at Family Tree DNA have clarified it as belonging to haplotype J12f2.1+, an ancient form of the Cohen haplotype. The + allows for one-step mutations of the gene over time.

Chief Red Bird's Y chromosome is not exactly matched by males living in Europe or descended from European or Old World emigrants, only by other Cherokee descendants.

Chief Red Bird's father, from whom he received the haplotype was a tribally identified Cherokee born about 1700 [since Red Bird himself was born about 1721 and died about 1811]. That time frame precedes the period of English/French/Spanish/Portuguese fathering of children by Cherokee women. The first European to marry a Cherokee woman was Cornelius Dougherty, an Indian trader born about 1668, who married Ahneewakee, a daughter of Chief Motoy 11, about 1745."

In his book, *Old World Roots of the Cherokee*, Yates writes the following: "Chief Red Bird's mother is unquestionably Cherokee, reportedly Paint Clan. The paternal line of this rare Cherokee Kohane can be traced in historical and genealogical records back to Moytoy 1, born about 1640. He married Quatsi {Patsy} of Tellico, a full blood Cherokee of the Wolf Clan. Before 1680, the Cherokee had little contact with Europeans, so it is unlikely Moytoy's father was a European. If he had been, it seems strange that he or his male descendants would have been promoted into positions of leadership in the tribe. His line includes Moytoy 11, Red Bird, Raven of Hiwassee, Tathtowe, Bad Water, Old Hop, Old Tassel, Doublehead, Tuckahoe and other Cherokee chiefs. Although most male Cherokee pedigrees were extinguished through warfare following

European contact, the survival of the Red Bird or Moytoy line in Brock Y chromosomal DNA is an exception" (Yates, Donald N., *Old World Roots of the Cherokee*, McFarland & Company, Inc. Publishers, North Carolina, 2012, pp. 129-130).

From the Cherokee DNA test, we can conclude that from the very conception of the tribe, the tribe was Hebrew from the ancient Middle East. The Cohen Modal Haplotype is the genetic signature of Hebrew high-priests going back to the Hebrew patriarch Aaron.

When and how did this tribe of Hebrews arrive to this continent? We will address this next. Because books have been written on this subject, what we write next will be a broad overview limited to one chapter. Whenever possible, reliable documentation will be used.

Because American Indians did not read or write in ancient times, they didn't keep written records. Events that happened in the past were expressed as "many moons ago" that make it virtually impossible to calculate a year associated with the event unless they lived in a place or in the midst of a society that had the ability to record the event in their historical records. Definitive accounts on who the Cherokee really are and their place of origin is not utterly lacking; you just need to know where to look. We know of only one ancient written record that tells of two Hebrew migrations to this continent along with the approximate times they departed and it tells of another much older third migration who were descendants of Abraham to the Land of Promise, the Americas. In addition there were three Mexican historians whose written histories back up the claims of the one ancient written record mentioned above. The name of that ancient written record....

(drum rolls please)....... ....is.......

The Book of Mormon

In the reference chapter titled, *The Beginning*, in Volume One, pages 4 and 5, we give a brief description of the Book of Mormon as follows:

The Book of Mormon is an ancient record that extends from 600 B.C. to 421 A.D. In or about the latter year, Moroni, the last of the Nephite historians, sealed the sacred record and hid them in a stone box in the ground. In 1827, the same Moroni, then a resurrected personage, delivered the engraved plates to Joseph Smith who translated them. The book is a record of a remnant of the house of Israel who was led by the hand of God to build a ship and cross the waters to the Promised Land, present day Mexico. First English Edition published in 1830. The Latter Day Revelation is part of the sacred scriptures used by the Church of Jesus Christ of Latter-Day Saints.

We would like to add the following: Contained in The Book of Mormon, is the *Book of Ether* that dates back to approximately 2700 B.C.

to 2600 B.C. and extends to some time beyond 600 B.C. The Book of Ether gives an account of an ancient people called the Jaredites. Jared, his family and an unidentified group of people described as friends of Jared, were led by God to the Americas shortly after the confusion of tongues and the destruction of the Tower of Babel in Babylonia. The Lord directed this group of people to build eight barge like boats, with peaked ends at the bow and stern, to cross the ocean to the Western Hemisphere defined as the Promised Land.

This is the first recorded migration of a people called the Jaredites to the New World. Archaeologists call them the Olmecas or Olmec but recorded Mexican history refers to them as the Quinametzin/Quinames or giants.

The Great Prophet Ether, the last of the Jaredite prophets, recorded the destruction of his people, estimated to be about one million souls, in arm to arm bloody tribal combat against each other. As far as he knew, the entire Jaredite/Olmec/Quinames race perished. He then hid up his records in a place that would be easily found by the next people to come. The great Mexican historian, Ixtlilxochitl, records the destruction of the "Giants," as the Jaredites were described as a large and mighty {strong} people, at 240 B.C. Because Ixtillilxochitl was so precise in his dating of other ancient Mexican events, his dating lends credibility to the Jaredite {Olmec/Quiname giants} 240 B.C. destruction.

Ancient historical Guatemalan records support this origin as found written in *The Lords of Totonicapan*, the original text of which was recorded in 1554, by Native American Guatemalans', in the language of the Quiche of Guatemala from legends centuries old. The sixteen Lords or important civic leaders of Totonicapan wanted to leave a written history of their people for their posterity written as follows:

"The three great Quiche nations…..are descendents of the Ten Tribes of the Kingdom of Israel, whom Shalmaneser reduced to perpetual captivity and who, finding themselves on the border of Assyria, resolved to emigrate…..

These, then were the three nations of Quiches, and they came from where the sun rises, descendants of Israel, of the same language and same customs…..They were sons of Abraham and Jacob…….

The three wise men, the Nahuales, the chiefs and leaders of three great peoples and of others who joined them called U Mamae [the ancients], extending their sight over the four parts of the world and over all that is beneath the sky, and finding no obstacle, came from where the sun rises, from a place called [in Mayan] Pa Tulan, Pa Civan.

Now on the twenty-eighth of September of 1554 we sign this attestation in which we have written that which by tradition our ancestors told us, who came from the other part of the sea, from Civan-Tulan, bordering on Babylonia." Note: The Mayan word "Pa" means place.

(Title of *The Lords of Totonicapan*, trans. Dionisio Jose Chonay and Delia Goetz, Norman, Oklahoma: University of Oklahoma Press, 1953, pp. 167, 170, 194).

It appears the two records, *The Book of Ether*, and *The Lords of Totonicapan* are in agreement as to the origins of their people; the same peoples who came in the first migration of three mentioned in the Book of Mormon. The *Book of Ether* speaks only of the family of Jared descendants whereas the Lords of Totonicapan are part of the descendants of the friends of Jared who immigrated together to the Americas on eight barge like ships, similar to the Ark of Noah. These ships had no sails but relied on furious winds that moved ocean currents to propel them to their destination, the Americas. The Pacific Ocean voyage was long and arduous, lasting 344 days, traveling nearly 15,000 miles. To avoid being repetitious, we refer you to Volume Three, *The Oldest City in the Americas*, pages 175-184, where we propose was their landing site; the northern coast of Peru, South America. In this Volume Four book, *The Twin Feathered Serpents* chapter, pages 63-73 gives greater insight on the Olmecs/Quinames and some of their grievous sins that led to their destruction.

Although the Jaredite prophet Ether recorded all the Jaredite nation was destroyed; he meant as far as he knew, all the Jaredites in the area were destroyed. This was a particular style of writing of the Hebrews that was used in the biblical scriptures as well.

Before the Jaredite destruction, many Quinames/Olmecs had moved, years before, to other areas where their descendants founded great religious city complexes. They founded the holy city of Cholula, one of Mexico's most ancient cities and one of the Lord's {Quetzalcoatl} frequented places to abide. After the Lord departed Mexico, the citizens of Cholula built their Great Temple in honor of the Lord Jesus, known to them as Quetzalcoatl. The word Quetzalcoatl translates in English to LORD. They also erected 365 smaller temples; one for each day of the year.

Cacaxtla, inhabited by the Quinames/Olmecs, was the capital of the region. Another nearby site, Xochitecatl was a Quiname/Olmec religious city complex built to honor the God Quetzalcoatl. Monte Alban was built by the Quinames/Olmecas who inhabited it for generations. After the great Jaredite destruction, the population of Quinames/Olmecs was reduced greatly, never to fully return; only the more righteous escaped the great destruction.

As written in the chapter, *The Oldest City in the Americas*, when the descendants of the friends of Jared multiplied, they would break away to form another tribe, take a different name, elect their own king and build a city. In honor of their first king, they would use the word Chichimec or Xhixhimec in front of their newly chosen tribal name. This identified them as the first settlers to arrive in the Americas. A few of these tribes were the Chichimec Maya tribes, the Chichimec Zapotecs, the Chichimec Toltecs, the Chichimec Aztecs, the Chichimeccas, the Chichimec Chontal tribes, the Chichimec Totonocas, etc. Later some tribes dropped the Chichimec and just used their tribal names being forgetful of their origins. There were many tribes, too numerous to name in this one chapter. These tribes had nearly 2,000 years to multiply and push northward into what is now known as America. We believe all DNA signatures of Native Americans whose blood samples confirm their ancient ancestors came from the Occidental areas of Asia, particularly China areas with some Mongolian and Siberian admixture, are descendants of this first migration; the exception being the Inuit tribes of Alaska, northern states of America, Canadian tribes and some Great Lake tribes whose DNA signatures confirm their ancestors were mainly from Mongolian and Siberian tribes that crossed through the Bering Strait.

We now know the people of the Hopewell mound building culture were descendants of people of the Adena mound building culture, who were, in turn descended from the local Archaic cultures [2000-500 B.C.]. To date, DNA has been extracted from the remains of seventy-three individuals buried at two sites, the Klunk mound group in Illinois and the Hopewell mound group in Ohio. Mitochondrial DNA was analyzed. The genetic DNA signature clearly indicates an Asian origin. The results demonstrated that 4 out of 5 new world haplotypes are present in the Hopewell Mound group. This is an indication of a mtDNA relationship between the Ohio Hopewell and other Native American groups in North and Central America.

The friends of Jared were most likely from the Tartary areas of China which is supported by DNA evidence. The Quinames/Olmecs were, for the most part, eradicated in the 240 B.C. destruction. Later the Spanish massacred the remaining populations of them in Cholula and surrounding areas. However, there remain a few descendants still in the Veracruz area of Mexico who look exactly like the Olmecs/Quinames for we have seen them. They are not black but resemble Polynesians however still a very large stocky built people. There is another small population of them living in Palmetto, Florida. Another people, the Chontal Maya of Tabasco, Mexico consider themselves descendants of the Olmecs/Quinames but are not related to the Oaxacan Chontal. They refer to themselves as the YoKot'an. YoKot'an was the area the Olmec/Quiname lived about 1400 B.C. to about 400 B.C. If a DNA sample could be obtained from these peoples and analyzed perhaps we would know more about the ancestral origin of Jared in the first migration as written in the Book of Mormon.

The Etowah mounds near Cartersville, Georgia were built by Chichimec descendants. Chichimec descendants, naming a few, are well represented in the Choctaws, Cussitaws, Chicasaws, Creeks, and the tribes of the Creek Confederacy.

The Cherokee **are not** descendants of this first migration. They are not a Chichimec tribe. It would be nearly two thousand years before the second migration would arrive as written in the Book of Mormon.

The **second migration** in the Book of Mormon gives an account of the Hebrew prophet Lehi and his family who left Jerusalem at the urging of God because of the imminent 599 B.C. Babylonian first destruction of Jerusalem during the reign of King Zedekiah/ Jehoiakim (1Nephi 1:4). The Prophet Lehi was an Israelite of the tribe of Manesseh, the son of Joseph who was sold into slavery. Lehi's family, consisted of his wife, Sariah, and his four sons, Laman, Lemuel, Sam, Nephi, and untold numbers of sisters. With them went Zoram, the servant of Laban, and Nephi's friend, Ishmael which included his wife, two daughters and their families, two sons and their families and three other daughters.

Together with this group of people, the Prophet Lehi led them out of Jerusalem about 601 B.C., through the wilderness to a fertile coastal region. There is much evidence that Lehi's family traveled along or parallel to the Red Sea through the Arabian Peninsula in a southeast direction then turned east to a lush fertile coastal region which they called Bountiful (1 Nephi 17:5-6). Most LDS researchers believe Wadi Sayq {River Valley} also called Khor Kharfot {inlet or port} in Oman meets all the requirements as described by Nephi to be the ancient site they called Bountiful. It is quiet easy to follow Lehi's family trail from the description given in the Book of Mormon, even in today's times. There Nephi was instructed by the Lord how to construct a ship that would carry them safely across the ocean to the Western Hemisphere, the Land of Promise. In all, this leg of their journey lasted eight years during which time Lehi and Sariah had two more sons, Jacob and Joseph. In Lehi's possession were brass plates that contained his genealogy, the five books of Moses and some of the Prophet Jeremiah's writings. Please note that The Prophet Jeremiah and the Prophet Lehi were contempories in Jerusalem. Nephi, on reading the brass plates, discovered that Zoram was a descendant of Joseph and his friend Ishmael was a descendant of the Tribe of Ephraim.

When the ship was ready to sail, Lehi gave the signal for all to board. The party of men, women and children along with their animals boarded the ship and sailed across the "sea," {the Pacific Ocean}. We are in agreement with some researchers that the ship reached the shores of what is now called Guatemala, Central America. On arriving to the fertile coastal plains of the Land of Promise, they began tilling the earth and planting seeds that they had brought from the land of Jerusalem. In addition, they began to raise flocks, herds, and animals of every kind.

Upon Lehi's death, his two oldest sons rebelled against their brother Nephi. Before Lehi died, he chose the younger son Nephi over his oldest son to receive the birthright blessing because he was righteous. Therefore the oldest son felt he was cheated out of what should have been rightfully his. Thereafter the oldest sons began to hate Nephi to the point they wanted to slay him. Hatred created a great division between Laman and Nephi that established two conflicting nations, the Nephites and the Lamanites. Being warned of God, Nephi and his family separated from those who sought his life. Leaving with him were Zoram and his family, his elder brother, Sam and his family, his two younger brothers, Jacob and Joseph, his sisters, and all those who would go with him. Nephi led this group of people into the wilderness for the space of many days until they settled in a place they named the Land of Nephi. There they planted seeds of every kind and raised animals of every kind. Nephi recorded they reaped in abundance and prospered exceedingly, and multiplied in the land. In time, Nephi built a temple similar to the temple of Solomon but constructed with local more plain materials.

It is the consensus of many researchers; the Land of Nephi is present day Guatemala City. This is supported by the archeological ruins of Kaminaljuyu, ancient name unknown, found there. Although urban sprawl has destroyed most of the 350 buildings and mounds, enough remains to study the architecture and artifacts removed to date the site to the times of Nephi. The main temple fits the description described by Nephi; the temple he built.

The term Lamanite was applied to those that seek to destroy the people of Nephi and those who were friendly to Nephi and the people of Nephi were called Nephites. So that the people of Nephi would know who the Nephites were and who the Laminates were, the Lord brought a curse of blackness upon the skins of the Laminates while the Nephites kept their much lighter white skin color. Critics of the Book of Mormon say the book is racist and scoff at the idea but if you will go to Volume Three of the *Ark Books*, page 367, you will see a picture of a Mayan Tree of Life with a light skin Nephite and a dark skin Laminate picking cacao or chocolate beans from the cacao tree. Most likely this picture came from the Land of Nephi area because the cacao or chocolate beans grow plentiful in that region. The picture came from a Mexican manuscript now in the British Museum (Le Plongeon, Augustus, *Sacred Mysteries Among the Mayas and the Quiches*). That picture settles the matter, once and for all. It did happen as written in the Book of Mormon (2 Nephi, 5:21).

Although the Book of Mormon doesn't identify tribes by name, we believe the Nephites were the Toltecs. The Toltecs are **not to be confused** with the Chichimec Toltecs. They were two different peoples from different migrations. Please refer to the *Update* chapter in Volume Three, pages 377-387, where we previously addressed this issue.

Nephi records he did teach his people to build buildings, and to work iron, copper, brass, steel, gold, silver, and of precious ores which were in great abundance (2 Nephi 5:15). The word Toltec generally means "craftsman of the highest level."

The Mexican historian, Alva Ixtlilxochitl, describes the characteristics of the Tultecas. "The Tultecas were great architects, carpenters, and workers of arts such as pottery. They mined and smelted gold and silver and worked precious stones......" (Chavero, Alfredo, *Obras Historicas de Don Fernando de Alva Ixtlilxochitl,* Editoral National, Mexico 1965, p.28).

Ixtlilxochitl's writings are in agreement with the Book of Mormon, therefore, with certainty, we can safely conclude the Nephites and the Toltecs are one and the same peoples.

In the above same previously mentioned *Update* chapter in Volume Three, we established the Nonoalca were the Lamanites who were constantly at war with the Toltec as early as 500 B.C. In later Mesoamerican writings, the Nonoalca Maya were also referred to as the Huaxtecas and the Mazatecs.

Nephi records that forty years had passed away and they had already had wars and contentions with their brethren (2 Nephi 5:34).

New research, in the absence of early written historical records, but in the presence of early archaeological records, we believe the following events happened in the Land of Nephi; also called the land of Lehi-Nephi. In approximately 187-160 B.C., the Land of Nephi had a population influx due to tremendous economic expansion. In essence, the town became a multi-cultural city which affected its political and religious climate. Prosperity, mainly from trade, affected the entire region however; wars, contentions and dissentions had remained a problem for centuries. These problems continued on until the people, all over the entire region, simply said enough is enough. There is archaeological evidence that a great many people left the southward lands and migrated into the lands northward where they settled. Part of that migration is recorded in the Book of Mormon (Helaman 3:3). Part of the Nonoalca Maya and Toltec Maya left with other tribes as well; the population shifted.

Those Toltec who lived in the land northward above the narrow neck of land or the Isthmus of Tehuantepec were simply called Toltec. Those that lived below the Isthmus of Tehuantepec in the land southward were called the Toltec Maya. The same was for the Nonoalca. They were either the Nonoalca or Nonoalca Maya.

The archaeological record parallels the 50 B.C. migration into many parts of the Valley of Mexico, particularly around the Teotihuacán region. Why that area? We believe the Toltec Maya had converted many people, from all tribes, to the Gospel of Jesus Christ and desired to leave the unrighteous to found a religious complex suitable to their ideology. Apparently they had great success among the Chichimec Toltec as it appears they worked in tandem to build Teotihuacán, original name unknown. The Toltec were master architects and builders, the Chichimec Toltec, being warlike, provided protection and were overseers of the many areas necessary to build the huge complex. A call went out to all of central Mexico's cultures to come and help build the complex. In exchange for their labor, they would receive food, housing, clothing and protection from their enemies. And come they did from all cultures. Some worked in the fields to provide food for the thousands of laborers, some worked as stone masons, some built cement houses for the laborers, some mixed cement for other buildings, some built roads and plazas, some raised cotton; the women made cotton clothing, raised children and cooked the food etc. Everyone had a job to perform as the task was enormous. The Chichimec Toltec organized and oversaw the many projects whereas the Toltec laid out the city complex and oversaw the actual building of buildings and pyramid structures. Because the Chichimec Toltec were more numerous than the Toltec, the Toltec became a subculture of the Chichimec Toltec. The Nonoalca who came to help as laborers were converts.

The great Pyramid of the Sun's first stage of completion was in 100 A.D. which was nearly the size as it is today. The second stage saw the construction of an altar atop the pyramid which no longer exists. Legends and traditions say the heavens opened up and Jesus Christ walked down pyramid like steps into the city's religious complex, no doubt to dedicate the Mountain of God Temple and light its eternal flame atop the pyramid as it was built in honor of Him (Volume Four, *The Aztec Sun Stone,* p. 116; *Etowah Mounds,* p. 97).

The beautifully decorated Temple of Quetzalcoatl was built in at least two stages and originally consisted of seven levels, like the ancient Sumerian Ziggurat temples (Volume Two, chapter *The Tower of Babel,* pp. 60-62). It was completed in about 250 A.D.

We will temporarily stop here and tell about the third migration, consisting of Hebrews, to the Land of Promise because the two Hebrew migrations intertwine.

The third migration in the Book of Mormon gives an account of Mulek, a son of King Zedekiah/Mattaniah, who led a group from Jerusalem, shortly after the departure of the Prophet Lehi, in about 587 B.C. and being directed by the Lord, came to the New World (Helaman 6:10). It was Nebuchadnezzar, King of Babylon, who captured King Zedekiah and gave judgment upon him by slaying his sons before the eyes of Zedekiah, then his eyes were put out, bound in chains, carried to Babylon and put in prison till the day of his death (Jeremiah 52:8-11). How did Mulek, son of Zedekiah, escape the wrath and fury of Nebuchadnezzar? Some speculate that Mulek was in the womb of his mother who had fled before Jerusalem was destroyed by Nebuchadnezzar's armies or perhaps Mulek was a young baby disguised as a daughter or perhaps he may have been born in captivity. We favor the first hypothesis which we will address later on.

Mulek's ship landed in the Land Northward which was near to the Jaredite/Quiname/Olmec heartland. LDS church members refer to the people of Mulek as Mulekites but new research indicates the Mexican historical records refer to them as the Xicalancas.

Fray Bernardino de Sahagun, a sixteenth century Catholic writer, records the following account of the arrival of a particular group of people in Mesoamerica:

"Countless years ago these first settlers arrived in these parts of New Spain {Mexico}, and they came in ships by the sea approaching this northern port; and because they disembarked there it was called Panutla, or Panoayan, place where they arrived who came by sea; now corruptly called Pantian {Panuco}." (Barnardino de Sahagun, Book Nine)

Panuco is near the present day city of Tampico, Mexico. After a period of about twenty-two years, some of these settlers traveled along the Gulf Coast of Mexico and eventually settled in the areas of Campeche and Chiapas on the southeast side of the Isthmus of Tehuantepec.

The *Lords of Totonicapan*, a native Mesoamerican document describes a group of people who were descendants of Abraham and Jacob and who crossed the ocean and settled in the area of the Bay of Campeche.

They were an agriculture based people who lived in houses made of sticks.

It appears the writings of Sahagun and the sixteen Lords of Totonicapan are in agreement that they are the same people who came by ships and landed in the Land Northward as described in the Book of Mormon.

Back to Mulek's mother. This is merely speculation but we think that Mattaniah may have fathered Mulek before he was made king at age 21, maybe at age 15-16, therefore no one knew about this son in the absence of marriage. Mattaniah certainly had a bad reputation. We also think that Mulek's mother may have left Jerusalem before her pregnancy was apparent, if indeed she did live there, because of scandal associated with unwed mothers. There is a good possibility that she went with a group of Hebrews from Jerusalem to the port city of Sidonina to live and give birth there; maybe saying she was a widow. Mattaniah may not have known she was pregnant with his child or if he did, he tried to cover it up by sending her out of town. After all, he was a teenager.

King Zedekiah/Mattaniah took the throne at age 21 and reigned for eleven years in Jerusalem and had legitimate sons. By that time Mulek could have been 16-17 years old still living in Sidonina, also known as Saida, Sidon or Zidon, located in what is today, Lebanon about twenty-five miles south of Beirut. Zidon or "Great Zidon" was the mother city and said to have been built by Noah's great-grandson, thus the name Zidon.

Tyre and Sidon were twin Phoenician port cities on the Mediterranean Sea, located about twenty five miles apart. These twin Phoenician cities were the leading trading hubs and ship builders in the Mediterranean. Their ships and navigation instruments were superior and capable of transoceanic voyages (Ezekiel 27). In fact, they were the first cities to send ships in the open seas. In order to expand their trading ports, the Phoenicians were colonizing far off lands at the time of the fall of Jerusalem to the Babylonian army. It appears that the Phoenicians had copies of the world maps that Noah's grandsons were commissioned to remap the world following the 9,500 B.C. cataclysm that nearly destroyed the world. And they were using the compass which the sons' of Noah re- introduced to this world (Volume One of the *Ark* books, chapter *The Brave New World*, p. 477).

According to the Book of Mormon, the hand of the Lord brought a Hebrew colony across the great waters from Jerusalem at the time that Zedekiah, King of Judah, was carried away captive into Babylon (Omni 1:15-16). They came in a Phoenician ship because, at that time, only the Phoenicians had the ability for transoceanic voyages. Although only one ship carried the Hebrew colony, there were probably more ships carrying other colonists to the same place at the same time as noted by Sahagun's account above. Not all colonists were necessarily

Hebrews but at least one ship brought a ship load of Hebrews to the Land Northward with Mulek, the son of Zedekiah/Mattaniah (Helaman 6:10).

After living around the Bay of Campeche area for a period of time, at least part of the Hebrew colonists went up a large river that flowed inland into the land southward. Finding a suitable place they settled and built Zarahemla, a city complex with a temple, and named the river Sidon after the city they had departed from across the sea.

The Hebrew word Sidon means "fish waters" or "waters of Sidon," as many tributaries flowed into it. In the Maya language waters were called Xocal Ha which means "fish waters," the same as Sidon in Hebrew. And there is the fact that the sailors of Phoenicia called themselves Sidonians. Some LDS researchers believe the Mexican Grijalva River is the Sidon River.

Mexican historical records indicate some of the colonists remained in the Olmec/Quiname areas in LaVenta and Monte Alban. Some of the other colonists may have been Asian or Orientals besides Hebrews (see carved stone picture, in this book, of a Mulekite/Xicalanca man, in *Update, Additions, and Correction* chapter).

Almost four centuries later, or around 225 B.C., the Toltec Maya from the Land of Nephi, in the Highlands of Guatemala, discovered the people of Zarahemla and found their ancestors came from Jerusalem about the same time as the Toltec Maya's ancestors. Feeling a kinship, the two groups of people merged as one with the Toltec Maya chosen to become their new leaders and thereafter both peoples became known as Toltec Maya (Omni 1:19). Zarahemla continued to have problems, both internal and external, with dissentions, contentions, and wars with other Nonoalca Maya tribes, resulting in the Amlicite **87 B.C.** war. According to the Book of Mormon, a Toltec Maya, named Amlici, united with a numerous host of Nonoalca Maya, and made war with the Toltec Maya because he wanted to be king of Zarahemla. While crossing the Sidon River, the Toltec Maya army encountered the Nonoalca Maya and Amlicite armies and gave ferrous battle whereon Amlici was slain by the sword. The Toltec Maya slew so many of the Nonoalca Maya that their bodies on the west bank of the Sidon River, were thrown into the river in order to make room to cross the river and contend with the Nonoalca Maya and the Amlicite armies before them, too numerous to number. The battle raged on until the Nonoalca Maya and Amlicites fled for their lives before the Toltec Maya into the wilderness of Hermounts. The Toltec Maya continued, for miles, in hot pursuit killing and wounding many to the extent they could not be numbered because of the greatness of their number (Alma 2: 27-38; Alma 3:1-6). After this war, the Toltec Maya returned to their homes only to discover that many of their women, children, flocks and herds had been slain; and also much of their crops of grain were destroyed by being trodden down by the marching armies.

Now the wilderness of Hermounts bordered on the Isthmus of Tehuantepec in the land southward. Fearing the wrath of the Toltec Maya, the survivors of the Amlicite War would have fled into the lands northward. Certainly a war of this magnitude would have had far reaching repercussions into ancient Anahuac {Mexico}. If not a written history, then a memory of legend. Thankfully the Toltec Maya record keepers recorded this event on thin golden plates that would eventually become known as the Book of Mormon.

About thirty seven years later or around 50 B.C., part of these Toltec Maya migrated out of the southward lands into the northern Anahuac lands, along with converted followers to found the religious complex known to us as Teotihuacán. On finding the survivors of the Amlicite war in the northern Anahuac lands, all was not forgiven; the Toltec and Chichimec Toltec drove them out of the land. Here is where written history and legend combine to tell the full story as follows: Constantine Samuel Rafinesque [1783-1840] was a naturalist, traveler, writer and somewhat historian of ancient Mesoamerica and its linguistics. He made a notable contribution to American prehistory with his studies of ancient monuments in America. In his writings, he wrote "When the Toltecas of Mexico drove away the Xicallens {Huichols, about 100 B.C.}, the bulk of that nation came to the Mississippi, and settled on both sides of it, above the Natchez;;....."

(Yates, Donald N., *Old World Roots of the Cherokee*, McFarland & Company, Inc., North Carolina, 1950, p.76).

That legendary statement was the missing part of the puzzle as to where these Nonoalca went after being driven out of Mexico. Rafinesque had the name of the tribes wrong but the date was right on. The Huichols are still in Mexico; don't think they ever left. Besides they were too shamanistic, mystical and steeped in dualism for the Nonoalca tastes. Today the Huichols, still for the most part, reject Christianity and cling to the old religion of dualism mixed with worship of the Life Force energy that outsiders wrongfully perceive as "nature worship." The only big war with significant losses that led to exile during that period of time was the Amlicite War which was recorded by the Toltec Maya record keepers. Rafinesque was relying solely on oral legends but the two combined records enable us to tell the full story.

There is some misunderstanding that the Huichols were the evil priesthood holders of Anahuac and may have come with the Nonoalca when they were driven out of Mexico. No, the descendants of the Chichimec Maya from the first migration had a caste system. One level of the caste system was the priesthood. One had to be born into the various levels and were expected to carry out their duties as relegated to them by reason of birth. Therefore, without exception, the priests came from within a tribe of people. Please understand the Nonoalca

Maya lived among the Chichimec Maya tribes and had adopted some of their ways and customs.

First, we want to note that these outcast Nonoalca were not traveling unchartered waters. They knew exactly where they were going because trade routes to that region were well known. The Nonoalca probably arrived in large canoes, having traveled up the coast of the Caribbean into the mouth of the Mississippi River. They would have arrived during the Middle Woodland Period [100 B.C. to 200 A.D.]. Perhaps they lingered for awhile among the Woodland people, along the Mississippi River, but not being religious chose to inhabit the land of now Arkansas along the Arkansas River. Fearing the Toltec's would discover their whereabouts; they dropped their tribal name of Nonoalca and chose another rather vague one or maybe even several different names. It seems strange that this tribe, even in the absence of a written language, could not remember who they were unless they wanted to be incognito. Isn't that the first thing people are taught; who they are by name and then is passed down for generations? Nevertheless, the Cherokee believe their original name was Aniyunwiya. Maybe but that is not a Nonoalca Maya or Chichimec Maya name. An alternate spelling of Cherokee is Tsalagi. In time, Tsalagi evolved to "Chelokee", a Creek word meaning "people of a different speech" then evolved to the most familiar name, Cherokee. Their speech was different alright; it was ancient Quiche Maya or even possibly Mam, a highland 5,000 year old Guatemalan Maya language which is still spoken in the highlands.

When the Prophet Lehi and his family arrived to the Promised Land, they would have spoken archaic Hebrew as their first language. Jerusalem was a multicultural city comprised of Hebrews, Greeks, Romans and Egyptians. Most of the citizens of Jerusalem were multi-lingual just as Europeans are today. So Lehi's family most likely was multi- lingual as well. The Book of Mormon bears out this fact in Mormon 9:32 which says the {Toltec} record keepers wrote in characters which they called Reformed Egyptian that was handed down and altered by them according to their manner of speech and implies that they wrote in Reformed Egyptian because it took less space on the golden plates than Hebrew and because of the evolution of the new language since the people left Jerusalem. The Prophet Nephi in 1 Nephi 1:2 states he kept a record in his father's language which consisted of the learning of the Jews and the language of the Egyptians. This tells us that the Book of Mormon record keepers wrote Jewish knowledge in Reformed Egyptian and that they indeed were multi-lingual in Jerusalem. Reformed Egyptian may be more of a pictorial language sort of like writing in short hand? Writing space was a premium on the small golden plates when everything had to be made by hand.

In time, they mixed with tribes from the first and third migrations and adopted their language and customs. The southern Nonoalca were

Maya speaking and probably spoke a dialect of ancient Maya from the Chichimec Maya descendants of the first migration that inhabited much of the area. Even today there are so many dialects of Maya that different villages separated by only a few miles cannot understand each other. It is doubtful if the Maya today could understand the Maya their ancestors spoke because language is evolving constantly. Nevertheless the Nonoalca Tsalagi spoke an ancient dialect of Chichimec Maya when they first arrived here.

We want to emphasize again that the Nonoalca Maya were Laminate descendants of the Hebrew Prophet Lehi who arrived in the second migration. They joined other Chichimec Maya tribes from the first migration and adopted their language and customs. By comparison their statue was taller than the first migration Chichimec Maya, their heads elongated rather than round, skins lighter in color but nevertheless reddish olive brown and their faces were more European looking. It is said that they had the long graceful stride and stance of noblemen due to their posture and tallness of statue. In other words, they were different in appearance from the average Chichimec Maya, with Asian roots, from the first migration.

As previously written in this Volume Four book, chapter *Etowah Mounds*, page 97, the Nonoalca Tsalgi priesthood abused their privileges to the point that the Nonoalca overthrew and violently massacred them, their wives and children. In essence they did away with the shackles of the Chichimec Maya caste system replacing it with a more egalitarian society with all religious ceremonies conducted thereafter with common medicine men.

The Creek, Choctaws and other related tribes have long maintained the Cherokee preceded them in coming to what is now called the USA from Mexico. Their legend is correct because the Nonoalca Tsalgi arrived in North America approximately 550-600 years in advance of the Muskogean tribes.

After living along the banks of the Arkansas River for nearly 200 years, part of the tribe migrated northward and after several wars, eventually made an alliance with the Iroquois, and merged together as one tribe.

We believe this Nonoalca tribe was the ancestors of the Cherokee. They were the descendants of the Hebrew Prophet Lehi. It was through this prophet that the genetic signature of the Cohen gene of Old Testament Hebrew/Jewish priests was passed to his male offspring who then passed it to every generation until Chief Red Bird received it and literally unlocked the mystery of the origin of the Cherokee. The Cherokee are the remnants of scattered Israel in America.

Dr. Anthony Jones, a full blood Cherokee, who holds a PhD. in both archeology and anthropology, believes the Cherokee originated in the Amazon River Basin, South America based on the facts that the Cherokee were the only tribe in North America who used the blow gun, named a clan "wild potato," or "wild sweet potato" and wove their baskets in a particular double weave, chain, and diagonal pattern styles used in the Amazon River Valley.

In response to these claims, first the blow gun was used through out Mesoamerica but without poisoned darts. Instead they used small clay balls for ammunition to stun small prey making it easy to bag them. Their use is pictured on many clay jars etc. and piles of these clay balls have been found in various locations through out Mesoamerica. The Cherokee and Mesoamericans favored river canes for blow guns while plank construction seems typical of the South American Indians. Second, the sweet potato grows wild in South America and all through Central America, Mexico and even North America. It was a delicious trade item and known through out coastal regions of ancient Mexico. Third, Amazonian baskets were also trade items. When the baskets grew old, they were dis-assembled and the natives learned how they were woven. Or maybe, some South American native Indian traders showed them how to weave that style of basket while tarrying in various ports of trade before returning to their homeland. If the Cherokee were ever in the Amazon River Basin, they didn't originate there but sojourned there briefly. It is to be noted that the Cherokee were not mound builders or potters but expert basket weavers. The Mesoamericans got around in their large trading canoes even to North America, Central America and South America.

The Cherokee today say that they were originally a white tribe but believe they got darker skins by intermarriage to darker tribes. They are right. Lehi's children were considered white, at least for a few generations. The full story is contained in the Book of Mormon; we just scratched the surface.

I don't like leaving a story hanging, so let us go back to Teotihuacán. After Christ made his appearance and dedicated his Temple, sometime around 100 A.D., the entire lands, both north and south of the Isthmus of Tehuantepec enjoyed peace and prosperity for 200 years. Then slowly the religious climate changed because of wicked priests who controlled the religious, social, and commercial activities of every day life of the people. In other words, they led the people astray and reinstated dualism or the worship of two gods instead of the one God of Israel as described in this book, chapter *The Twin Feathered Serpents,* pages 63-73. To oppose these wicked priests meant imprisonment or even death. Reverting back to the old ways brought back spiritual darkness, hatred, atrocities, many wars and dissentions as was done three hundred years previous. The Nonoalca and the Toltec continued to engage in many vicious wars until the final battle in 385 A.D. when the Nonoalca, being in greater number, defeated the Toltec in a tremendous battle where 230,000 Toltec soldiers were killed. Those who escaped to the Land Southward were hunted down and sacrificed to the sun god

(Mormon 6:8; 8:2). All whites, including women and children, were slain or sacrificed.

The archaeological and Mexican historical records bear witness that in the years 350 A.D. to 900 A.D. the society was steeped in idolatry, apostasy, mysticism, and spiritual darkness; the same time of the Classic Maya period. The white skinned Toltec were no more; only the Chichimec Toltec remained (Volume Three, chapter *Update*, pp. 377-387).

According to the Book of Mormon, a white skinned Toltec named Moroni, the last of the Toltec record keepers, did survive. He recorded this last battle on the plates of Mormon, wandered for ten years carrying the plates of Mormon into North America where he buried them in a stone box in a hill, located in what is now called the state of New York. Centuries later, the now angel Moroni, told Joseph Smith where the plates were hidden. Joseph Smith retrieved and translated them into what is now called The Book of Mormon. Buried with the plates of Mormon were an urim and thummin or seer stones that enabled Joseph Smith to translate the record into English. The Prophet Jared, from the first migration, brought the urim and thummin from a Babylonian port to the Promised Land. These seer stones were passed down through generations of prophets until the Prophet Ether received them. When Ether finished his record and concealed it, he left the urim and thummin seer stones with the golden plates. In 121 B.C.,

540 years before Moroni's time, Ether's 24 golden plates and urim and thummin were discovered by the people of King Limhi. King Limhi and his people later escaped from the Lamanite Nonoalca Maya in the highland land of Lehi-Nephi to Zarahemla where they merged or intertwined with the people of Zarahemla as recorded in Mosiah, Book of Mormon. Limhi and his people were descendants of the Prophet Lehi. Thereafter Zarahemla and the lands of Zarahemla were occupied by two Hebrew populations; the descendants of the Prophet Lehi from the second migration and the descendants of Mulek from the third migration, collectively called Toltec Maya. The golden plates were translated by use of the urim and thummin, and kept thereafter by Moroni's ancestors. In essence, the Bible is a record of the Jews {Hebrews} in the Old World and the Book of Mormon is a record of the Jews {Hebrews} in the New World.

We do want to emphasize that there were other migrations to Mesoamerica but the three mentioned in the Book of Mormon were the most significant.

Next we want to remove the shroud of mystery associated with the mound builders that will help you understand more about them and their religious beliefs. Previously written in this chapter, it was established that the Adena and Hopewell cultures originated in Asia, descendants of the first migration as friends of Jared. They migrated early into North America and established earthwork burial mounds along the Ohio and Mississippi Rivers. Amidst the mounds were small earthen platform temples and archaeologists have found holes in the ground where previous was a wooden henge, similar to Stone Henge, used to time the equinoxes and solstices. We believe the people of those cultures held to the same religious beliefs as of the people of Stone Henge and of the Irish who built the passageway tombs. They built their burial mounds near large bodies of water and rivers which flowed strong with the Life Force energy because it was believed this energy enriched soil would guarantee them a good resurrection on the last day. They were timing the winter solstices just as Stone Henge and the Newgrange Ireland Site had done. The same was done at the Lamar Mounds site in Georgia only their site was almost an island being surrounded by Life Force Energy. These sites were religious complexes and cemeteries only. Few, if any, lived on the site but lived in surrounding areas. During this period of time, small platform temples were usually erected to honor this energy being equated as the power of the Holy Ghost and were considered sacred. These people were early Christians having received their knowledge like the early Irish and early people of Britannia {England}. We have already written in this book about *Stonehenge*, pages 108-109, and about the *Newgrange Ireland Site*, pages 110-115. A good review of this energy is in Volume Two, chapter *The Spiraling Life Force*, pages 117-131, and in Volume One, chapter *The Interaction of Universes*, pages 137-141. More will be said in the next chapter as to where this doctrine originated.

Further evidence that these people were early Christians is the fact that in **all** mound builder burial mounds the deceased were buried with their heads facing toward the East direction. Today most Christian cemeteries bury the dead facing East in the same fashion because on the day of resurrection that is the direction the Lord will come; from East to West (Ezekiel 44). They want to rise up {resurrect} and greet Him at his coming.

It was during the Middle Woodland Period [500 B.C.-400 A.D.] that the construction of bigger and more elaborate earthworks appeared from the Great Lakes to the Gulf Coast. These sites functioned for the same purpose as the Hopewell and Adena cultures. Then a new religion swept through the region, the religion of Quetzalcoatl. Larger platform temples, like the Great Temple Etowah Mound, were erected in his honor. Each had an eternal flame.

Flat topped mounds were used as the base for temples with huts on top for housing for priests who maintained the eternal flame 24 hours around the clock. The high priest was usually a chief who presided over the people. He usually had a separate hut on the temple mound as well. Each morning the high priest would greet the morning sun, with hands and head lifted up toward the sun in prayer. They were not sun worshippers of our star but offered prayers toward the sun because the sun was the symbol of Quetzalcoatl, the Lord of heaven and earth. The high priest was called, the Sun. The title of the Sun or the Great Sun meant the same as High Priest, a title held until his death, and then a new high priest was selected from the priesthood who maintained the eternal flame. This new religion incorporated the Life Force earlier religion into one because the newer larger temple sites were still being built along rivers and lakes with burial mounds in the Life Force energized soil. These places were holy and sacred places. Games and ceremonial festive events were held in the plaza areas.

During the Middle Mississippian Period [1200-1400 A.D. or C.E.], the largest and most complex Mississippian site, Cahokia was built. Cahokia is located near East St. Louis, Illinois, and is the largest pre-Columbian settlement north of Mexico. Because it was the most influential of the Mississippian culture centers, it can be compared to the Vatican for the new religion.

During excavation of burial mound #72, south of Monks mound {the huge pyramid temple}, archaeologist found the remains of a man in this 40's. The man was buried and lying on a bed of more than 20,000 marine shell disc beads arranged in the shape of a falcon. The man was placed over the falcon image with its wings and tail beneath the man's arms and legs. The bird's head was beneath the man's head; he was a "birdman" which is a common symbol in the Mississippian culture. This man was a Great Prophet. Because the Mississippian culture didn't have a written language or written religious scriptures of any kind, they didn't have a word for prophet. The closest they could come to expressing the word prophet was using the birdman symbol for prophet. The birdmen were prophets who carried messages between heaven and earth or carried messages from God to men on earth and from men on earth to God.

Who brought the religion of Quetzalcoatl to these cultures? We can only speculate. Perhaps it was the Chichimec Chontals, later known as Creeks, who built the Etowah mounds. It seems everywhere they went, they converted other tribes to this religion; call them early missionaries. Maybe Moroni, during the Middle Woodland Period [ca 500 B.C.-400 A.D.], taught them on his way to the New York area carrying the plates of Mormon? Better yet, maybe the Lord himself came when he walked the Americas and later dedicated the temple built in his honor; then lit its eternal flame. The truth of the matter is the entire culture was so impressed by who ever came; they converted fully to Christianity (Volume One, chapter *The Brave New World*, pp. 480-481).

According to Cherokee oral legends, the tribe left the Great Lakes region and the Iroquois tribe migrating to the site of an ancient earthwork burial mound, located near a fork in the Tuckasegee River southwest of Cherokee, North Carolina, thought to have been built by the Mississippian culture about 1000 A.D. They settled there sometime after 1000 A.D. and named the site Kituwah. The Cherokee today believe all Cherokees originated from the Mother Town of Kituwah. It is their tradition this is the location where God gave the sacred fire and laws to the Cherokee and established them as a people. Based on those traditions, it appears the Cherokee converted to the new religion of Quetzalcoatl and became early Christians. Perhaps they were converted by the Creeks? After their conversion, the burial mound probably served two purposes, a temple and a burial place. We believe that Christ came to this temple, gave them a set of laws {Ten Commandments?} and then lit their eternal flame which was maintained for centuries. As previously written in this Volume Four chapter *Etowah Mounds* pages 97-105, the Lord did the same thing at the Great Temple Mound in Etowah. Kituwah's burial mound is located near the Life Force charged Tuckasegee River and Life Force charged soil along the river; a perfect burial site for early Christian believers in a future resurrection. As the Cherokee have long maintained, Kituwah is a sacred site; the place for a new fresh start for born again Cherokee people, now established as a nation.

Thereafter, the sacred fire or eternal flame was a constant reminder of the Great Spirit or Creator who was the source of all their blessings. It was the centerpiece for different ceremonies and festivals and an opportunity to thank the Creator. For example in late September the Cherokee celebrated the Ripe Corn by a Thanksgiving ceremony where Thanks were offered to the Creator for the bountiful fall harvest. As practiced by the Maya in Anahuac, New Fire ceremonies were practiced by the Cherokee where all the hearth fires were extinguished, including the eternal flame which was reduced to live coals. At the end of the ceremony or festival, all Cherokee homes from far and wide came to get fire from the coals of the Eternal Flame and rekindle their hearth fires. It was a time of refreshing and purification by immersing themselves seven times in a row in the Life Force charged river. It was a new start for the New Year. Whenever the Cherokee migrated or were gone on long trips, a few coals of their sacred fire or Eternal Flame were carried with them, in a Hebrew ark like basket, so they could restart hearth fires where ever they went. The ark like basket was carried on two staves exactly like the Hebrew ark that contained the Ten Commandments. If ever the sacred fire should become extinguished, it could only be restarted from another temple sacred fire that was dedicated to Quetzalcoatl; a sacred fire that He lit. This meant traveling long distances to the Etowah temple mound or temples along the Mississippi River mound builders, maybe even to temples in Mexico. One legend says they once traveled to Peru to obtain sacred fire.

By 1350-1400 A.D., the Cahokia site went into decline and by 1500 A.D. the population of most areas had dispersed to other areas. We believe the same thing that happened at Teotihuacán happened here because *The Annals of the Cakchiquels*, an important native Maya document states:

"The invasion of the Serpents from about 700 A.D. onward, coming up the Mississippi in their long snake-painted dugouts, carrying their sacred fire, brought an end to peaceful living, and brought with them war, pillage and the priesthood of the sacrifiers."

Who were these serpent priests? We can only speculate that the most likely candidates would be the Chortis Maya, descendants of the 1st migration, whose chiefs compared themselves to the Cumatz {means serpent} head of a serpent or Chan and the serpents body were people under the jurisdiction of the Chan or people of the Chan. The Chorti community regards itself as a serpent. Apparently the Serpent People of the Chan were migrating to new territory to escape the spreading civil rebellion wars. Their priests did human sacrifices, had sacred fire and the Chortis' in general were warlike. As mentioned before, more study is needed on the subject to positively identify the Chortis Maya to the 700 A.D. serpent invasion (Volume Four chapter *Etowah Mounds*, pp. 97-98).

Once these Serpent priests were accepted by the Mississippian Culture to be their priests, the priesthood was empowered to become evil, controlling, extracting heavy tax burdens on the population and adulterous. They demanded total support from the people and may have wanted to bring back the old religion of dualism that required human sacrifice to Tezcatlipoca (Volume Four, p. 70). In a civil rebellion, the population, being followers of Quetzalcoatl, simply walked away and the culture collapsed. Whereas in Teotihuacán the civil rebellion resulted in all out war that progressively spread all over Anahuac including the Yucatán, Petén and Highland areas of Guatemala. The surviving populations of those areas didn't leave but simply walked away and vanished into the thick jungles in civil defiance, and then their religious complexes simply collapsed. The Maya never disappeared but built many villages in the jungles far away from the stone city religious complexes their ancestors built. Descendants of those Maya have returned to the archaeological ruins of the stone cities to become tourist taxi cab drivers, tour guides, restaurant owners, food vendors and souvenir shop owners etc. The Maya are still there; they never left.

According to the historical writings of Ixtlilxochitl, the Toltecas had a bible called the Toltec Bible or Teoamoxtli which is a Nahuatl word that interpreted means the Divine Book of Moses. Teo means 'Divine', amotl means 'book' and moxtli means 'Moses'. The *Divine Book of Moses* is probably the Hebrew Torah or the first five books of the Bible. Lehi, the prophet, would not have left Jerusalem without the Hebrew Torah. Upon his death, these scriptures would have been passed down to the Toltec record keepers. The *Divine Book of Moses* was in use as late as the seventh century A.D. by the Chichimec Toltec then, at a later date, presumably destroyed by the Aztecs and Spanish.

(*Antiquities of Mexico*, Vol. VI, p. 204)

As previously pictured and written in Volume One of the *Ark* books, chapter *The Union of the Polarity*, pages 250-251, A Star of David symbol was found in the Mayan ruins of Uxmal, Yucatán, Mexico and carvings have been found on granite stelas in Compache, Mexico that clearly show a star of David on ear spools covering nearly half the side of the model's face dated 700 A.D.

A four-horned incense burner was found at Monte Alban dated to 500 B.C. to 100 B.C. is similar to the types of urns from Jerusalem from that same time period. It is on display in the Oaxaca Valley Room of the National Museum of Anthropology in Mexico City.

Archaeologists have found jug or pear shaped underground cisterns, to collect and store rainwater in the Yucatán. These chaltunes were hand hewn in solid lime bedrock with a narrow opening. Those bottle-shaped cisterns were then plastered with a layer of hydraulic plaster to prevent water loss seepage through the bottom and the walls. These same style ancient cisterns are found in Israel and the Middle East.

Along the coast of Israel is a small sea shell snail creature, the murex trunculus, used to extract the rare purple blue pigment that dyed clothing. The pigment was extracted from the sea snail by cracking its shell. So rare is this pigment, it became the mark of royalty. Along the Gulf coast of Mesoamerica, this same process was done to extract the same rare purplish blue pigment. It takes hundreds of these small sea shell snails to produce a small amount of purplish blue pigment, a color so beloved by the ancient Middle East royalty and the ancient Mesoamericans'.

In the *Update, Additions and Correction* chapter in this Volume Four book is a hand drawn reproduction picture of a Mulekite/Xicalanca man that was carved on a piece of basalt stone found in an Olmec area. It has been titled "the walker" because of the foot symbol located next to the man on the left side. The original basalt stone is found at the Olmec Museum in LaVenta Mexico. Reproductions can be purchased there.

In the *Update, Additions and Correction* chapter in this Volume Four book, we wrote about the Yucatán Tulum site being built like the Jerusalem Temple of Solomon complex. All the above things hint at a Mesoamerican Hebrew presence in ancient times.

Writing this chapter took on special meaning for one of your authors, E. J. Clark, because she is a double descendant of Chief Red Bird on her maternal side. She has another Cherokee lineage on her maternal side and a Tuscarora {Lumbee} Native American lineage on her paternal side.

Understanding the migration patterns in the Toltec/ Book of Mormon record is the essential key to understand the peopling of Mesoamerica and North America. When the second and third migrations arrived, these lands were already teeming with hundreds and thousands of descendants of different tribes from the first migration who were Asians. Their ancestors were the friends of Jared. Jared's family were probably Israelites as they came from the "great tower" region of Babylonia. The second and third migrations were Hebrews from Jerusalem. Early Mexican historical and archeological records plus modern day DNA evidence all confirm these findings that support the Toltec/Book of Mormon record.

For further information on the Cherokee, Donald N. Yates books listed below may be of interest.

Old World Roots of the Cherokee and *Old Souls in a New World.*

December 21, 2012 and Beyond

December 21, 2012 came and went without much ado leaving a lot of people wondering what happened if anything. Some events happened as written in *The Ark of Millions of Years* book series and some did not.

Did a cataclysm happen as many believed would happen? No, however many ancients did believe a cataclysm could happen at the end of a Sun Year of 104,000 years. Nostradamus, the ancient Egyptians, the Hopi, the Maya and the Aztecs all believed this date would bring a cataclysmic destruction because December 21, 2012 was the end of a Sun Year and the end of a Great Year as well.

Based on those predictions we wrote our physical planet could experience a cataclysmic destruction during its three day transit of the Milky Way dark rift. We believed it was far better to be fore warned and prepared than to be caught off guard and unprepared. Many people did take heed and prepared in various ways with emergency food storage, survival gear, basement safe rooms and underground shelters. Was this all for naught? **NO!** We still advise to be diligent in all things and maintain emergency preparedness in the event of a natural disaster because we are living in the last days of the end times.

Did the Spirit Earth separate by process of rapture from the Temporal Earth and go into the fourth dimension on December 21, 2012? Yes, we believe that it did.

It departed as it arrived without much ado or fanfare. On December 21st, high winds blew across the continental United States. In East Tennessee, blizzard conditions mixed with high winds started around 7 am. The winds increased to 11 am then slowly decreased after 1 pm. In our opinion, the winds may have been caused by the Ouroboros portal being opened to allow the Spirit Earth to enter into the 4th dimension. Although the Ouroboros portal is located about 28,000 light years from the Temporal Earth, the portal will remain open until the Spirit Earth arrives and passes through the portal gate into the 4th dimension. And, it is quiet possible that there are other portals much closer.

Quiet frankly, I, E.J. Clark, was dismayed that very little appeared to happen on December 21st, yet I knew my research on the subject was solid. I felt something was missing so I decided to review my five volumes of the *Zohar* books and other ancient texts once again. Guided by instinct, I found the proverbial needle in a field of haystacks that opened the eyes of my understanding.

As previously written in Volume One in the *Garden of Eden* chapter, pages 160-164, Adam was given, by God, ten scrolls that collectively were called *The Divine Book of Wisdom* or *Adam's Book*. When Adam was expelled from the Garden of Eden, these scrolls flew out of his hands but they were given back to him by the angel Raphael by God's command to do so. Thereafter these scrolls were called "the flying scrolls" for generations. Briefly, these scrolls were God's handbook of heavenly wisdom that revealed inscriptions of higher mysteries that whosoever was privileged to peruse them could learn God's knowledge of how to create, how to control heavenly forces, and learn what will occur in all time.

Adam left *The Book of Divine Wisdom* to his son, Seth, who transmitted it in turn to his posterity, and so on until it was received by Enoch, the seventh generation from Adam. After Enoch was taken by God, *The Book of Divine Wisdom* was hidden until the coming of Noah who was favored in the eyes of the Lord. The Lord sent forth the angel, Raphael, to deliver the holy book to Noah to make known to him what will be and what to do. In time Noah received understanding of the knowledge therein. From the knowledge in the book, Noah, son of Lamech, built the Ark and understood all the words under the guidance of the angel Raphael and other heavenly beings. Noah learned and understood of future things to come. Shem, son of Noah, handed down the book to Abraham, then from Abraham to Isaac, from Isaac to Jacob, from Jacob to Levi, from Levi to Kohath, from Kohath to Amram, and from Amram to Moses. From Moses it was passed to Aaron, from Aaron to Phineas, from Phineas to his son, and then to all generations coming after. Only those who were righteous and reverent of the Lord were afforded grace to gain the understanding and knowledge contained in the book.

Copies of the book were also passed from Moses to Joshua, from Joshua to the Elders, from the Elders to the prophets, and from the prophets to the Wise Men {Magi}. Thus this continued in every generation, until Solomon, the king received the book. By the power and knowledge contained in the book, Solomon became the wisest of his generation.

Solomon made copies of *The Divine Book of Wisdom* then placed his original passed down copies inside the hollow brass columns at the entrance of his temple. Centuries later, the Knight Templers, who were searching for the fabled "flying scrolls," found them in Solomon's temple ruins. From there copies were made by the Templers and Solomon's original copies were taken to France and then to Scotland. Upon returning to France, the Templers began building magnificent European cathedrals using new architectural methods revealed in the scrolls. Readers are referred to Volume Three, pages 331-332, for more on Templar cathedral building.

There is much evidence that William Sinclair carried King Solomon's original copies of the "flying scrolls" in trunks to his home in Scotland which were later removed to underground vaults under Roslyn Chapel. A picture is found in Volume Two, page 273, of a stone carving of a

Nephlim, in Roslyn Chapel, carrying the "flying scrolls" that contained the instructions for rebuilding the Earth after the cataclysm that nearly destroyed this planet from a near miss interloper, consequently causing the oceans to flood the world (Volume One, chapters, *The Cataclysm* pp. 195-208 and *The Arrival of Noah* pp.209-239). In Volume Three, page 158, is a picture of your authors standing at the side entrance to Roslyn Chapel, Scotland. Later these scrolls were carried to America by the Freemasons to the Freemason city of Washington D.C. while it was being built and most likely are now stored in an underground vault in the House of the Temple which is a Masonic Temple in Washington D.C. The Temple's cornerstone was laid in the northeast corner on October 18, 1911. The city of Washington D.C. was laid out by the city planners from esoteric knowledge found in the "flying scrolls." Most of the city planners, if not all, were Freemasons.

According to the *Book of the Angel Rezial*, the great prophets were not able to make prophecies until they had studied *The Divine Book of Wisdom* or *"flying scrolls"* sometimes called the *Jerusalem Scrolls, the Book of the Angel Raziel* and *Adam's Book*. When righteous true prophets read the *Jerusalem Scrolls*, they are filled with the Spirit of the Lord that enables them to prophesy. The prophecy that America was destined to be the New Jerusalem came from *The Divine Book of Wisdom* (Volume One, pp. 256-257).

The *Book of Ether* is one of the books that make up the Toltec/Book of Mormon record. Ether was a direct descendent of Jared and was the last in a long line of royalty. He was the last prophet and record keeper of the Jaredites. Ether declared that the New Jerusalem would be built upon "this land" meaning the American continent (Ether 13:2-6). Remember the Jaredites {Olmecas} were led by God to cross the ocean to the Promised Land about 2600 B.C. The Toltec/Book of Mormon record is silent on the *Jerusalem Scrolls* {*The Divine Book of Wisdom*}.

Jared's brother was the first Jaredite prophet. He led his people from the great "tower" in Mesopotamia to the Promised Land, the Americas. Because he was a Great Prophet of God, he would have had copies of that record and surely brought them to the New World. No prophet could be called "Great" until he had read and studied *The Divine Book of Wisdom*. So great was this prophet's faith, he could see the spirit body of Jesus with his mortal eyes. The sacred scrolls would have been passed down through the royal lines until it was received by the Prophet Ether who studied the scrolls and learned the New Jerusalem would be built upon the land they now possessed by the seed of Joseph who was sold into Egypt. Ere how else would he know this? The Jaredites rejected his teachings concerning a "New Jerusalem" causing him to hide in caves for his protection. Centuries later, the Prophet Joseph Smith revealed the name of the brother of Jared as Mahonri Moriancumer. When Ether studied the *Jerusalem Scrolls*, he was

348

filled with the Spirit of the Lord that blessed him with godly powers of seer ship. He saw from the beginning to the end of the world. What happened to the record Ether received is unknown because Ether witnessed the destruction of his people, the Jaredites, and recorded the event in the *Book of Ether*. Ether finished his records and hid them away, where they would eventually be found by the people that God sent next to receive this Promised Land. Ether's final words entered in his record were: "*Whether the Lord will that I be translated, or that I suffer, the will of the Lord in the flesh, it mattereth not, if it so be that I am saved in the kingdom of God. Amen.*" Nothing else was recorded by him; he simply disappears from the record. Elder Neal A. Maxwell stated that Ether was a very special prophet who might have been translated. If so, then Ether would have taken the record with him.

The first prophet among his people in the Toltec/Book of Mormon was Lehi, a Hebrew prophet, who led his family and followers from Jerusalem to a Promise Land in the western hemisphere, the Americas. He was a descendant of Joseph, who was sold in Egypt, through his son Manasseh (Alma 10:3). The thirteen "shining ones" came down from Heaven and went forth upon the face of the earth. Their first visit was to the Prophet Lehi; and the first came {the premortal Jesus} and gave him a book {note it was probably a scroll but translated as book} and bade him to read it (Volume Three, chapter, *The Grand Finale* pp. 307-308) (Volume One, chapter, *The Brave New World* pp. 478-481). As

Lehi was reading the book, he was filled with the Spirit of the Lord. The book revealed that Jerusalem would be destroyed, the inhabitants thereof should perish by the sword and many would be carried away captive into Babylon. The book revealed many upcoming future events (1 Nephi: 9-15). No doubt this book was a copy of *The Divine Book of Wisdom* personally delivered to the Prophet Lehi by the Lord. Thus this is how Lehi came to possess the *Jerusalem Scrolls*.

Upon the death of the Prophet Lehi, his youngest son, Nephi, became the next prophet who would have received the book. Upon reading the *Divine Book*, Nephi began to prophesy concerning the future of the American continent. He sees Columbus crossing the ocean to the seed of his brethren in the Promised Land; he sees the arrival of people fleeing from Europe to settle in America; he sees a record from the Jews, the Bible, would be brought with them; that the new settlers would overpower Europe {the Revolutionary War}; that the new settlers would drive the indigenous people out of the land; he saw the discovery and translation of the Book of Mormon; and that the Apostle John would write concerning the final days {in his Revelation} (1 Nephi: 13). Nephi made record of the prophecies concerning the birth, life, and death of the Savior in more detail. Chapter 13 in First Nephi is an amazing chapter. Nephi's prophecies extend from the destruction of his people in 385 A.D., to the 20th century. Like his father, he was a Great Prophet.

Most likely, *The Divine Book of Wisdom*, continued to be passed down to future prophets and writers of the Toltec/Book of Mormon record however the record remained silent on this matter until Third Nephi, a 7th generation descendant from the Prophet Lehi, wrote the land they {House of Israel, meaning the Hebrew Nephites}, now lived in would become a New Jerusalem and the remnant of Jacob should build a city, which shall be called the New Jerusalem (3 Nephi 20:21-22; 21:23-24). So it does appear that *The Divine Book of Wisdom* was being passed down as this Nephi was writing about future events found written in the book. Most likely this record, along with others, was hidden up by Ammaron in a hill called Shim in about 321 A.D. Ammaron had kept the Nephite/Toltec records for the previous fifteen years when he was "constrained by the Holy Ghost" to hide up all the sacred records because the Laminates/Nonoalca were destroying every record containing God's word (4 Nephi 1:48). When Mormon was ten years old, he was instructed by Ammaron to **only** recover the plates of Nephi and to leave the rest until he became 24 years old (Mormon 1:1-5; 2:17). He revealed to Mormon where the sacred records were hidden. When Mormon was 24 years old, he took **all** the sacred records (Mormon 4:23). Near the time of the final battle between the Toltecs and Nonoalca, Mormon re-hid up the sacred records on the Hill Cumorah; keeping only the golden engraved small plates to give to his son Moroni (Mormon 6:6). Perhaps *The Divine Book of Wisdom*, first given to Lehi by Jesus, still remains there in the Hill Cumorah, Mesoamerica along with the other records. What happened to the golden engraved small plates of Nephi that Mormon gave to his son Moroni? Eventually they became known as the plates of Mormon because Mormon did an abridgment of the record which later was translated into the *Book of Mormon* (Volume One, chapter, *The Brave New World* pp. 481-482).

Centuries later, the Prophet Joseph Smith, while living in Navoo, Illinois had many Jewish friends who possessed copies of the *Zohar* scrolls. This group of Jews, along with Joseph Smith, met twice a week to study the *Zohar* manuscripts. The record was written in archaic Hebrew but Joseph learned to read the language with help from his Jewish friends. The *Zohar* is what remains today of *The Divine Book of Wisdom* although the scrolls Joseph studied were by far more complete. Joseph learned of the New Jerusalem prophecy from that record. The LDS Tenth Article of Faith, written by the Prophet Joseph Smith in 1842, declares that the New Jerusalem will be built upon the American Continent. He learned this from 2 sources: (1) As he translated the Toltec/Book of Mormon record and (2) from studying the *Zohar* manuscripts (D&C 57 1-3). It does appear that the Prophet Joseph Smith's seer power was greatly enhanced from his study of the *Zohar* manuscripts.

As you now see, *The Divine Book of Wisdom, Jerusalem Scrolls, Adam's Book, The Book of the Angel Rezial* or the *"flying scrolls"* have greatly impacted the formation of this great nation, America, even to the city design of this nation's capitol, Washington D.C. The prophecy that America was destined to become the New Jerusalem came from *The Divine Book of Wisdom.* Christopher Columbus, a Jew, had access to the *Jerusalem Scrolls,* in possession of his father. That prophecy spurred him on to try and find the new land across the "great waters" destined to become the New Jerusalem. This prophecy allowed the American colonies to defeat the British in the Revolutionary War and win their independence from England (Volume One, chapter, *The Union of the Polarity* pp. 255-261). The Constitution of the United States of America was divinely inspired by God. Included in the *Jerusalem Scrolls* were a set of instructions on how to form democratic governments based on freedom of the people. The Freemason founding fathers used these instructional guidelines to draft the Constitution of the United States, and it still remains the oldest written national constitution still in force anywhere in the world. The main reason the Confederates lost the Civil War is because this nation and its citizens, namely the Negro slaves, were to remain free whose freedom was promised by God by virtue of living in the Promised Land. The ancient inhabitants of Mesoamerica learned from their prophets and writers of the Toltec/ Book of Mormon record of the divine destiny of this continent and the role they and their descendants, if they remained righteous, would have upon this Promised Land, a land given to them forever that would remain free. This promise extends to today's times depending on the righteousness of its citizens and to all of the Americas. Ether added one more stipulation to the promise; **they would remain free "if they will but serve the God of the Land who is Jesus Christ"** (Ether 2:12).

The needle in the haystack that was missed during the writing of The *Ark* books was **that all of God's knowledge and source of power was contained in *The Divine Book of Wisdom*, extending to revealing all upcoming future events.** It develops that Noah learned how to go about building the Ark in advance of the flood from studying *The Divine Book of Wisdom,* he learned in advance where the spiritual creation would "fall" to unite with planet earth in another universe and what would befall his descendants there. **It was revealed in the book when the last day of the spiritual creation would be in this dimension or December 21, 2012.** In other words, **Noah knew all things from the beginning to the end in advance of his arrival to this planet.**

According to the *Zohar,* Noah and his descendants were permitted a longer duration of life in order to preserve knowledge. Noah and his sons had to study the constellations, in this universe, to understand Precession in order to know when the end of the age or the Great

Year would occur (Volume One, chapter, *The Arrival of Noah* pp. 230-231). He learned about the equinoxes and winter solstices and knew, in advance, the end of age date of December 21, 2012 would occur on a winter solstice. He and his sons had to rethink time on this sphere as to minutes, hours, days, months, years and ages so as to measure time accurately for future generations. **In addition he learned from *The Divine Book of Wisdom* that the first resurrection of the righteous dead would occur on the same date as December 21, 2012!** Nothing was withheld from Noah. As soon as they could calculate and measure time accurately upon the Temporal Earth, Noah began to prophesy and teach about the end of the age events to all who would listen.

When Noah's descendants were "scattered," some of his sons went to ancient Ireland and converted the early Irish kings to Christianity and taught them about the Union of the Polarity, and the end of the age events concerning the departure of the Spirit Earth and first resurrection of the righteous dead due to occur on the winter solstice of December 21, 2012. The Irish kings then built their megalithic passageway tombs to reflect this knowledge and express their Christian belief of a resurrection on December 21, 2012. They designed their tombs to illuminate, in the inner chambers, on winter solstices so they would resurrect in sun light (Volume Four, chapter, *Newgrange Ireland Site*, pp. 110-115).

One thousand years later, this knowledge was carried to ancient Britannia {England}. Thousands were converted to Christianity. Stonehenge and many other henges were built all over the country to mark the equinoxes and solstices to herald the resurrection on a future winter solstice (*Stonehenge* chapter in Volume Four, pp. 108-109).

Apparently the sons of Noah scattered to parts of Asia and taught these people the same message. Part of those people came in the first migration to the Land of Promise with the family of Jared, called the friends of Jared. Upon arriving to the western continent, they went northward and settled along the Ohio River areas and were the ancestors of the Adena and Hopewell cultures who built wooden henges in the same manner and religious beliefs of Stonehenge and the Newgrange Irish site.

There is a tomb that illuminates on the winter solstice in Monte Alban and the main plaza in front of two tall tombs in Tikal illuminates on that date. Their ancestors came in the first migration to the western continent and were Asians who were taught by the scattered sons of Noah. Anywhere in the world where the winter solstice is illuminated by the sun on henges, in tombs, on rock carvings etc. is first and foremost a reflection of Noah's teachings and second a calendar tracking the time of seasons.

It is evident that Flavius Josephus {c. A.D. 37-100} had access to *The Divine Book of Wisdom*. He was born to an aristocratic Jewish family and became a noted first-century Jewish historian. His detailed accounts of the Jewish war that led to the destruction of Jerusalem and the Temple in A.D. 70 have survived whereas the full biblical account did not. His historical accounts supply us with much more additional insight to the biblical scriptures and have been published as *The New Complete Works Of Josephus*. In that book, under the section of *Jewish Antiquities*, on page 55, Josephus quotes directly from the *Divine Book of Wisdom* manuscripts relating to Noah as follows "….for those ancients were beloved by God and made by God himself and besides God afforded them a longer time of life on account of their virtue, and good use they made of it in astronomical and geometrical discoveries, which would not have afforded the time of foretelling {the periods of the stars} unless they had lived six hundred years; for the great year is completed in that interval."

We want our readers to understand that the manuscripts/scrolls of *The Divine Book of Wisdom* did exist for over two thousand years. Josephus even quoted from those manuscripts/scrolls, word per word. In Volume One of *The Ark of Millions of Years*, in the chapter *The Arrival of Noah*, pages 230-231, we quote the exact same words which were taken from the now published *Zohar* texts.

Did a resurrection occur on December 21, 2012? Yes.

You will not find graves ripped open because the souls of the deceased do not dwell in graves but are in the Spirit World or Paradise. The righteous souls who qualified there were given bodies terrestrial to reside on the Spirit Earth now removed to the 4th dimension. When Spirit Earth received its Terrestrial glory in the 4th dimension that was the renewal of Earth, the original and true Earth spoken of by the prophets (Isaiah 65: 17-19; 13:13).

For these resurrected souls, bodies' terrestrial is a temporary state much like translated beings until the final judgment when they will receive glorified bodies designed to live on the Celestial Earth and other Celestial Worlds in a higher dimension or Heaven. At the same time, many kinds of animals, birds, and insects such as butterflies were resurrected to fill the Terrestrial Spirit Earth. Resurrected wild animals such as lions, tigers, bears etc. are now docile grass eaters. None shall hurt anything or anyone on the spiritual Terrestrial Earth. All will live together in harmony with mankind in a kingdom of peace where the most powerful of beasts shall submit to the control of a child (2 Nephi 21:10). There cities and homes are provided for all resurrected terrestrial beings to dwell. There they will prepare for the arrival of Christ and for his one thousand year millennial reign.

Because Noah was a Holy man and a Great Prophet of God, we believe the Spirit Earth departed into the 4th dimension and a resurrection occurred on December 21, 2012 as foretold in *The Divine Book of Wisdom* and prophesied by Noah. Those two events were spiritual in nature, therefore could not be seen by mortal eyes. In addition is the fact that God always honors the words of his holy prophets. We also believe that this was one of many plain and precious truths removed from the Bible.

Did the Day of Retribution or wrath of God occur on December 21, 2012? Yes.

Remember a day with God is one thousand years. This means from December 21, 2012 until the return of Christ and beyond, God will use the natural forces on this planet to bring people near to him. God will use earthquakes in diverse places, hurricanes, cyclones, typhoons, tsunamis, drought, wildfires, severe weather, flooding, famine, avalanches, pestilences, plagues, tornadoes, mudslides, volcanic eruptions and climatic changes to bring about repentance of iniquity and salvation of souls. Included in the above list is war. War is brought about by sin and unrighteousness. In time of trouble who is there to turn to except God? These great destructions are Retribution.

Those who have emergency preparedness ready such as food storage, underground shelters, safe rooms in basements, etc. may need them. So be prepared for the unexpected.

Did Christ make an appearance on December 21, 2012 as many expected? No.

The *Zohar* prophecy states the knowledge of the one mystery or Union of the Polarity would be restored back to the Earth right before the imminent return of the Savior (Volume One, chapter, *The Future World* pp. 520-521). We might add that the true earth, now in a higher dimension, has been renewed by receiving its terrestrial glory.

The Ark of Millions of Years, Volumes One through Four, proclaim the knowledge of the Union of the Polarity to the world. We are the only authors on the subject in the world to do so. Readers are referred to page 54 in this volume. There you will see a picture of Nostradamus in figure 5: Plate 72. He is holding an empty blank book for all to see denoting the departure of the spiritual creation from this universe. Below that illustration is a picture of a deer, which represents Christ, looking at two women who represent the world. Another meaning could be interpreted as follows: After the departure of the Spirit Earth at the end of the age, Christ will soon make his appearance to the world. Please review pages 53-58 in this book for more information.

In this Volume Four on page 146 is a picture of the Symbol of Tibetan Buddhism. Located in the center of the picture are the twelve ages contained in a circle that represents the heavenly vault containing the constellations. The circle is complete denoting the completion of a Great Year of 26,000 years which ended on December 21, 2012. On either side of the circle of ages are two deer representing Christ symbolizing the expected return of Christ at the end of the age.

Most of the Mesoamerican cultures expected Christ to return at the end of the age as evidenced on page 75, Volume Three, figure 27. Here Christ is shown returning to Earth on his serpent rope on December 21, 2012. To date He has not returned but we remind our readers that we still are at the end of the age and will be so for a few years more because the wheels of time move slowly; exactly 71.5 years per one degree in the equinoctial precession cycle.

The Ark of Millions of Years Volumes One through Four restored the knowledge of the Union of The Polarity to the world in fulfillment of the *Zohar* prophecy. After the restoration of this knowledge, in accordance to the *Zohar* prophecy, the imminent return of the Savior is expected. Since this Volume Four is being revised, the time will be after this Volume Four becomes "live" or published which is expected to be around January 2015.

The scriptures say only God, not even Jesus, knows when the return of Christ/Jesus will be. The date was not given in *The Divine Book of Wisdom*, and only alluded to in the *Zohar* prophecy as written above.

Fragments of the *Zohar* are part of the *Divine Book of Wisdom*. Therefore we believe the time for Christ to return is very close. Maybe Christ will return after the occurrences of the four blood moons beginning on Passover 2014 and ending on September 28, 2015 after the Feast of Tabernacles in 2015? The blood moons occur on two Jewish Passovers and two on the Feast of Tabernacles. Texas Pastor John Hagee has written and published a book on the subject titled, *Four Blood Moons*. He contends it is a signal that something big is about to happen or something big is about to change.

Another popular book written by a Messianic Rabbi, Jonathan Cahn is *The Harbinger*. The author contends the Hebrews and Jews were commanded by God to give the land a Sabbath year of rest meaning every seven years the land was to lie in fallow in commemoration of God creating the world and on the seventh day, He rested. It was a rotating cycle of seven years. The seventh year was called the shemitah or shmita. Failure to keep the shmita would result in retribution from the Lord the following year. Rabbi Cahn has linked World War 11, the great depression, 911 collapses of the twin towers, the collapse of many global economies etc. to the shemitah. His book ties into Hagee's book, the *Four Blood Moons*. Many Messianic Jews who observe the shemitah believe tribulation started in 2013 and believe the second coming will occur in the middle of 2015 or 3 ½ years from 2013, during or after the four blood moons? This would be a mid-tribulation rapture and is based on the fact it is also the time of the Year of Jubilee. The Year of Jubilee occurs after seven shemitahs or 49-50 years. It is a time of release, liberation or cancellation of all debts. Release and liberation can apply to release or liberation from earth by rapture around 2016-2017. Rabbi Cahn's book seems to be well researched judging from his many television talk show interviews. Those dates bear watching as well as the date of 2039 when Christ/Quetzalcoatl received a vision of the year 2039 during one of his visits to pray upon Mount Popocatepetl in Mexico. He received a vision of the year 2039, when the land would be reborn for the millennial age (Volume Three, chapter, *The Grand Finale*, pp. 320-321).

In our *Ark* books we used the Babylonian model of five world ages, the same as modern astronomers use today. Using that model, we said it takes 26,000 years for the sun to move through all the constellations called a Great Year. Like many others, we used the rounded off number of 26,000 years but the actual time period is 25,092 years. If you divide that number by five world ages, each age would last about 5,000 years.

In Volume Two of the *Ark* books, pages 146-147, are pictures of the Aztec Sun Stone. One picture is a stylized drawing and the other is an actual photograph taken by your authors. We did an update chapter in this Volume Four book pages 116-117 on the Aztec Sun Stone where we concluded the stone was not Aztec but Toltec/Nephite and may have been fashioned by the hands of the Lord/Quetzalcoatl or He caused it to be made for the Toltecs/Nephites. Sometimes the Toltecs are called Tultecs but we have consistently used the name Toltecs, however the name is used interchangeably in Mexican history. If you look closely at the center of the stylized picture on page 146, you will see four world ages surrounding the head of God located in the very center. The Toltecs/Nephites believed in a four world age model. Being great astronomers, they calculated it took 25,740 years for the sun to move through all the constellations called a Great Year. If you subtract 25,092 years from 25,740 years, there is a difference of 6 years and about 4 ½ months. Who is correct? Modern astronomers say they are but remember the Toltec/Nephites had access to records that we do not possess. In addition the Lord presented this stone to the Toltec/Nephites so that they would never forget the far off winter solstice date of December 21, 2012 based on a solar four world age time table as follows below:

One degree of a 360-degree circle equals 71.5 years in the equinoctial precession cycle. Twenty-four degrees of a solstice to equinox cycle equals 1,716 years. Fifteen 1,716-year periods equal the full equinoctial precession cycle of 25,740 years (Yorgason, Blaine M. *New Evidences of Christ in Ancient America*, Book of Mormon Research Foundation, 1999, pp. 14-15). With the use of modern day computers, exact Gregorian dates were able to be calculated. We will list the four world ages noting that each world age, in accordance to their belief, ended in destruction.

1. **Water Sun: Beginning of age to the flood: 4841 B.C. to 3126 B.C.**

   Age destruction: Sunday, 6 October 3127 B.C.

2. **Earth Sun: Flood to earth destruction: 3126 B.C. to Age destruction**

   Tuesday, 6 April 1412 B.C.

3. **Wind Sun: Earth destruction to wind destruction: 1411 B.C. to A.D.   305.**

   Age destruction: Sunday, 24 September A.D. 305

4. **Fire Sun: Wind destruction to fire destruction: A.D. 305 to A.D. 2019.**

   Age destruction: Saturday, 31 August A.D. 2019.

(Tultec Four-Solar Age System Table, Blaine M. Yorgason, Bruce W. Warren, Harold Brown, *New Evidences of Christ in Ancient America*, Book of Mormon Research Foundation, 1999, pp..14, 15)

As of this date, Sunday, 31 August 2014, that event is exactly five years away! Could it be that date is the true end of Precession and the true End of the Age? Note it is seven years from 2012 to 2019, the length of the tribulation years. The Old Testament Prophet Jeremiah, calls the first half of tribulation "Jacob's trouble" because it primarily centers on the Jews in Israel but has ramifications extending to other nations as well (Jeremiah 30:7 KJV). Are we not seeing this now? After a pre-tribulation rapture {if there is one?}, the terrible time of the Great Tribulation will begin when the gates of hell shall burst open and evil spirals out of control, lasting three and one half years {ISIS?}. If our timeline is correct, 2015 will mark the first half of tribulation, each half being the length of 3 ½ years, followed by a pre or mid-tribulation rapture {if there is one?}. At the end of the Great Tribulation period, the heavens shall catch on fire and the elements dissolve and melt in the heat when Christ returns (2 Peter 3:12). One third of the earth will be destroyed as the angels pour fire from the four corners of the heavens and one third of the world's population is prophesied in Revelation to perish. The only problem with the Age destruction of fire due to happen on Saturday, 31 August 2019, is the date of the second coming of Christ, which is supposed to be known only by God. That produces a dilemma with no clear answer.

The Book of Revelation is full of visions of tribulation and of things to come till the second coming of Christ. Christ gave these visions to John of Patmos, traditionally believed to be the Apostle John, who authored the first, second, and third epistles of John, as well as the Book of Revelation so that the servants of God may see what shortly must come to pass before his return.

The End is near is a cry that has echoed throughout human history. So far, these predictions have come to naught. Maybe this is because we have misunderstood what the book is all about? The Book of Revelation is all about the eternal conflict between the forces of Good and Evil. Consider this, there are many prophecies concerning the House of Israel for the last days. According to the New Jerusalem prophecy, the continental United States, Canada and Mexico are the new House of Israel, under the authority of Ephraim and Manasseh that have become great nations, under God. Descendants of all thirteen {Ephraim and Manasseh received a double portion}, (Volume One, chapter, *The Union of the Polarity* p. 258) tribes of Israel are to be found there, even though most do not know that they are literal descendants of the 10/ thirteen lost tribes and the majorities are Christians or House of Israel. The House of Judah is also well represented. On the back of the US one dollar bill is pictured a 13 step pyramid with the "All seeing eye of God" symbolizing God watching over the descendants of the 13 tribes in the New Jerusalem. Perhaps when the New Testament Bible is speaking to the House of Israel, it is speaking to the United States and other nations whose people are true followers of Christ.

When the House of Israel was conquered in 722 B.C. by Assyria and later scattered throughout the Northern Gentile nations, the House of Israel forgot they were part of God's chosen people and began to view themselves as Gentiles. These lost tribes have never returned. The House of Israel was made up of the 10 lost tribes, called "the Israelites," and the House of Judah consisted of the 2 remaining tribes, Judah and Benjamin or Benjamites as they sometimes were called. A few Levites were included to preside over temple ceremonies in accordance to Mosaic Law.

The following is a short history review of ancient Israel. Shortly after the death of King Solomon, Rehoboam, his son, took the throne and levied heavy taxation on the people. The 10 northern tribes refused to submit to Rehoboam and walked away. This created a division in Israel. The northern kingdom was called the House of Israel or Israelites. Their capitol was Samaria.

Around 586 B.C., the Babylonian King Nebuchadnezzar deported the prominent citizens of Jerusalem to Babylon. The poor and weak citizens of Jerusalem were left behind.

The southern kingdom was called the House of Judah with Jerusalem as its capitol. In 539 B.C., after the fall of Babylon to the Persian King Cyrus the Great, the exiled Judeans began to slowly return to the land of Judah following 70 years of captivity. At first the return was a trickle but always remained a gradual process over many years and many of those in exile, including their descendants, did not return. Those that did return to the land of Judah were no longer called Judeans but shortened to "Jews." According to Josephus, only 42,400 and 62 Judeans returned (*Jewish Antiquities*, Book 11, chapter 2, p.360). After their return, the second Temple was completed in ca. 521 B.C. during the 6th year of King Cyrus the Greats reign.

Jeremiah the Prophet foretold to the exiled Judeans that they would serve Nebuchadnezzar and his posterity for 70 years because Israel violated or didn't observe 70 Sabbath years {the shemitah/shmita} (Leviticus 26:31-35) (2 Chronicles 36:21-22), then God would restore them again to the land of their fathers, and they should build their Temple and enjoy prosperity. After 70 years of servitude, God stirred up the mind of Cyrus and made him write the following decree throughout all Asia:

"Thus saith Cyrus the King: Since God almighty hath appointed me to be king of the habitable earth, I believe that he is that God which the nation of the Israelites worship; for indeed he foretold my name by the prophets, and that I should build him a house at Jerusalem, in the country of Judea."

According to the Jewish historian, Josephus, the Persian King Cyrus was given a **book** which Isaiah, after he died, left behind him that was prophetic. Isaiah was a close relative to those who were kings during his lifetime who likely passed Isaiah's copy of the prophetic book down to the Prophet Jeremiah. The king most likely to have received a passed down copy of Isaiah's book, who gave it to the Prophet Jeremiah, was King Josiah. It was under the support of the prophets, Zephaniah and Jeremiah that King Josiah sought to seek God, purged the land of all idolatry, cleansed and repaired the Temple and reformed Temple worship therefore there was a close relationship between the king and Jeremiah. The only book, that was prophetic and in the possession of prophets, was *The Divine Book of Wisdom*. Now Isaiah died about 150 years before the Babylonian invasion but his copy of *The Divine Book of Wisdom* most likely wound up in the possession of Jeremiah the prophet, who probably had his own personal copy of the book. When Nebuchadnezzar seized Jerusalem in 586 B.C., he ordered that Jeremiah be freed from prison and treated well. Jeremiah probably gave the Prophet Ezekiel Isaiah's copy of *The Divine Book of Wisdom* while he was imprisoned in Jerusalem because Ezekiel was a contemporary of Jeremiah in Jerusalem. Ezekiel went into captivity with the Judeans while Jeremiah remained in Jerusalem. Most likely the Prophet Ezekiel delivered to King Cyrus of Babylon, Isaiah's copy of *The Divine Book of Wisdom*. After King Cyrus read the book, he was seized upon him to fulfill what was so written; so he gave the Judeans leave to go back to their own country, to rebuild their city Jerusalem and the Temple of God. On top of that, Cyrus said he would assist them by writing to the rulers and governors in the area to contribute to them gold and silver for the building of the temple and to supply beasts for their sacrifice. He even returned the vessels of God, which King Nebuchadnezzar had pillaged out of the temple, and had carried to Babylon.

King Cyrus had been given a copy of *The Divine Book of Wisdom* that formally belonged to Isaiah wherein it was written by God that the Judeans would serve 70 years in servitude, then King Cyrus would give them leave to return to their own country, the land of Judea, to rebuild Jerusalem and their 2nd Temple. Furthermore, King Cyrus, after reading *The Divine Book of Wisdom* prophecy specifically naming him, was moved by the Spirit of God to provide those means to enable them to do so as the bulk of the expenses for the re-building of Jerusalem and the Temple were to be taken out of the King's revenues. So it appears that Jeremiah also had a copy of the divine manuscript where he was prophetic to the Judeans as to the length of time they would remain in exile (Josephus, *The New Complete Works of Josephus*, Kregel Publications, 1999, section *Jewish Antiquities*, Book 11, chapter 1, p. 359). That book changed the course of history for the Judeans who were in exile in Babylon. And, the most amazing thing is very few people even know about the existence of that record until *The Ark of Millions of Years* brought knowledge of that ancient record to light.

What happened to Jeremiah's copy of *The Divine Book of Wisdom*? Well it appears that while Baruch the scribe, reading from Jeremiah's scrolls, proclaimed God's judgments which were to befall Jerusalem to then King of Jerusalem, Jehoiakim, that the King of Judah took a knife and cut up the scrolls and threw them into his winter quarters firepot, which consumed the entire book. After that, Jeremiah had to rely on his memory and re-write all of God's words since the time of King Josiah, on new scrolls which thereafter were called Jeremiah's book of prophecies. Note that Jeremiah was called to be a prophet under the reign of King Josiah. It appears, from time to time, God spoke to Jeremiah and had Jeremiah to write His words on scrolls. These prophetic scrolls were added to Jeremiah's copy of *The Divine Book of Wisdom*. God spoke to the Prophet Isaiah in similar ways and had Isaiah to record His words on scrolls. Isaiah's scrolls, like Jeremiah's scrolls, became known as Isaiah's book of prophecies; in truth these scrolls became part of *The Divine Book of Wisdom* and some of these same books of prophetic scrolls, that once were part of *The Divine Book of Wisdom*, were selected to become included in the *Bible* such as the books of Jeremiah, Ezekiel, Isaiah, Amos, Joel, Obadiah, Jonah, Micah, Nahum, Habakkuk, Malachi, Haggai, Hosea, Zechariah, Daniel and Zephaniah. Every prophet, worth his salt, had a copy of *The Divine Book of Wisdom*. When God spoke unto them, they recorded God's message on a scroll and added their book of prophecies to their existing copy of *The Divine Book of Wisdom*. However, Jeremiah had a scribe, Baruch ben Neriah, who recorded his dictations on scrolls. According to early rabbinical literature, Baruch ben Neriah is included among the prophets, and state that he prophesied in the period following the Roman destruction of Jerusalem in A.D. 70.

Josephus records that Herod the Great completely rebuilt or remodeled the Temple in 20-18 B.C., thereafter called Herod's Temple. The House of Israel and the House of Judah are two separate houses. It was with the House of Israel and the House of Judah that God made covenants. In Matthew 15:24, KJV, the Lord answered and said *"I am not sent but unto the Lost Sheep of the House of Israel."* It was prophesied that sometime in the future, the House of Israel and the House of Judah, will unite as one (Jeremiah 3:18). The first fulfillment of the prophecy was undoubtedly the Judean return from the Babylonian captivity. On May 14, 1948 the establishment of a new nation, the State of Israel, was proclaimed essentially restoring Israel's ancient homelands back to the original twelve tribes and their descendants. Following the collapse of communism in the former Soviet Union, there was a wave of immigration to Israel consisting of about 300,000 Christians {Israelites} and one million Jews {House of Judah}. In addition some 200,000 foreign workers reside in Israel on a permanent basis that are overwhelming Christian {Israelites}. The majority of Christians are Catholic, Protestants, Eastern and Oriental Orthodox. A new phenomenon is occurring in the Catholic churches as the Catholic priests have rooted in Israeli society. They now observe the Jewish liturgical calendar and observe many Jewish holidays. Christian life is flourishing in Israel especially in areas in close proximity to holy sites. Maybe the two houses of Israel are now walking side by side in partial unification with more to come later? Or, if America is the New Jerusalem, perhaps the two houses of Israel have already united unbeknownst to each other? The capitol of the New Jerusalem is Washington D.C. Just food for thought but it does make sense.

We recommend studying the Old and New Testament Bible with particular emphasis on the Book of Revelation with those thoughts in mind. Maybe then, the Book of Revelation can be better understood. The Bible is an Israel book throughout and the Lord's servants are his people Israel now called Christians. Bear in mind, the main prophecy that has not been fulfilled, that is if you accept scripture at face value, is the Third Jewish Temple will be rebuilt on Temple Mount before Christ returns. As of now, the Dome of the Rock Islamic mosque occupies the site of the former Jewish Temples on Temple Mount. Something has to give. When Bill Clinton was president, he suggested sharing Temple Mount with the Muslims and Jews. Lately this suggestion is being seriously considered by the two faiths. This solution would be in accordance to Isaiah's prophecy that the Temple Mount should be "a house of prayer **for all nations**" (Isaiah 56:7; Mark 11:17) instead of a source of discord and conflict. Regardless, at least you will be familiar with the chain of events and what to look for, in the end times, as tribulation does appear to be a world wide event that will absolutely scare the Babylon out of you!

Our advice, take heed and be viligent because time is short. It's later than you think. As previously written, the years 2015, 2016-2017, 2019 and 2039 all bear watching.

Concerning the end times and tribulation, perhaps Luke 21:28 says it best as follows: "And when these things begin to come to pass, then look up, and lift up your heads; for your redemption draweth nigh."

Does *The Divine Book of Wisdom* still exist today? Yes but only in fragments noting that some prophetic scrolls in the Old Testament were once part of the *Divine Book of Wisdom* that were included in the Bible. The House of the Temple in Washington D.C. most likely has a copy of these divine scrolls but they are not available to the general public; it is a well kept secret. Readers are referred to Volume One of the *Ark* books, chapter, *The Books*, pages 287-328 for an entire chapter on the subject. In the event that a copy of *The Divine Book of Wisdom* {scrolls} should be found, it would be worth millions, if not billions, on the rare book market. Please bear in mind, some ancient scrolls could be 120 feet long, unrolled, or even longer. Therefore, 10 scrolls could easily fill a trunk. In addition, these scrolls were divided by topics such as The Creation Scrolls, Architectural Scrolls, Scrolls of Magic etc; many scrolls, many topics.

Did a rapture occur among the living on December 21, 2012? No, that remains to be a future event.

What will happen to the Temporal Earth now that its spiritual counterpart has departed into the fourth dimension?

Planet Earth is no longer a co-dimensional planet as it has lost one of its tetrahedrons (Volume Three, chapter, *The Tetrahedron*, pp. 185-204). In essence it has lost its feminine gendered soul mate from which it, Planet Earth, was nurtured and sustained. Simply stated, the Yin or feminine gendered counterpart has lost its Yang or male gendered counterpart. Planet Earth has lost its opposing force that kept things in balance and harmony. In this situation, the two opposing forces are good versus evil. Please review pages 39-40 in this Volume Four book, chapter titled, *Volume Three Additions,* and Volume Three, chapter, *The Other Worlds*, pages 213-214, where we established the Spirit Earth is ruled over by God and the Temporal Earth is ruled over by Lucifer (Matthew 4:8-10; John 12:31; John 14:30; 2 Corinthians 4:4).

With no opposition from the opposing good force of the Spirit Earth, Lucifer now has free reign to do as he pleases. Therefore, we see the Temporal Earth becoming more unrighteous. Christianity, Jews, families and democracy will be under assault as well as our freedom and civil liberties. The US Constitution is under attack as never before. Corruption, fraud, greed, crime, immorality, war and radical Islamic terrorism will increase. Political correctness is the vehicle Lucifer uses to silence opposition. Face it; we are now sitting ducks on a planet ruled by a fallen merciless evil prince known as Lucifer, the Prince of Darkness. The harsh reality is the future looks bleak for Planet Earth until the Millennium.

We recommend re-reading all four volumes of *The Ark of Millions of Years* because these books contain so much end time knowledge that it is impossible to reference every necessary point. The eyes of your understanding will be opened, just as mine were when I re-read many ancient texts; the principle is the same.

The Divine Book of Wisdom knowledge has flowed through all the pages of *The Ark of Millions of Years* series and has coursed through the veins of Old Testament, New Testament, and Mesoamerican prophets, including the modern day Prophet, Joseph Smith, like a river of living water sparkling with the fire of crystals that shower new light on the creation bringing us greater understanding of God's workings in His Plan of Salvation for all of mankind to understand. The book was God's handbook of creation that was prophetic of future events. God gave it to Adam who passed it down until it was received by Noah. Noah passed it down to his children who subsequently made scribed copies that were re-scribed many times throughout all generations until we have received what is left of the divine manuscripts; fragments. From these fragments, your authors were able to reconstruct the Union of the Polarity to tell a new story of creation and much more; even to the very end. After the apostles of Christ died, the Spirit of God withdrew from mankind leaving the Divine Book of Wisdom manuscripts powerless to inspire. Therefore the book fell into disuse leaving mankind in spiritual darkness called the "Dark Ages". Without being re-scribed over and over again and passed down to the next generations, in time the book was forgotten and nearly lost save for a few fragments. The world wide rise of Christianity marked the end of the "Dark Ages". In modern times God now inspires righteous men, women and prophets through the gift and power of the Holy Ghost. The fragments that remain of this remarkable document are now contained in the Zohar. Those who are fortunate enough to find and read parts of the Zohar manuscript fragments now receive inspiration through the gift and power of the Holy Ghost according to their righteousness.

The Ark of Millions of Years series began with *The Divine Book of Wisdom* and four volumes later ended with *The Divine Book of Wisdom* knowledge. We hope that you have enjoyed these books as much as we have enjoyed writing them.

The End

Anyone interested in this type of underground 2012 shelter, contact E. J. Clark at <u>maengland@frontiernet.net</u>.

E. J. Clark's underground shelter being installed at 1500 feet elevation on her farm.

The End

Brooks A. Agnew grew up in Pasadena, California around JPL and Cal Tech. He entered the Air Force in 1973, where he graduated top

in his class in electronics engineering. He was one of the most successful scientists with ground probing radar technology in the world for oil and gas exploration. Similar technology is currently utilized in the Mars Express program. He received his bachelors in

Chemistry from Tennessee Technological University with honors. He continued his education with a Masters degree in statistics and a Doctorate in physics in 2000.

He is the author of thousands of technical papers, seminars, documentaries, or books on precision measurement and exploration into the mysteries of the universe and of the Earth. He is the host of X-Squared Radio, one of North America's most widely listened to internet paranormal radio programs. He is also the Expedition leader of the greatest civilian expedition in history to the Arctic Circle to examine the theory that planets form as hollow spheres. The team's hypothesis was Japan's Genes of Galileo Winner in 2007. He is currently the President & CEO of Vision Motor Cars designing and manufacturing affordable electric vehicles.

EJ Clark is the consummate archeologist with more than 30 years of experience researching ancient civilizations. She has personally crawled through pyramids, tunnels, traveled by canoe down jungle rivers and climbed temples to find her evidence. Her understanding

 of the ancient writings such as the Zohar, Sefer Yetzerah, the Popul Vuh and many more adds priceless perspective to the book. Her discoveries have corrected some of the biggest archeological blunders of modern times.

As a female medical professional, she has had the income to feed her desire to see these places and find the truth for us. She knows where the ancient halls of records are located. She recovered the secrets of the Freemasons and knows why they were so important. And, because she knows this, you can learn about it in the book.